To Sir & Denis

Best wish

Ripon Lodge
Bear's Hill
9/8/06

NO ACCOUNTING
FOR PARADISE

Selected works of William Oxley

Poetry:

The Notebook of Hephaestus (Lomond Press, 1981)
A Map of Time (University of Salzburg, 1984)
The Mansands' Trilogy (Keepsake Press, 1988)
Mad Tom on Tower Hill (Stride, 1988)
Forest Sequence (Mammon Press, 1991)
The Patient Reconstruction of Paradise
(Acumen Publications, 1991)
In the Drift of Words (Rockingham Press, 1992)
The Playboy (University of Salzburg, 1992)
Cardboard Troy (Stride, 1993)
Collected Longer Poems (University of Salzburg, 1994)
The Green Crayon Man (Rockingham Press, 1997)

Translations:

Poems of a Black Orpheus (L.S. Senghor)
(The Menard Press, 1981)

Prose:

Of Human Consciousness (University of Salzburg, 1982)
The Idea and Its Imminence (University of Salzburg, 1982)
The Cauldron of Inspiration (University of Salzburg, 1983)
The Inner Tapestry (University of Salzburg, 1985)
Of Poets and Poetry: Letters between a Father and Son
ed. Patricia Oxley (University of Salzburg, 1988)
Distinguishing Poetry ed. Glyn Pursglove
(University of Salzburg, 1989)
*Completing the Picture: exiles, outsiders and
independents* (Stride, 1995)
Three Plays (University of Salzburg, 1996)

No Accounting
for Paradise

AN AUTOBIOGRAPHY

William Oxley

Rockingham Press

Published in 1999
by
The Rockingham Press
11 Musley Lane,
Ware, Hertfordshire
SG12 7EN

British Library Cataloguing-in-Publication Data

A catalogue record for this book
is available from the British Library

ISBN 1 873468 65 2

Printed and bound in Great Britain by
Biddles Limited
Guildford & Kings Lynn

CONTENTS

ILLUSTRATIONS

*This book is dedicated to
poetry and friendship*

We have forgotten the old high modes of loving
— John Heath-Stubbs.

Infected minds infect each thing they see
— Sir Philip Sidney.

For he on honey-dew hath fed
And drunk the milk of Paradise.
— Samuel Taylor Coleridge,
Kubla Khan.

CHAPTER ONE
Encounter with a Hare

We called it the Jungle because half a whole field covered by tall green bamboo-like shoots with bright red leaves, some thick as a man's thumb, deserved to be called a jungle. In its densest part close to the Road – another obvious name – I lay panting, hidden. Far away I could hear the Enemy crashing about in the undergrowth. If they found me I would most certainly be shot. Best I lie doggo, chest heaving, blood roaring in my ears, face flushed among fronds of wet grass.

It was not my enemies who found me but a large, grey hare. Like a furry alarm clock. It had been disturbed by the pitched battle of the Cowboys and Indians and the rich undergrowth being combed for one escaped outlaw – me. With a look of terror, then of curiosity, the hurrying hare halted a few inches from my face. In all its long, hunted animal experience it had never come across one of the pale furless animals skulking in undergrowth in a state that resembled its own fear and alarm.

For a moment, hare and human eyed each other: the small dark beady eyes of the hare, its fur dew-wet, its ears sharp and its nose twitching; the boy red-faced and wide-eyed. Deep down in Nature, close to the grass-roots where the earth of summer is always cool, there was a moment of accord. The hare forgot all the bloodstained history of its persecuted tribe; forgot, too, the chases and horrors of the fields, and emergency conferences in deep, mud-smelling warrens. Similarly, the solitary child, the lonesome outlaw whose friends were out to get him, forgot everything in the wondrous proximity of a furry animal.

In that moment I saw a warm sweet creature – one that appealed to a child yet which had an air of independence, a certain eccentricity of manner (a 'madness' as I was later to learn from *Alice in Wonderland*). Then, with a single bound, the hare leaped right over me; and I rolled over trying desperately to clutch it in my arms. The wet grass was cool on my neck. I saw the white fur of its belly. Then there was only the empty sky above me and the sound of the animal crashing away through the green jungle.

From then on, I lost all interest in Cowboys and Indians –
somewhere in the summer of '51 that was – for I had in that instant of
creature closeness seen many things. A small and beautiful world
both near and real. Then mankind forever fleeing in terror. And
perhaps my own future? Well, whatever, for days afterwards I lived
on that moment of vision, of great pause.

I returned often to that very spot. I climbed our highest, windiest
chestnut tree that overlooked the same wilderness, to survey the whole
world – as it seemed to me. Or I would lurk under a green leather
canopy of rhododendrons hoping to meet some other member of that
rare kingdom. But the hare never came again, and all I encountered
was the occasional, not very interesting, frog.

I still remember that hare; and remember what I felt about it as
clearly as I recall the strangely exotic place where I met the creature:
that miniature jungle which some retired ex-colonial must have planted
with seed picked up in Java or Malaya, just as his ancestors had brought
us rhododendrons. And though that summer of childhood now seems
remote and like another world, yet there was in it, even then, another
world that was real. One I had dimly perceived in that moment in the
undergrowth beneath sky-high trees. A world of perfect life reflected
in that hare's eyes; and a feeling of creaturely oneness trapped in the
evil haste of this thing called time. The look of unspoken fear in man
or beast which begins in terror, ends in apology, and reveals the
instinctive knowledge of Paradise in every living thing.

So that now, years on, nobody will convince me of the 'rose-tinted
lies' of memory. Rather that memory strips away all superfluous
detail, leaving us only the warm bare bones of truth. For another
world exists behind the physical world we see. But –

> In this world's long night of hiding
> Only what is felt is what's abiding.

The encounter with the hare – just as years before a real snake had
taught me fear – had left me with clearly illuminated feeling. And as
I grew older I remained aware of 'that other world', and still wanted
it. And though I loved this world, I found myself forever looking
everywhere for some intimation of that other. In fact, what I think I
wanted in my way was 'the best of both worlds' – as do most people.

CHAPTER TWO
A Look Further Back

Some of my earliest remembrances go back to the years we lived in a cul-de-sac called Buckland Avenue in Blackley, North Manchester. The Second World War was only just over, and much of my infant life was coloured by local prejudice and easily remembered phrases such as 'Black Market', 'blitz' and 'spiv'. 'Black Market', in my childish imagination, was a sort of shop run by spivs in the dead of night, 'Spiv' being the ultimate wartime insult in England – or so I thought having heard it so often being used in that sense by the adults of that period.

The district where we lived was known as 'the Hill', and fell into three distinct areas . At the bottom was a wide poorly-frequented road that wound past in the direction of Old Blackley, running parallel to the filthy, dye-choked River Irk. The recognizable part of, let's call it Area One, was that fish-infested and reed-bearded lake with small cul-de-sac known as 'the Avenue' built above its margins. Area Two consisted solely of 'the Crescent' which encircled No-Kids'-Land – a space of waste land oddly named 'the Croft'. The population of these two zones were solidly English middle-class, save for a sprinkling of Jewish families which had been forced out of Cheetham Hill by the Blitz. Area Three, at the top of the hill just where it levelled off in a plateau, was where the planners had sited an estate of neat-ugly war-time pre-fabs. Set well away from the dwellings of the bourgeoisie lower down the Hill, the Pre-fabs, nevertheless, came to dominate the district.

The Pre-fab Gang were refugee children who had been driven out of Ancoats and Collyhurst, Old Trafford, Levenshulme and other parts of Manchester courtesy of Hitler's slum clearance programme. Their leader was Craig who, at the ripe age of nine, had grown into a formidable little fighting machine. Because of his skill with fists and feet, and possessing a kind of bullying adventurousness in excess of the other children, he had been elevated to position of chief of the tribe and had become the terror not only of the Pre-fab Estate, but of the whole district as well.

The Gang came and went wherever they pleased and effectively ruled everywhere on the Hill. Their reign of terror continued for so long it seemed almost a normal dimension of life to the children on the Hill. But, as is the way, even in childhood rebellion eventually began to stir. A plot was afoot centred on a house in the Avenue and another just round the corner.

It was while we were living in the Avenue that I'd spent three years in and out of hospital with several serious illnesses. Despite my mother, with varying degress of success, trying to teach me good manners, politeness and other social graces, I was very strong-willed for an eight year old – due no doubt to being spoilt while ill. But despite not being physically strong, with a larger, more loutish pal called Ian, I first conceived the notion of organized rebellion against tyrant Craig.

That other children were capable of rebellion had been proven by a short skirmish in which Gabriel, a very un-angelic Jewish boy, had led the 'Goodies'. Regrettably, the Goodies had been both too few in number and woefully short on weapons.

In conjunction with Ian, I called on all the local children to ask them to gather among the nettles, the pits and potholes, the rusted prams and builders' materials, on the disused Croft on the following Saturday to do battle with Craig's gang.

However weapons constituted a real logistical problem. But Ian realised that Craig had no archers! Ian, one of life's practical children, made excellent bows and arrows, so we set to in his back garden, producing fifteen bows, only two of which snapped during trials. We also made a large quantity of arrows out of stripped slender branches. So, after meeting on the Friday evening to discuss tactics, we felt sufficiently confident to ascend the Hill the following morning carrying the official declaration of war in a sealed envelope. A technical difficulty arose because no one could properly read the 'joined-up writing' of Ian's older sister. But this was quickly resolved by me simply naming the time and place, 'Two o'clock this afternoon on the Croft!'

About forty kids, both boys and girls, finally turned up at the Croft. Führer Craig appeared with the kids from the Pre-fab Estate who streamed across the road to the Croft. In the guise of pirates, cowboys, American G.I.'s, red indians, etc., they came whooping and screaming with the delight of impending battle. When in the ensuing fight I spotted Craig, I insulted him as best I knew how, calling him a 'dirty spiv' before firing an arrow at him at point blank range.

To my surprise – and, I confess, to my guilty horror – the arrow stuck right in his arm drawing blood immediately. He let out a fearful yell and burst into tears before he sobbed out those immortal words of childhood: 'I'm gonna tell us Mam of you!' And Craig ran off down Windermere Road in the direction of his pre-fabricated home. Which meant we'd won. For a moment, I didn't give a hoot about what grown ups thought. We'd won!

Of course, I got into trouble over the battle; it wasn't just the fighting, though my mother objected to such natural boyish behaviour. At that time I wasn't supposed to indulge in hardly any physical exercise at all and it was explained to me yet again how I had to 'be careful'.

I'd just been through a period when I'd been almost continuously ill, and of which I still have the strongest and least pleasant memories; a period which has always led me to claim, truthfully, 'I started school aged five, and I left aged five!'

It was in those unhealthy years that, on at least one occasion, I visited death's open and gloomy door. I was twice incarcerated in the clinically murky, depressive prison of a hospital: a near orphanage world into which rheumatic fever with heart complications precipitated me out of a happy home, a condition of freedom. Nine months at a stretch seems to a child a whole consuming life-time. I was in a world of smelly bed-pans, hypodermic syringes, stethoscopes, temperature charts – o their sinister wavy red ink! – thermometers, bloody swabs, nice nurses and night nurses, horrid nurses, hospital porters who looked as unhealthy as any patient, remote white-coated doctors and formidable matrons ... all the clean and febrile atmosphere of hospital in fact. Then afterwards, the way I was severely coddled, bossed, forbidden games, nagged at to 'be careful' and subjected to prodding and poking medical examinations ...

People often ask me now, how far has the experience affected me in the long term? Why am I not a hypochondriac or a medical neurotic? I think, perhaps, the experience was so profound that its effects could be too deep for me to detect? Who knows? A few years ago I was asked how I managed to find time to write when I had a full-time job, a young family, was involved in editing at least four magazines and also trying to write novels. My glib reply was that by being so ill as a child and being confined to bed for long periods, I'd 'acquired a distaste for sleep'. So perhaps there has been a subsconscious reaction to that period of my life? I've also been told that I have a subconscious desire for freedom and doing everything I possibly can in the open air, and that this arises from my long stays in hospital at a formative period of my life? It's true that I do like being outside, but I can honestly say that being sent to an open air school certainly wasn't the cause!

After I'd been in hospital, I spent about a year in a recuperative school for delicate and, I dare say, backward children. A kind of asylum school that gave only rudimentary lessons and believed so much in the curative properties of fresh air that it was called, officially, 'The Open Air School'.

Each day for an hour the entire school was forced to lie down out of doors in a sort of open-ended hanger. We lay on camp beds, wrapped in thin grey blankets. Sometimes, snow flakes would tumble and drift across the concrete playground and reach the outermost beds of the huddled figures of pupils; and often in winter there would be a film of frost on the floor. It was a crazy set-up and perhaps Teutonic in origin. I think even the army did better in those days.

The sole happy recollection I have of that place of open windows, closed minds and windy verandas is that, in a moment of anger, I smashed the power of the school bully, and his spectacles as well!

But before my tenth birthday, less than a year after the Battle of the Croft, my family was on the point of leaving the Avenue and moving to a no less exciting place – the Road. It was a place which was to have a more wonderful and paradisial side to it altogether. It was to change me as no other place has ever done.

CHAPTER THREE
Humour is not Enough

My father had four distinct interests or passions in life. These were good literature, commerce (his job of work which he took very seriously), comedy, and the fight game. He began his boxing career in the ring via the old-fashioned fairground boxing booth. Then, later, he joined the Manchester YMCA boxing team. He often told me how he'd fought his first three fights 'in one evening at Jack Smith's boxing booth' for which he'd received, as victor in each bout, the paltry prize money of seven shillings and sixpence. But his proudest moment was when he won the North of England featherweight boxing title at the Free Trade Hall in Manchester. And once he was even billed to fight the British and Empire champion Nel Tarlton at the Liverpool Stadium, though this fight never took place because of the champion's illness.

Most of his fights he won on points. Only once did he ever speak of being defeated and that was against a Canadian cowboy though, of course, he may have lost others. A combination of fast footwork, a good left jab, and a fair punch in either hand plus, above all, a quick brain usually kept him out of trouble.

A man possessed of a great sense of humour, perhaps the most intellectual man to step into a boxing ring, but neither humour nor intellect could save him one evening at Liverpool Stadium.

'You're doin' nicely Harry! Come on, just keep that straight left goin' an' the Cowboy won't getcha!', his second had whispered urgently to him half way through the first round as his opponent had briefly backed him up into a corner. The crowd roared and his second's words kept drumming rhythmically in his head as he jabbed away: 'The Cowboy won't getcha ... the Cowboy won't ...' But 'Cowboy' Jackson was sure gonna try. And the Canadian just kept coming at Harry, his bullet head down like a charging animal's.

By the end of Round Two: 'I knew I was ahead on points,' he always insisted afterwards, '... but the Canadian was tough, very tough. Like a grizzly bear from the Rockies. And although my left jab had been going into his mug as regular as a piston, he was still unmarked. And not slowing down at all. So I knew if I was to win I'd just got to stay out of trouble – daren't have started mixing it with him.'

How often I heard him reminisce about that particular fight! It was his thirty-third bout. Yet the way he told it was still so fresh and vivid, though it must have taken place twenty to thirty years before I first heard the story. He told it so vividly that one saw the clouds of cigar smoke swagged beneath the arc lights, and the wealthy animal faces, animated and sweat-shined in the ringside seats – one could feel the excitement vibrating as he recounted the story of that fateful match.

'The Cowboy was an ugly customer, and he went for me right from the first bell. Right from the moment we touched gloves I had to back-peddle and just keep my left snaking out. It was exactly like the time Tunney fought Dempsey. You know Tunney used to practise running backwards for two miles each day? Well, I wish I had. I knew I'd got to stay well out of trouble with the Canadian if I was to have a cat in hell's chance of surviving. He was bigger and heavier and he punched a lot harder than me. So I kept moving about the ring and pushing out my left. I knew all I had to do was to keep cool and I'd stay ahead on points because I was a much better boxer. Just jab, jab, jab ... and the points would keep piling up until I won. But Cowboy Jackson was a wild one and no mistake. He kept coming forward, trying to rush me, get me off-guard and, well, I suppose I got tired of it in the end ...'

How calmly he used to tell that story! Yet there was always a note of regret in his voice, in his grey eyes beneath those curling eyebrows.

'Yes, I suppose I lost patience. Shouldn't have, mind you. A boxer should never lose his patience. It invariably proves fatal. Anyway, the big fellah came swinging in at me – brushing aside my left as if it was a feather. But then, just once, I saw an opening – saw he was off-guard. Immediately, I side-stepped and let go with a right-cross intended for his chin. But instead it caught him on the side of his head – full on the ear to be exact. A terrific punch which, had it found its proper target, would have put him down for the full count. Evidently the thought stung him badly for the next second, wham! Something hit me so fast I never knew where it came from. And that was that. The Cowboy won the fight, and I'd almost no recollection of the remainder of that evening. My thirty-third fight and I'd never been knocked out before. What's more, I didn't really start to come round till I was on the train home and it had reached Bolton ...'

My father might just have made the big time in boxing but for the fact that his employers did not approve of his engaging in such a rough sport. The directors of the firm of cotton manufacturers and merchants, where my father was employed by day, did not like to see black eyes and scarred eyebrows or bruised cheeks in their city office. It was not considered 'good for business'. In retrospect the firm's attitude towards this sport seems excessively narrow; especially as another member of that company was, at the time my father was boxing, the reigning world motor cycle champion – and that seems to me an infinitely more dangerous sport. But then, I suppose, the latter employee being the managing director's son may have had something to do with it.

Fighter though he was, my father never quite found the courage to give up his job and take up boxing full time. This was, in a way, understandable for, as father often said, in those post-First World War years 'one did not lightly throw up a good job ... on whatever suspicion of personal talent.' There was just too much unemployment about. So, instead, he continued for a while as a covert amateur under the pseudonym of 'Harry Clay', until, finally, he abandoned the fight game altogether. I think he always regretted he had not pursued it further. Instead, he settled for being a faithful servant of one commercial firm for over fifty years, yet without ever being really happy with his employment.

His deep and wide acquaintanceship with books made him exceptionally erudite – especially as he possessed a remarkable memory. Commerce provided his livelihood. And his strong sense of humour – he was a natural comedian – put him in great demand both socially and as a public entertainer at clubs, pubs and masonic lodges. Keen on physical fitness from a boy, he would 'work out' in the back yard of the terraced house where he was born. Of a winter's morning he'd use milk bottles as indian clubs and finish up his exercises by dousing himself with water that had been left out all night in the freezing air in a tub. He was also an intellectual, steeped in the works of Nietzsche, Sir Thomas Browne, Carlyle and Montaigne. Yet he was never a prig or your customary effete intellectual but a free thinker and an open-hearted extrovert easy with all who met him. And as a man who only had the occasional beer, he would most decidedly have appreciated the anecdote retailed about him by my friend John in later years who said, 'My mother used to think your father drank a lot. For she reckoned that no one could be always so cheerful and not be a boozer.'

My father, too, was a great retailer of jokes and quips. Some I recall like the one about the 'octogenarian who married a girl of seventeen ... old men will try anything for rheumatism!' Others went for ever with the death of my father, being only kept alive in his memory.

Conversely, though, my father could write bitterly and more profoundly in his notebooks: 'Those who believe in the fantasies of Truth and Justice and try to live up to their ideals find the road of life tough going – a bitter struggle for existence with little peace, hope or contentment'; and similarly: 'No one can tell why we are here, from whence we come, or much less where we are going. Even those on whom Nature or blind Chance have bestowed their most splendid gifts must, in the end, die and leave but a short memory behind – just a legacy on the wind'.

As a young man my father had little time for social activities, being tied up with training for five nights a week and reading his beloved books in the rest of his spare time. But around 1924 he met the woman who would eventually be my mother. By all accounts Catherine Steele was a very attractive young woman with a profusion of red hair and an inclination towards the fashionable in dress. She had been a classical pianist and dancer but was, by the time she encountered father, reduced to earning her living as a secretary with another Manchester cotton firm. Again it was a question of talent sacrificed through financial necessity.

One day mother delivered a letter to my father's office in Cannon Street, Manchester, and there she met him. On her own confession she found him at that first encounter a 'somewhat conceited and off-hand young man' and she was not at all attracted to him. But, a few days later, she was having a cup of coffee by herself in the old Lyons' restaurant in Market Street when my father went in. After pushing his trilby back on his forehead in the way he – and Jimmy Cagney – always did, he surveyed the tables. And, seeing mother, he decided to join her. Apparently she found him less off-putting at this, their second meeting, and as a result their relationship began.

My mother came from Hale in Cheshire and her father was employed by the banking firm of E.D. Sassoon & Co. as manager of their Persian and Arabic departments. Her mother came of Irish farming stock, never worked, and was a lifelong sufferer from asthma. By all accounts this lady was the cause of her husband's – my grandfather's – huge drink problem. Though as a child I was always given to understand that it was owing to the 'bad company' he was inclined to keep. But marriage to a hypochondriac Catholic cannot have been much fun.

As a child, mother was used to servants and carriages and strange monied relatives. But the family had come rapidly down in the world partly through the outside assistance of bookmakers and partly through the inside help of booze. Whilst there was still money available, however, my mother had studied the piano under the internationally renowned music teacher Edward Isaacs, and had even given solo performances attended by such well-known figures in the music world of those days as Neville Cardus, Sammy Langford and William Archer, the music critic of *The Times*. She had also received tuition at the Madge Atkinson Dancing School in Manchester in Greek choral dancing and ballet. This odd institution had connections with the London theatre world and people like Forbes-Robertson. But by the time she met my father she was in other employment as the secretary of a somewhat eccentric cotton merchant and race-horse owner. And though by her own account she was more than happy to work in an office, one sensed that she regretted not having gone on to become a concert pianist 'like Eileen Joyce'.

In marked social contrast to the natal ambience of mother, my father had grown up in the dull environs of a mean little street of houses in Old Blackley, patriotically named 'Nelson Terrace'. It was an area known locally as 'The Hollow' and was dominated by the awful presence of a huge and smelly chemical works. A dismal world of cobbled streets, smoke-smeared skies, gas streetlamps and scrap metal yards.

But for all its pessimistic skyline, its Victorian schools and harsh-faced preachers at the local church, it had not altogether depressed my father's natural ebullience. He was too many-sided and resilient to ever be entirely overborne by any single strand of experience. A bit like myself in this. Though he would certainly have been happier – as his letters to me in old age testify – to have matured in less gloomy surroundings. Indeed, one feels that if only he had had a little more luck and encouragement he might well have gone on to achieve important things, not only in boxing, but perhaps in literature as well. As it was, however, even academic achievement had been denied him at an early stage. For, despite the fact that he was always late for school because he helped with a milk delivery round in order to earn money for his mother, he still managed to get a scholarship to that brainiest of English schools – Manchester Grammar School. Incredible as it may now seem, he had been denied that opportunity. He was not allowed to take up the scholarship because the headmaster of St Alfred's Primary School was able to persuade his parents (and maybe they did not need much persuading?) that it would not do a boy from his background much good going to grammar school and they should accept instead the prize-in-lieu of forty pounds. A prize, no doubt, aimed at dissuading poor parents from sending their kids to 'mix with their betters', for forty pounds was a considerable sum in 1911.

Paradoxically though – for my father never forgave his parents nor the school for the decision – it acted as a spur to his intellectual growth. Though he never attended university or other such training establishment, he avoided the customary development into the well-schooled philistine and became genuinely learned in many fields. Even so, he never received the least opportunity to put to use his vast natural scholarship or his not inconsiderable skill with words – except that he always wrote his own scripts for his various roles ('turns' as he called them) as stage comedian, compère, monologuist or after-dinner speaker. Nor did he ever have the opportunity to enjoy the company of other learned men or intellectuals, but had to content himself with the crass levels of society in which he was forced to dwell.

Though my mother was no intellectual, there was clearly a bond inherent in their relationship – a small pact of despair – bred of equally unsuccessful struggles to develop their very different talents. Beyond this, of course, only Venus may presume to guess at their mutual attraction. But, as all children sometimes must, I have often speculated on the matter. Above all I have wondered if my mother or, indeed, any of the people who knew my father as a wit and comedian, ever really appreciated the truth that lay behind the laughter and the *bonhomie*? Ever understood the true message which emerged with disturbing clarity time and again in his personal letters and talks with me (a late flowering of his final years), and in the chance remarks thrown out for others' benefit? Namely, that as a human being and a parent one needs to contribute something more to life than facetious indifference. To give some touch of personal vision, to help foster it in others, and above all to make some effort, however small it may be, to uncover through oneself the true meaning of this life: which life, for better or for worse, we all share. To realize that humour is not enough.

CHAPTER FOUR
The Road that was Paradise

An immemorially-shadowed, unpaved road that ran through the hearts of all who knew it, 'the Road', was really a lost lane. In days gone by when a peasantry had lived the land, it would have been a winding cart track with pools of sunlight lying in its ruts and hedges on either side, a path along which an agrarian people had come and gone with that essential regularity of old humanity. But from the time of the Industrial Revolution it was doomed, sooner or later, to change. From being a cart track, and then a lane, it would finally become a minor road with houses to replace the grey Lancashire cottages and farmhouses. The Road curved down to a hollow filled with a nest of defiant trees from whose umbrageous canopy were thrust up roofs of large late-Victorian houses. From this point in time memory sees the Road still plunging curvedly down into the obscurity of this fertile spot, overgrown and dominated by dictatorial trees. And a cold wind bites the eyes as I think of that last generation which enjoyed the undisturbed years of the Road.

Still cut off from suburban North Manchester and separated from the neighbouring mill towns, a curious little community thrived there in blessed isolation; a three-fold class community that occupied different kinds of dwellings. First, were the farmers who lived in decaying farmhouses with tumbledown barns and muck-spread cobbled yards. Then there was the so-called working-class who occupied either the six new and incredibly small semi's beside the duck pond, or the small terrace of houses round the back of Dunnocks' orchard – down the Loop Lane. Lastly, and most significantly, were the supposedly better off middle-class citizens who lived in the fading graciousness of the imposing tree-imprisoned houses. High houses with small haughty occupants.

A wide black-cindered road, then, beneath a great green roof of trees: it was a place of shadows and contrasts. Contrasts between the tall pointed-roofed houses with sagging eves and elaborate doors – some like ours with a glass vestibule of cathedral-like proportions that had stained-glass windows and exotic flowers on shelves and a potted palm tree to greet milkman and postman – and the diminutive semi's with their red brickwork and garish paintwork, dwellings as tasteless as their occupants were thought to be by the rest of the Road.

Again, there was contrast in the gardens. The big houses had elaborate acreages of orchards and kitchen gardens, and wide smooth lawns on which croquet – that game of Empire – was still played. Whilst the smaller dwellings had hardly any gardens at all; and what there were, when not eaten up by ramshackle hen-runs, were usually ill-kempt.

In some ways least typical of the locals, the Dunnocks were also the most typical residents of the Road, especially in their contribution to the snobbery fund. They were a couple who had retired from some far part of the Empire, accustomed to servants and drinks on the veranda in the musical twilight. Mrs Dunnock, older than her husband, bore some resemblance to Queen Victoria, while her husband, it was rumoured, fancied any nice- looking young woman and, equally, he fancied she fancied him. They had two eccentricities. Mrs Dunnock was for ever riding about the district on a silly little sit-up-and-beg motor scooter, carrying a corgi dog in a basket on the handlebars. The other peculiarity in their lives was their adopted son Nigel.

Nigel was one of my closest friends, because his house was across the Road from ours. What distinguished him from the other children was his treachery. Every game or adventure would end in some sort of betrayal on his part, even when circumstances were in his favour as, for example, at his birthday party. Somehow, we managed to survive the dangerously provocative rigours of several party games without major incident. Then, wisely, Mrs Dunnock seated us at a big table where we piled into the birthday tea. We had barely got through the sandwiches before Nigel said to John: 'Would you like some jelly?' The very politeness of Nigel's manner should have put John on 'red alert'. As he replied eagerly, 'Jelly, goody!', Nigel picked up the red wobbly jelly and toppled the whole thing onto John's lap, from whence it slid with a horrid plop onto the wooden floor. Screams and yells and demented laughter brought Nigel's mother scurrying into the room. But Nigel blandly informed his mother that John had 'tried to pinch all the jelly for hisself!' At this some of us began to protest, but Mrs Dunnock never believed anything bad about Nigel, and it was poor John who received the telling off. I persisted in taunting Nigel over the matter of the jelly and eventually he threw a bun at me. I leapt away from the table and rushed across the room to retrieve the missile intending to return the messy compliment. But as

I did so John yelled, 'Look out!', and in the nick of time I ducked to avoid a knife thrown at me by Nigel which sailed over my head harmlessly but smashed the window into the garden. Sensibly, if somewhat unjustly, Mrs Dunnock severely admonished all present, then terminated the party abruptly by packing everyone off home.

We used to play out a lot in the evenings those days. There were golden summer evenings in abundance, as there always are for those who spend a good deal of time outdoors. Golden summer evenings, the sun silently sawing away at the edge of the hills or, like a huge apple, glowing in the orchard of sky. Twilight coming, in covetous streaks of green and brown and yellow through tall trees, sneakily anointing huge stone gateposts, porous walls, the twisted boughs of the trees. The sun also making last flashes of tremendousness on big-faced windows before the final dark: an unrolling velvet of another universe imbued with secret scents.

And among all this real, true and imagination-splendid world, the cries of kids playing 'hide an' seek', 'cowies an' indians', and other games involving wild chases through long deep shadows. From six until as late as ten in the evening it would go on uninterrupted: till, one by one, the children were called in from their ditty-loud and dirty-faced pursuits – their happiness. The Carters and the Emersons were the last to be hollered home, for they were the children of the 'working classes'. How I envied them! And how I heard, and deliberately unheard, that their parents were 'irresponsible' or 'did not care'. How could they not care, giving their offspring such delicious extra minutes of freedom?

Very different from the Dunnocks, and light years away from all the other adults in his eccentricities, was Farmer Johnny. Where the Dunnocks thought of children – except for dear Nigel – very much as they must have thought of their servants back east, as creatures to be indulged but gently and firmly kept in their place, Farmer Johnny had no time for kids at all.

A tough-looking crow of a man, Farmer Johnny sported a greasy flat cap, a crumpled collarless shirt, a filthy unbuttoned waistcoat, a jacket with the shoulder padding coming out, and torn trousers tucked in manured gum boots. He owned a few acres of useless green hillside that sloped down to the unsavoury River Irk; and he dwelt in what passed for a farmhouse with dirty curtains over half-boarded up windows. A great permanently shut gate blocked the entrance to the farmyard. No child ever penetrated there because Farmer Johnny hated kids like vermin, and he kept a horrid black dog to advertise his displeasure. Let any child so much as set foot on his land, and Farmer Johnny would be heard running over the hills towards the intruder. I say 'heard running' because the most famous aspect of his character was his voluble swearing. It was like the language of a trooper born of a harlot. The air would go blue around his wild head as he steamed up his sloping fields at a great rate, or stood by his broken down fencing swiping about with stick and tongue. Parents never tired of warning their children to avoid Farmer Johnny. Yet despite their efforts, this gruff and totally anti-social man was one of the most fascinating figures of the Road.

Of altogether more gentle disposition was Farmer Martin who owned the farm at the other end of the Road, just past the giant pylon with its red lettered notice that read: DANGER: 124,000 volts. Farmer Martin, a handsome but innocuous man seldom intruded into our lives in person. Though I associate his farm with a number of still intrusive memories, like the occasion I went to see the milking of his cows or to help with haymaking.

An ordinary enough experience milking cows, basic and smelly, almost like a birth, except that it once became unusually vivid for me when the farm boy dipped a sort of circular disc of blue glass into a milk churn and showed it to me and my friend Gordon. A thin film of milk was spread over its surface and, miraculously illuminated, Gordon and I saw – ugh! – thousands of microbes crawling on the glass. As we gasped, the farm lad leered, 'Them's worrus drinks wi us milk!' Strange as it may seem, though, my liking for milk or cream was not noticeably diminished.

Through the agency of my pal Gordon Carter, whose little house with its large hen run and black duck pond was slap next to Farmer Martin's land, I went to haymaking the first summer we lived there. I was conscious of a dripping sun that seemed to fill all the sky, and of sweating men in waistcoats and rolled up sleeves working with pitch forks loading a couple of ancient horse-drawn carts with freshly mown hay. I helped by carrying great armfuls of the stuff, whilst at the same time wheezing asthmatically from the clouds of pollen. The prick of the yellow stalks on sunburnt arms, the flittering of butterflies and insects, and the scuttling away of mice – all come back still! I remember, too, wrestling with freckled Gordon whose hair was like a miniature cottage thatch, and recall the resultant short quarrel betwixt us that was to be the forerunner of many ultimately friendly bouts.

Farmer Martin had finally to separate us and threaten to send us packing.

Equally vivid are the two cart horses, maybe shires, with their nicotine-brown fetlocks and jingling bridles and fascinating blinkers, that drew the creaking carts. But most of all there returns the sense of fun and joy which the combination of hay, pollen and haze of hot light produced in Gordon and me. Somehow, instinctively, I was conscious of the best of this world, and of how its beauty and joy feeds our human sense of a better world – a world identical to our own but perfected. Like at my encounter with the hare, this day of infancy among the mellow-sweet scented hay beneath an awesome sun, seemed to awaken in me intenser knowledge still of perfection. It was a landscape humming with a feeling that was of a decidedly spiritual sort. The world showed a perfect face and I loved it ... and was to keep on loving it.

Even so, there was another equally real side to this rural life. A raw and violent face that appeared when, for example, a mouse was speared deliberately by the pitchfork of a brutal farmhand. Or when, on another day, a stray dog invaded those same fields. The creature turned up first at the duck pond where Gordon and I were messing about. The dog didn't give us any trouble to start with. But when it suddenly charged round the pond and scattered the hens, ducks and geese that belonged to Gordon's dad, we had to drive it off with stones and shouts. Next thing, we saw the dog going for Farmer Martin's cows in the nearby field. This was better fun for us, watching the poor black and white cows running about in terror, their great udders swinging like bald bagpipes, and now and then stopping abruptly to try and butt the mongrel. For Gordon and I had no responsibility for the cattle. Unlike Gordon's dad's poultry the cows were not 'ours'. Out of the corner of our eye we saw Farmer Martin appear at the distant white gate of his farmyard. He began shouting at the cur, but it was to no avail. The dog ignored him and continued with its persecution of the cows. So after a few minutes of arm-waving and bawling the mild-mannered farmer appeared to give up and retire to the farmhouse.

We had just begun to tire of watching the dog's senseless game – after all, a dog couldn't eat a cow, could it? – when Farmer Martin re-appeared carrying what, at that distance, looked like a large stick or even a club. It was too far away for us to think of it as anything else. Suddenly, however, there was a bang – a single loud noise. And we saw the dog lie down abruptly.

Slowly the significance of what we were watching was borne in on us. Wonderful! Amazing! Gordon turned to me and said in excited reverence: 'He ... he's goned an' shottit! That's ... that's a real live gun!' Almost immediately we jackassed it off across the open green fields in the direction of the dog, and in a state of breathless excitement we arrived at the fatal spot just in time to see Farmer Martin giving the cur a hefty kick to make sure it was dead. To our combined delight and horror we saw blood: the farmer really had shot the black and white dog. 'Killed it dead!' as we tautologically repeated for hours afterwards. And we would have feasted our eyes on the sight for an eternity, but for the fact that Farmer Martin told us with unaccustomed brusqueness to clear off. So we reeled away from the scene dreamily stunned by the wonderful reality of it all. Going straight home first to relate the event to our respective sets of parents, and then to as many of our friends as we could find. For, then, death was just about the most wonderful thing in life.

The only other animal I had seen killed before that day was a hen by Gordon's poultry-loving dad. Gordon's dad was the local coalman: he drove a lorry delivering great sacks of coal to people's houses and had a perpetually black face grimed with coal dust. He wore the customary waistcoat, collarless shirt, muffler and flat cap. He had a messy garden full of hens, geese and ducks, as well as several pigeon cotes on wooden stilts. The pigeons cooed all day and the hens laid wonderfully smooth white or brown eggs which had lime and bits of straw sticking to them.

One day Gordon and I watched his dad strangle a hen, stretch its neck by standing on its head with his hobnailed boot and pulling it till it was like an ostrich's. After which torture, O wonders, the hen still managed to get up and run round despite the fact that Gordon's dad had lopped off its head with an axe. As usual, I was both delighted and horrified at the same time; and I related it with gory relish to my parents at meal time – the traditional hour which kids unfailingly choose to mention horrors to their parents. But I found it easier to accept that event than when my friend Ian from the Avenue had boiled a frog alive in an old kettle. That act put me off cruelty for life.

Owing to the geographically enclosed nature of the Road – that area which my mother so aptly termed 'a children's paradise' – it had, as I have said, something of the aura of village life about it. Indeed, the Road and its subsidiary, the Loop Lane, seemed more clearly defined, more possessed of a spiritual identity than other roads

I have lived in either before or since. It had a 'dream quality' even my pragmatic friend John Wilson has since confessed.

Three things about the Road stand out. Its people. Its snobbish social hierarchy. And its seasons. I have since come to appreciate that, especially with the advent of the motor car, people have, for the most part, lost touch with the seasons and are growing progressively out of harmony with Nature.

But the seasons. First then: its summer face. The Road in the hillside hollow always wore a maternal shading. Its surface was cracked, wrinkled, ash-filled – but the friendly trees made it maternal. A dust bowl. A warmth. Its crumbling garden walls along one side were draped with catmint that had a following of bees and butterflies; and there were crazy, pointless-seeming fences where flowers tumbled. The muscular boughs of the trees were bowed with the weight of leafload and possessed of a silent wrapping of humid heat. In summer.

In summer, too: ash, benign oak, warm chestnut, elm and sweet female silver birch – all seemingly supporting the somewhere sky. A sky of blue fragments with snatches of tree-sniffed clouds like trailing beards under the sun. (It's all true this description.) And all round the flaking houses, the green fields drying and steaming in the hot sun. With dragonflies zooming the Duck Pond and the slimegreen pool by 'The Willows'; midges in the soporific twilight; and other, flower-searching insects forever threading and re-threading the wide days of light. Summer.

But when winter gripped the Road ...brrr! Winter penetrated, permeated, drenched that symbolic way. Entered its every crack and crevice. The first rains turned all to mud, to wet trash, to a black porridge of grit-stone-cinder. Made it an unofficial river with many snotty little tributaries. It was finally a scribble of crude streams and a tangle of awkward puddles. The weather: over all a drizzle as fine as wet net curtains; or a heavier mesh of cold rain like an icy breathlessness. Then storms: big tracer bullets of wet racing across the fields, blasting roofs and leaves – the drops 'big as half-crowns' my mother used to say. And sometimes a sleet that pelted the winter road and its surrounding slopes till everywhere was sunk in that cold monotonous Lancashire damp.

Winter. Finally, the snow would come. An iced winter world. So cold the wind on the hill by Martin's Farm. Wind fingering through the thickest of clothes to get at the chest and legs. And John and I stumbling home from school down the whitely invisibled Road, through the dark and the drifts – no lights save the star-ringed moon, though but half four in the afternoon: the winterdeep premature evening. Me with new shoes on ... oh fatal error! I falling continuously as my friend walks on. Snow so deep and smooth and frozenbananaskinhard that I fall an unbelievable number of times, the great stark branches above coldly gleeful at my plight. I slip. I slide. I fall. On back. On side. On face. Yet we are still choked with laughter. Damn, blast, bugger ... I lie there laughing, paralysed by laughter in all that beautiful snow, in that inexplicable joy of winter. Aware once more of that other world ...

The copper knight of Autumn clanking by on a yellow charger, his lance of purple couched to the coming Winter; or Springs of brightening elderberries and the flowery glow of universal loving, that Road which was Paradise knew these seasons, and instilled a part of every season into the souls of us, the Children of the Road.

*   *   *   *   *

In the Road, as though by some predetermined accident, there sprang up a sudden generation of children like those mythic warriors sown from a king's teeth. The Children of the Road were all in some measure children of the Earth. There was pragmatic John, his downtrodden younger brother Bernard, and his happier sister Cecilia; there was the awful Nigel; and Hayden the beautiful boy who also had a pretty little sister whose name I have forgotten. There was my plumpish, fair-haired sister Jean; and another freckled and more attractive Jean. Tough little Gordon, the coalman's son; and two attractive and full-of-life sisters Joan and Anne, both flirts. There was another Joan, too, who died and whose memory is forever associated by me with lilies and a goldfish pond. There were the Matthews' girls, Barbara and her littler nameless sister. Then from down the Loop Lane came my pal Trevor – unwanted by his real parents, dwelling with his old aunt. And, of course, next door to Trevor lived that fearsome brood of roughnecks, the Emersons, who moved in and out of the dilapidated backyards at the rear of the terraced cottages all day long – a family composed of several sons plus their remarkable sisters: one tall as a small tree and nicknamed 'Bony' and her younger sister known far and near as 'Daft Audrey'. Whilst from the first house in the Road, from The Willows, with its hidden orchard and greenslime willow pond, there was Caroline.

Caroline, aged ten and acknowledged First Lady of the Road, a beautiful little minx with long coils of golden hair, deep blue eyes and plenty of self-possession. She it was who showed any new children round the Road, and if she approved of them they might even be permitted to call at The Willows occasionally. Caroline's mother had taught at the infants' school which, years before, I had briefly attended prior to my long educational lay-off due to bouts of hospitalization. I could only have been five when Caroline's mother brought her to school to be perched on a front desk and 'shown off' to impress on us rough little brats what a nice, decently turned out and properly behaved child should look like. And, indeed, I had been duly impressed – so much so that when my sister repeated: '*she* lives here, in this road!' I had felt my ten-year-old heart bound. To my lasting shame as an individualist, I remember feeling honoured by the news: that the daughter of a local dignitary was coming to call on *my* sister!

I recall still the moment I caught sight of Caroline in our wide Victorian hallway with its long ruddy carpet. We were introduced; but I was tongue-tied before that vision of golden ringlets, a redlipped bow of a mouth and the neat figure in white swagger coat. Yet, even then, I was not altogether blinded by the little lady. Though spellbound, I recall resenting immediately a certain coldness in her. When she and my sister departed together, I was left with a clutch of inarticulate thoughts. I was determined to resist the dominance of Lady Caroline, as I inwardly called her. My mother, whose social sense made her a poor woman's Jane Austin, wrote off that first encounter with Caroline in down-to earth cynicism: 'She only came to see what the house was like inside. To see if we had money!' And I suppose she was right. For it was, as things turned out, the sole time Caroline ever set foot in Penrhyn, as our house was named. But occasionally Caroline would abandon the seclusion of secret gardens and the company of select friends, and decide to bestow her presence on the common ruck of kids.

The Dingle was a deep valley in the form of a Y-shaped fissure caused by the confluence of two streams whose waters cut through a hillside and ran swiftly away to pour eventually into the horrid River Irk ('the Styx', as John and I named it). It was situated at the far side of a level plateau of waste land, just behind Penrhyn. This tree-lined glen was the heart and paradisial abyss into which much of my childhood joy was gladly poured. Its dual streams ran and sang through sandy clefts, meeting at a point where the central island of land formation ended in a biscuit-coloured cliff of downward sloping sand. This spot, so many miles from any sea, made a marvellous substitute beach. Trees grew at crazy angles overhanging the clear bed of the stream; bluebells and daffodils were there among ferns and creepers; and the steep embankments were covered with tough moorland grasses. It was a beautiful spot, made more beautiful still by the fact that no adult was ever known to visit it.

We all trooped behind Lady Caroline, our self-appointed leader, down to the spot where the two streams noisily met. The rougher elements among the children like John, Nigel, Gordon, Bernard, Derek Emerson and myself, and others too, raced and tumbled madly down the slopes like self-propelling infantile Dervishes. With Bony Emerson resembling a broomstick in a dress flapping and striding forward with her sister, Daft Audrey, the latter's mouth perpetually open 'catching flies', hobbling awkwardly behind. And many another child made up the seething mass and mess of mucky infancy there – all wild, wild, wild ... yet temporarily prepared to submit to the orders of Caroline. We were an army of kids, little workers carrying stones, wood, branches, junk, flotsam and small logs – using shovels, trowels or just small bare hands to shift heaps of sand. Children all now busily building the great dam.

Hear the gurgle of protesting waters: waters not used to being civilised. See the occasional shaft of solid sunlight or the ominous shadow of a great cloud darkening all the gully. Above all note Lady Caroline: legs akimbo, arms folded, directing with clear sharp childish words the whole operation. Even I, rebel, conformed. Periodically, as the dam rose steadily higher, some young child would wander thoughtlessly away from the metaphorical chain gang. Immediately, he or she would be admonished by Caroline and ordered back to work. Similarly, I recall Gordon and I accidentally getting in each other's way. Of course neither of us saw it as 'accidental', and in seconds the proverbial knives were out. We rolled over and over in the sand and mud screaming, suffering pain but aware of our audience and secretly pleased we were the centre of attention and much of it female. But she scolded us in no uncertain terms. 'Stop it!' The amazing thing is we did stop it. And there we stood ... feeling ashamed! Stood with our heads hung low listening to the words of a schoolm'am mother coming out of a schoolm'am's daughter's mouth.

Though other dams were to be constructed in the future at that selfsame spot, none ever equalled the one built that day. Every child who took part would confirm that. And no one doubted it was really due to the vision and organisational skill of Lady Caroline. Not only was it an event typical of the life of the Road. It was something more – a sort of simulacrum of adult life. And W.H. Auden expressed it aptly and perhaps prophetically:

> Clocks shoo the childhood from its face,
> And accurate machines begin
> And concentrate its adults in
> A narrow day to exercise
> Their gifts in some cramped enterprise.

But 'cramped enterprise' or not, we children derived enormous pleasure from building that dam.

And I something more too. For the first time I became aware of the presence of unattainable woman. I was drawn, instinctively, to her presence; I loved her beauty – the looks that I and others saw she possessed – yet, at the same time, I loathed the subjection that this fascination seemed to impose upon me. Of course, with a poet's hindsight, I now see Caroline as the first occasion on which the Muse manifested Herself to me. But I was no poet then and had no way of understanding the fact. I merely suffered the agonies of conflict in a world charmed by infancy, and yet one growing more beautiful and more ugly by the hour.

*   *   *   *   *

The great wall of flame seemed to climb higher each second as it swept towards the raised gardens of the houses. It was an alarming spectacle that Old Grimshaw saw from the end of his garden as he watched the black coils of smoke stain the sky. He knew somewhere a child was peering delightedly at this awesome spectacle of fiery destruction – a child whom he could probably name.

Even more sure of his suspicions was my father as he scrambled up the embankment. He knew for certain John and I were the arsonists. Out of breath and with soot smudging his forehead, he shouldered his way through the rhododendrons into the Wilsons' garden, crossed the lawn and yanked open the summer house door. 'Out!' he barked – and John and I crawled into the sunlight. As we emerged we could hear the roaring of the fire. This time, even we felt we'd probably overdone things. If the roaring and the thrumming were anything to go by, it sounded a more devastating affair than when we'd accidently burned the pig farm to the ground – the illegal piggery built by the Emersons.

With a false calmness and not much humour in his eyes for once, my father surveyed us. Then, giving a sigh, he pulled out his pipe. 'Either of you two got a match?'

I remember quite clearly thinking that I couldn't believe my ears as my father stood there, a pall of smoke drifting over the bushes behind him, and asking nonchelantly for a match.

'No,' we both replied, hoping he wouldn't search the summer house.

'Alright. Did you two start this?'

'No!' we shouted, both of us lying through our teeth.

'Don't give me that!' he retorted then, trying unsuccessfully to appeal to our better natures, he added, 'You do know, don't you, that you've nearly given old Grimshaw a heart attack? The old cock's frightened out of his wits, and his dogs are going barmy.' We stared sheepishly at an interesting patch of lawn in front of our dirty plimsoles.

Without any further words of warning except 'Just watch out!', my father turned on his heels and disappeared back through the bushes. Moments later, John and I saw him talking to Old Gimshaw who was looking very agitated by the fire.

'Dunno what they're all worryin' about – the fires never get nowhere near their precious gardens!' spat out John in gleeful disgust, speaking from the knowledgeable position of expert fire-raiser. I agreed with him. We'd done this many times before and knew that the ribbon path and the high banks below the gardens always proved an effective barrier ...

But it was at cricket that my father's presence was most felt. The game itself became a ritual in that paradise. Shortly after moving to the Road he and I had begun to play in earnest: always on the plateau of waste land beyond our garden overlooking the deep Dingle. Though unsuitable for cricket, sheer enthusiasm had worn a tolerable pitch across the area's brutal surface. Although we diligently cleared away stones and junk and rubbish, nothing could be done about the shrubbery nor the hazardous little hillocks which made the game so risky.

Our 'team' consisted of most of the boys, and some girls, in the

Road plus, always, my father. In his old red cardigan with its broken zip, his gardening trousers and Home Guard boots, he doubled as bowler and umpire. Hour after hour, through spring, summer and autumn that patient and cheerful man – by then well into his fifties – would bowl over after over to us selfish batsmen. A great believer in fair play, my father sought to impress on us the need to 'give the other fellow the benefit of the doubt'. On and on we would play, day after day, in the school holidays and most weekends. The sun would boil down over the trees, the fields and hills around would shimmer in greening heat; a breeze would fan and tan our faces; and father would always be there. Mother, too, would make ice lollies in our first fridge and hand them across the jagged fence to the members of England's infant team.

My dad would be forever urging us to 'keep your eye on the ball!' and 'play a straight bat!' But keeping one's eye on the ball in those circumstances meant several things: for a start with the lumps in that home-made pitch, to take one's eye off the ball could be fatal. One also needed to watch exactly where the ball went. A scrubland of semi-jungle surrounded our little Oval; and many hours were spent looking for lost cricket balls.

Oddly, this task imposed as a by-product of the game became a pleasure for me. I would often wander about in the undergrowth with its wet sharp-edged grass brushing my ankles, hosts of tiny frogs forever leaping out of the way. Well into the evening and after the game was over I could be found there searching, just searching for the pleasure of it. Sometimes, I would be there before breakfast, with the cool morning air and awakening sun blending with my movements. Always I was looking for a red ball. It was in those deeper searching reveries that it seemed as if I was lost and seeking for more than some mislaid cricket ball. It was as though I was, at such times, learning to think; or somehow remembering that all I really was in essence was a thinking being, a unique spirit.

*   *   *   *   *

The life of the Road reached its zenith in the Coronation Year of 1953. That summer was to be one of long warm days and delicious twilights. Everything was forgotten in the news of the forthcoming Coronation of Princess Elizabeth. Also it was known, or I should say rumoured, that preparations were under way to celebrate the great event in our own little world.

This meant, firstly, that the annual garden party which the Smiths – as the leading family of the Road's establishment – always gave for us children, would be the best ever that year. Those garden parties meant so much to us. There were always long tables stacked with rich food and drink; croquet on the lawns; party games and sports; fancy dress, laughter, tears, quarrelling, running in and out of tents on gracious lawns, and joy and misbehaviour in abundance. Such excitement! Such colour added to life ... oodles of it! Super! Terrific! Great!

I remember Coronation Day somewhat inaccurately as an immaculate summer's day. The Road itself wore an especially festive air and was closed to all visitors. An unnecessary precaution really for few people ever ventured that way. The residents went from house to house visiting in friendly fashion. Significantly it was those houses possessing a T.V. set, two in number if my memory is correct, that received the most visitors: the whole Coronation ceremony being transmitted live throughout the day. It all made for a sudden eruption of village-style life. Never before in the Road had so many of its worthies been seen fraternizing in public all at once.

The smartly attired Mr Fielding, a schools' inspector and Caroline's daddy, strolled benignly about chatting to everyone and giving the 'inferior' members of the community the rare benefit of his presence. By contrast there was Old Man Carter, Gordon's dad, dressed in his best bib-and-tucker and sporting a new spotted red necktie and red braces. He wandered to and from nowhere in particular, trying to appear to be on familiar terms with everyone, especially what my mother called 'the upper crust' of that little society, and straining his larynx – already half-throttled by the spotted necktie – to avoid speaking as though his mouth was full of its usual coaldust.

For some reason Mr Dunnock began the day by ostentatiously mowing his sunken front lawn. A performance that lasted for most of the morning (it was a very big lawn). Red-faced Mr Matthews made a point, too, of standing outside his front door in his morose fashion. Even normally there wasn't much room in the Matthews' tiny semi', especially when Mrs Matthews was inside for she was beyond all question the largest woman in the Road: a rolling and titanic heap of flesh. But there was even less room that day for, though not himself one of the 'upper ten' of the Road, Mr Matthews' house had become very important. It possessed one of the only TV sets – especially hired for the day. So it was for him a day of personal glory, if a somewhat uncomfortable one.

Then there was Mr Fentem whose pretty and naively friendly daughters were very popular with everyone. Fentem was a mouse of a man who had graduated from the job of making cardboard boxes in a factory to that of schoolteacher, second grade. As a result, he was of more social consequence than the rest of his immediate neighbours who dwelt in the six diminutive semi's that some phantom builder had shoved up in the Road one pre-war night. This sense of having 'made it' may also have something to do with why Mr Fentem wore a trilby whatever the weather.

Around, too, would have been Mr Martin (not Farmer Martin who, like Farmer Johnny, never appeared in our society). Martin was an elegant Welshman who sported a very English blazer and corduroys that always had knifelike creases. Though small, Martin was a dashing figure. Always short of cash, the Martins were good-livers who smoked and drank a lot and took great care of their personal appearances. They always had about them an after-the-party ethos, a sort of good-natured hangover. Yet for all his good looks and slender figure Martin never looked healthy even to me, a child: I thought him debauched, without quite knowing what the word meant. Though apart from my father, Mr Martin was the only grown up who really had any time for kids, and would even, now and again, play cricket with us.

That day one even saw Old Grimshaw, with whom I used to play chess. He was the most ancient personage in the Road, except for his wife who may have been older still. 'Grimmy' had clicking false teeth and his wife's manner was as prickly as a thornbush. Similarly, Old Man Emerson – who seemed nearly as ancient as Grimmy – abandoned his hen runs, pig sties and allotments, and became uncharacteristically gregarious just for the day.

As for my father, I can't actually recall how things were with him. Such occasions sometimes made him unreasonable and unsociable; he went a different way to the crowd. Normally a friendly and gregarious man of much vitality and physical strength, my father was in many ways the Road's greatest extrovert and certainly the one adult thoroughly liked by all the children. But that day, everyone having become convivial, I suspect he was hidden away behind our house, down past the great holly bush digging furiously at the hard clayey soil with his biceps heaving bellicosely and getting something deep and inexplicable out of his system. Never a lover of the truly public occasion, he would have become suddenly perverse and anti-status-quo. My mother, who was not a good mixer, would only appear reluctantly when the official celebrations had begun.

By three o'clock in the afternoon everyone was in their best attire and on their best behaviour – even some of the kids began that way – and drifting nervously into the walled grounds of the Smiths' domain. There was an air of expectancy that seemed to affect even the gnarled oaks and chestnut trees that were hung with coloured streamers and all kinds of bunting.

So there we all were, young and old residents of the Road, packed indoors for a short space of time. Everyone who was anyone and, that day, everyone who was no one, was present. The Smiths' house overflowed with guests chattering vigorously amongst its well-kept Edwardian elegance and its Empire-flavoured ethos. Mr Dunnock with his neat moustache brushed and bristling importantly; Mrs Lang with her eyes like dismayed prunes; Mrs Matthews, her meaty face and body, if not her personality, dominating the drawing room; and Nancy, her long nurse's legs fascinating more than the little boys. And what an opportunity it was for the women to examine each other's habiliments; to paw the household ornaments; and to commit ocular rape upon the fine décor of the place with their lewd domestic eyes. Most of the ladies had never set foot in the house before, so it was a case of God Save Her Majesty for providing the opportunity.

Attached to the rear of the Smiths' grand house was a spacious sun-lounge. It was all glass and yellow and green painted wood; and inside it every child who lived in the Road, and some from the Loop Lane too, had been rehearsed for the pageant to be enacted in honour of the Coronation of the new queen. In accordance with my passion for cricket, plus the need for the Empire touch (one didn't use the word 'Commonwealth' in those days), I played Don Bradman, the great Australian batsman. Equally appropriately Caroline was an engagingly superior Britannia in little Empire-style dress and wearing a coronet made of cardboard overlaid with silver paper, carrying, as well as her shield, an impressive gilded spear.

The children's pageant began around half-past three. Caroline in her splendid Britannia outfit delivered her long prologue, and also had the task of providing a running commentary to link the rest of the plebeian efforts together. But I was stricken with fear as the moment drew close for me to speak. It was not exactly that I forgot my lines. But I spoke them like a horse auctioneer selling a prize racehorse, that is, at about a thousand words a minute! There I stood, in my white shirt, trousers and batsman's pads, leaning on a cricket bat and holding a red ball in my right hand. I never once glanced at the audience after I had begun to speak, but gazed steadfastly up at the ceiling; and this all because in rehearsals I'd been constantly admonished for staring fixedly at my toes! Sad really, yet a perfect instance of my awkward and volatile nature. One minute bubbling over with confidence, and the next a victim of crippling and miserable shyness.

Only when I had finished my high speed recitation did I unscrew my eyes from the ceiling. The audience clapped me just as they did each childish effort. It was while I was doing some knock-kneed bowing as per instructions, that I looked at Britannia and was disgusted to observe that she had her lines pasted onto the back of her shield. It was quite a shock I can tell you to see that Goddess of the Eleven-Plus, and all possible other childish achievements, up to such deception. Especially since it had been her mother who, throughout rehearsals, had been most insistent that we children learnt our lines 'orf by heart'! Yet there was Caroline the brilliant and beautiful, the paradigm of all possible childish virtues – pulling a fast one, cheating, by reading her lines off the back of that infernal shield. Naturally enough, it never occurred to me that, whilst the rest of us kids had scarcely more than a handful of lines apiece – even those brave ad-libbers – Caroline had several hundred. It was simply cheating on her part, and that was that!

Afterwards, we all trooped outside to play games on the emerald lawns and to gorge the food that had miraculously appeared on the long tables after a brief shower of rain. We ate – scoffed is a more exact term – cakes, meat pies, sausage rolls, meat or fish paste sandwiches, egg sandwiches, cheese sandwiches, and many another sandwich containing ham, tongue, beef, chicken and so forth; we had lettuce, tomato, cress and onions; buttered scones, iced buns, éclairs, truffles, jam tarts, trifle, jelly, apple pie and fruit of various sorts. The whole banquet being washed down with orangeade, cherryade, lemonade, dandelion-and-burdock, Tizer or raspberryade.

In childish hunger we ate and drank to excess. Then followed the laughter, the gaiety, the silliness, and the occasional quarrel. There was racing around and upsetting things and people; and a huge amount of showing off. There was hysterical giggling and spilt juice – oh the memory of a large spreading stain of raspberryade down the front of a pretty party frock! – or a tomato shoved down a neck. And, of course, there occurred those niggling little snubs that are a part of childish communication; a sad but accurate reflection of petty parental snobbery and ill-feeling. Again, under the simpering gaze of our fond parents we gallivanted about, or were organized into foolish games like egg-and-spoon races, sack races, three-legged races, human wheelbarrows, high-jumping, skipping ... or, later, we had to take part in musical chairs and one fiendish charade after another that it was assumed we all enjoyed.

Yet let it not be thought for a moment that this longed-for occasion, this event dreamed of and dramatised for so long in our tiny minds, was anything but wonderful on the day. It was wonderful. Especially when the sun came out. Then everything was just right, perfect, paradisial. The world was positively magical. The garden flowerbeds became vibrant with streams of colour. There were purply-blue bursts of early lupins; the plum trees ripe with rain-fed and sun-sucked juice; the apple trees crabbily agog with small leaf and coming fruit; and the warm lawns, sun-singed, and freshly razored – the brief shower serving to emphasise their haylike odour. With the earth all over sweating with new warmth.

The sky was warmblue after the brief passage of galleon-sized clouds that had sent a million silver wires slanting across near fields, lanes and gardens. Now the paths were steaming and the terrace boiling quietly. A cat darted in and out of the rose bushes, all black and white soft-pawed fur and a glittering suspicion of yellow eyes. The damp grass, as it dried, murmured grassy words. The clayey soil turned to light brown blotting paper, and already dust was being formed to await the next sweeping breeze. The trees were heavy with hanging-tongue leaves that were still as thirsty as ever despite the recent rain: their warm boughs cracked and scabbed. Lastly there was the big house: a distinguished stone diplomat imposing amidst lawns and privet hedges. The silent imperial backdrop to good living, its doors and windows polished in the same renewing sun. – This is how it was that day for all who had eyes to see.

Adults in groups. Some falsely jolly. Some genuinely happy. Coming and going. Touching. Standing and talking. Being sensible, sad or sentimental by turns. There, in that moment in time. In 1953. Ageing mouths and aged mouths. Thin lips and thick lips. All moving to the crude tune of words. Affectation choking some: 'Oh, my deah, it was quite the most marvellous thing!' or 'But she's a real commoner!' ... And the 'real commoner' (whom Mr Dunnock couldn't take his eyes off) sucking on a straw with red lipsticky lips, or bellowing across the genteel lawns, 'Eric! Our Eric ... come 'ere this minute willya?' And ungainly Eric shambling dutifully away from a group up to no good by the marquee.

Adults in groups. The gentlemanly Mr Reynolds, the suave Mr Martin, and the shrewdly-pious Mrs Wilson, together discussing the obsessive mysteries of compulsory education. Coalman Carter there too. Strictly out of all conversation on 'heddication': 'Ah knows nowt about heddication!' was his proud boast. Not far away would be Mr Dunnock, Nigel's dad, hearty as ever in plus-fours, with a glass of beer in his well-fed hand and his pipe sticking out of the corner of his mouth, just waiting for the moment when – the ladies out of earshot – he would be able to move in and tell Carter a dirty joke. One could see the dapper Mr Martin too, fancying himself with the ladies like any good Welshman, whilst dead scared that his pretty little wife might at the same time be making dimples at the men. Where Dunnock was an amorous tank, Martin was the spruce seducer of scented dance halls.

Yet ... again what about my father? Was he there? Or not? If he was, if he had finally capitulated and joined the garden party, then you may be sure he would have been drunk ... though not on alcohol but on 'company'. Perhaps he would have been reciting an embarrassing verse or two of some risqué ballad or saying something vaguely bawdy, this time within delicate earshot of the ladies; or attracting a group of kids with his idiosyncratic remarks. If my father was in evidence at that grand garden fête, he might well have been reminiscing about his days as a boxer; or narrating some commercial traveller's tale; or talking about 'life at the Mill' for which he worked as a sales representative. Equally, and with that ease of manner he could turn on at will, he may even have been expatiating on some favourite author or literary topic to an audience of mostly baffled adults; or he might have been whistling or, well, just being himself ... which was regarded as his worst social failing of all!

That great day was truly representative of the little enclosed world we knew simply as the Road. The outside world – never more than a distant murmur (and then it was only boring old Manchester) – had now ceased to exist. Beyond the walls of those gardens, past the

Dingle, the Sand Hills and Farmer Johnny's forbidden acres, we knew there were other places and other people, but they didn't seem to matter. There was literally no spirit of 'it's always greener on the other side of the hill' in the Road. For, apart from the fact that it clearly wasn't any greener over the hill, it was just fine in our somewhat isolated Road. And the garden parties of summer – of which the present one was the finest ever – only made the place more enjoyable: only increased our sense of security. I cannot think there was anyone, young or old, who was totally insensible to the spirit of that Road. Its security, its peace, its timelessness was a hovering presence. I think the spirit of that place affected everyone in some degree, existed for everyone.

I know that for me it existed. It came and dwelt in me, forming and nourishing the vague vision of perfection that was to be with me always despite the very real passage of time. I had seen its presence in the greenwet moss of underbush roots; I had seen it in broken pools and clinging to spider-webbed doors; or lurking in corners of old insect-infested walls and among strange exotic weeds near our house. I had found it in dank cellars; I had heard it in the drip, drip of water from broken taps; in cupboards at night; in attics and lofts among junk and dust; and outdoors in bird-song and leaves, and in the blue and grey skies of forgotten days. It was a presence in the rain and in the white-velvet snow of winter. For it was in things and images of things as a quality outside time: it was in the mind which heard its urgent silence. It was a dreaming harmony that linked all things, this spirit of place. And that Coronation party, those Empire Days, Christmases, had merely made it into a communal experience – at least for those with eyes to see and hearts to feel.

CHAPTER FIVE
Educating the Uneducable

(i) The Gift of a Tutor

Anyone glancing at Miss Cawthorne would only have seen a tall, elderly spinster. Yet a closer look might have revealed traces of the beauty she once had been. But all her long life Miss Cawthorne had been something more; she had inherited a fine mind. Classical and independent, she had thrown herself into teaching, rising quickly to the position of headmistress. Then, after retirement, she had become a special tutor employed by the city's education authority to teach children who, for one reason or another, were unable to attend school. This was to be her final term, that autumn she was to retire for good.

Yet as Miss Cawthorne made her way to our house, the prospect of teaching a backward ten-year-old boy did not altogether appeal. She had always been used to girls and, whatever their faults, she felt they provided a more gentle and sensitive environment than boys seemed to do; boys were rougher, somehow cruder, and noisier; they were also much more difficult to get to concentrate. For *most* of the time she was my tutor, I did little to help dispel her prejudices.

As she turned into the drive of the house, Miss Cawthorne would have noticed that the whole place was surrounded by stately chestnut trees whose pink candles would soon begin to appear. My mother greeted her and soon a cup of tea was being drunk and a chat taking place in the kitchen, from where the two ladies could see me seated somewhat moodily at a bare wooden table in the shade of a great tree.

After a while I heard my mother observe, 'Well, Miss Cawthorne, I, er, expect you'd like to meet your new charge? He's been waiting patiently like a good boy for half an hour now. I put him outside as it's such a lovely day and the doctor says he should get as much fresh air as possible. And he's forbidden anything energetic for some time yet. No rough games or things like that.' She spoke with that flatness of accent one finds among people who live in the Manchester area.

Miss Cawthorne returned momentarily to the hall to collect her briefcase, then my mother led her round the side of the house to the wooden table placed on the velvety green law. But to their surprise it was now deserted. I was nowhere in sight.

'Oh dear me!'exclaimed mother, 'Where can he have got to now?'

A look of misgiving came over Miss Cawthorne.

'This is most inconsiderate of him!' Mother sounded peeved. 'He knew you were here. He's been sat there all this time waiting. And now, just as he's needed, he's disappeared!' She looked around in exasperation and then called out, 'William?' There was no answer. 'William?'

I must have shifted my position somewhat for a handful of chestnut twigs crashed down onto the garden table.

'Oh William! You're not up that tree *again*? How many times do you have to be told? You know you're not supposed to climb trees!'

Mother looked at my prospective tutor in exasperation. 'It seems impossible to get it into his head that he must not do such energetic things. He just doesn't seem to appreciate how ill he's been. You know, he was so delicate we didn't dare tell him when it was time to leave hospital because the doctors feared the excitement might kill him.'

Eventually I was persuaded down the tree; and mother, after a few more words of admonition, retired indoors. Then the tutor's struggle began.

'Sit down properly, boy!' commanded the elderly spinster suddenly amazingly stern.

I'd never been called 'boy' before and was so surprised I did as I was told. Miss Cawthorne seated herself opposite, surveying me carefully.

I'm not sure what she saw in me. I'd been spoilt by mother after being in hospital and was inclined to look moody and peevish at times. Yet I'd also heard people say that I was handsome with a sensitive appearance – though I wasn't quite sure what that meant then.

Eventually Miss Cawthorne decided to begin, and took some books out of her case. 'Now William, what subjects interest you most?'

'I like war best.' I replied simply but candidly.

'War?' she echoed. 'Don't you mean history?'

'No – war. You know – fightin' and shootin'!' I replied enthusiastically. All those months in a hospital bed, plus being forbidden all physical exercise, had stirred my appetite for such things.

The tutor pressed on. 'But *history*, William, is not only about *wars*! It's about countries and their kings, queens and governments. It's

about ordinary people too like you and me. History concerns itself
with how people lived in days gone by, with the things they did for a
living, the kind of houses in which they lived and the cities and
buildings they worked in. Take the churches they built ...'

'But it's wars I like!' I insisted doggedly.

'William! It's rude to interrupt when a lady's speaking.'

This was a tactical error. But before she could attempt to seize the
initiative again, I asked abruptly, 'Miss, do you know anyone what's
bin in the War?'

'No, I do not. Furthermore, it's not "Do you know anyone what's
been in the War?" but "Do you know anyone who *has* been in the
War?" Do you understand? Your grammar is very bad!'

'Yes, miss ... but *I* know someone who's bin in the War. Sid has ...
he's the man what come to paint our house.'

Thus the struggle began in earnest. A struggle that was to last for
most of the six months until she finally retired. Yet, Miss Cawthorne
had an ally in her struggle, an unexpected and somewhat unpredictable
ally: Nature. She intuitively sensed, even before that first morning
was over, that I was strangely mesmerized by Nature and all the green
things surrounding me. But it soon became obvious that I was only
mildly interested in drawing pictures of toads, chaffinches, foxes or
sheep; or in preserving flowers between pages of books. Somehow
I stubbornly refused to be stimulated.

Eventually, my obsession with war was replaced with an equally
strong pre-occupation with cricket. Miss Cawthorne was growing
equally tired of this new obsession when she suddenly recalled a poem
in a book she possessed. She knew she had the book somewhere at
home and was determined to look it out and bring it along as soon as
possible.

The following day, at the small wooden table under the giant
chestnut trees, a bright sun embracing everything with its poured
loveliness, she began to read the poem:

> Willow, King Willow, thy guard hold tight!
> Trouble is coming before the night,
> Hopping, galloping, short and strong
> Comes the Leathery Duke along ...

Though used to my father reciting verses both serious and comic,
this was the first time I had *consciously* heard poetry read aloud and
I remember the almost mystical feeling it inspired in me. I also

remember that after she'd finished reading the poem, she said nothing, allowing the sound of the birds and the rustling of the branches to continue the sentiment of the moment. I sat there mesmerized. In my mind all the garden birds sang with ever-increasing intensity. The great trees breathed and delicate white clouds like fluffy burrs moved through the high heavens above the garden. It was for me a moment of great purity.

At length, however, Miss Cawthorne ventured to speak. 'Did you like the poem?'

When there was no answer she repeated, 'William – *did* you like the poem?'

'Er ... yes,' I answered distractedly. Then, recollecting myself, asked, 'But what was it about?'

'Why ... it was about cricket, of course!'

I must have looked at her blankly, for she went on to explain in her precise manner that 'King Willow' was, of course, 'a cricket bat'; and that the 'Leathery Duke', the 'cricket ball', and so on. But it seemed to make little difference.

I was listening – listening for ... something? Some echo beyond the poem perhaps? And, for a moment, it was as if I had ceased to be at the table with her, and was slowly becoming merged in the green and blue and gold of the light-dappled background. Then I wanted her to read another poem. Then another. And the whole time I gave her my undivided attention.

When lessons were over for that morning Miss Cawthorne began to pack her things away. Suddenly she asked me if I would 'like to keep the book of poems?' I replied enthusiastically that I would 'like 'em very much'. So she gave me the book. I still have it, *The Silver Book of Children's Verse*, edited by Frank Jones. I can't remember if I could actually read by then, but whether I could or not, the book became instrumental in helping me with the task. Later, she also gave me *The Boy's Book of Verse* edited by A.M. Phillip which I also still have, though for some odd reason it has my sister's name in it. But as my sister immediately professed a dislike of poetry, once she knew that I liked it, I've always thought of it as mine.

Miss Cawthorne's choice of a farewell present proved spot on. I was overjoyed to receive from my tutor a real Indian tomahawk, something she'd inherited from an uncle in Canada, and I went whooping round the garden like Geronimo. That – and the gift of poetry – was all I could ever have asked from any teacher.

(ii) The Academy for Young Gentlemen

After Miss Cawthorne left, I was sent in the autumn term of 1949 to
Professor Hoffmann's 'Premier Academy for Young Gentlemen'
(which also catered for young gentlewomen, though it was considered
less important to advertise that fact) which was situated on the fringes
of a strange park ominously called 'Boggart Hole Clough' – a boggart
being a malevolent spirit. The school consisted of a large Victorian
house with a high-walled garden to the rear dubbed 'the playground'.
The chief drawing room had been converted into a classroom, whilst
on the opposite side of the gloomy hallway, was the music room.
Apart from a tiny cloakroom with a row of coat pegs, the only other
room that formed part of the scholastic set-up was the dining-room-
cum-kitchen at the back of the house.

The classroom had several rows of the most decrepit blackly-
varnished desks imaginable. They resembled rejects from some
monastic chapter house, and had woodworm-eaten and elbow-
furrowed sloping tops. Opening them was like opening the hatches
of an old- fashioned sailing ship. A faded blue carpet, threadbare
from generations of little feet, covered most of the floor and there
was a surround of oily brown linoleum. Net curtains filled the windows
and the walls were a shiny cream colour. The plentiful woodwork of
sills, doors and panelling matched the desks with the same black
varnishing. Boggart-coloration for baby boggarts!

The entire complement of the academy was only about fifteen
pupils. That was at its height and doing a roaring trade in learning.
When my sister and I attended the Premier Academy there were,
besides ourselves less than a dozen others.

Old Hoffy, a gothic figure, would preside heavily over the class,
white hair, parted by a clearing of speckled baldness, tufted and prolific
over his ears. He wore a stiff winged-collar with exposed tie and
either a green or black suit. He made the perfect caricature of the
absent-minded professor; except he wasn't particularly forgetful. Nor
did he have the expected scholar's pallor, for old Hoffy possessed the
high colouring of a country parson and, as if to emphasise a link with
fields and open air, he would often stand outside his back door on
frosty mornings doing a ridiculous series of deep-breathing exercises.

Those pupils who did not go home for lunch brought sandwiches.
Consequently, I remember vividly lunch hours spent with the

Hoffmann family. The luncheon room, which was really the family kitchen, containing a large black cooking range and big table which dominated the room. There a dozen pupils, plus the entire Hoffmann family, would lunch uneasily together. Old Hoffy presided at the head of the table. With a gold watch chain across his midriff and the usual green tie holding his neck in, he would solemnly keep everyone, most of all his pupils, in fearful good order. Often he would lecture us on our table manners, or, I should say, lack of them.

Naturally, as children, it was difficult to curb us entirely and we chattered incessantly. Television, then the newest and most wonderful invention, often came up. Some pupils were from homes which already had the magic box; others, like my sister and myself, were not so fortunate. I was impressed with how my sister used to suffer whenever the subject came up! And how she dearly wished we had a T.V. set so as to be 'like everyone else'. Alas, I doubt she will ever forgive me for when, out of a mixture of devilment and impatience , I committed the cardinal sin of admitting: 'We haven't got a television because we're too poor to buy one!' Which wasn't strictly true but, unlike my sister, I cared very little for social appearances.

Speaking of my sister and those lunch hours spent at the Hoffmanns' table, she recalls one in particular – probably to get her own back on her dear brother! A subject that came up now and again was what we budding citizens would like to be when we grew up. On the occasion in question Old Hoffy evidently asked each of us in turn what our ambitions for the future were. The boys' replies varied from such roles as cricketer, footballer, engine driver or fighter pilot to that more nebulous pursuit of 'dunno!' As for the girls they, with greater unanimity if not greater humility, invariably saw themselves as future film stars.

When my turn came Old Hoffy, polishing his spectacles, asked gruffly: 'And what do you intend to become, Master Oxley?' To which question, according to my sister, I answered without any hesitation, 'I want to be immortal!'

Despite many 'tellings-off', most of which I considered unjust, I mostly remained silent. I did not dare answer him back. No pupil ever did. Not through fear of a beating or a thousand lines or anything like that, but under Old Hoffy's iron law the penalty for 'answering back' was immediate expulsion. And it was a privilege to attend the Premier Academy; there was a long waiting list of children eager to become young gentlemen, all eager to seize our places ... or so we were assured. Consequently few were prepared to run the risk of Old Hoffy's ultimate sanction.

Despite that, however, I was expelled from the Academy. Not just once but twice. Which was a miracle if one considers the 'waiting list'. I have no real idea how I came to be taken back on either occasion – though it clearly must have had something to do with the eloquence and persuasive charm of my father. The circumstances of my first expulsion I have forgotten; but I remember vividly the second time I was shown the door.

We used to have to queue up to have our books marked before Old Hoffy's big desk in front of the tall mantelpiece. One day, there were just me and a sweet-and-sour girl called Margery standing in front of the Professor's black desk. All the rest of the class had their noses in their books. I was about to have my book marked first when Old Hoffy gave a loud sniff, scratched himself and decided he must first answer a call of nature. As soon as the old man's back was turned this was, as usual, taken as an excuse for everyone to relax. So Margery and I started arguing! She began to pull faces and bait me, until, losing patience, I took a kick at her. Which proved to be an error for two reasons: first of all it was not the sort of conduct expected of a young gentleman; secondly, at the precise moment I kicked out, Old Hoffy re-entered the classroom. Naturally, the roof was pulled down over my ears – one of which was grabbed by the teacher. I was stood in front of the class and subjected to a lecture on cowardice and the ungentlemanliness of hitting girls. It lasted about a quarter of an hour, at the end of which Old Hoffy trusted I was duly chastened. I wasn't, of course, even for a moment. As punishment I was sent to the back of the queue of two and made to wait to have my damned book marked.

Margery, eventually, went back to her desk. Before dealing with me, Old Hoffy lifted up the big top of his desk and shoved his head beneath it. For what could only have been a moment or two, all that was visible were the white tufts of his hair and the bald middle dome of his head. Thinking he couldn't see me, I stuck my tongue out at Margery and sniggered. The next second ... wham! The lid of the desk was thumped shut, the book wrenched from in front of my face and my vile smirk exposed. Old Hoffy roared. He yelled. He shook me. 'I ... I will not be sniggered at behind my back! I will not tolerate insubordination!' His voice was deafening. It thundered over the varnished desks as he frogmarched me to my place.

'I do not like smirking boys!' he shouted over and over as he systematically emptied the contents of the desk into my satchel. 'And ... I will not have them in my school!' Then, still holding me by an ear, he led me to the cloakroom. After which – hey presto! – a few moments later I was descending the short flight of steps to the street ... and freedom. The door of the Academy was slammed firmly shut behind me.

At first I was, I confess, a little bemused by the speed of events. But as I walked towards the bus stop I suddenly realised I had, unwittingly, joined a very select band of schoolkids again: the Brotherhood of the Expelled. I immediately began to fill with a great sense of joyous freedom. It was scarcely mid-day and I was out of school! Free of the hated place. And, in a curious sort of way, legally so. I reached the bus stop opposite the old red-brick Blackley library building and, on impulse, stuffed all my schoolbooks into a litter bin. I was convinced this time I could not possibly be returning to the Academy.

Rarely have I felt more light-hearted in my life than when I climbed aboard the red bus a few minutes later. It was one of the happiest rides I ever took. I had no thought of the future, or of what my parents might say. Anyway, father would be at work and mother was out that afternoon. So I had a glorious free holiday to look forward to, no matter of how short a duration it would be.

I knew, of course, that when mother came home she would be most upset. As, true to form, she was. And, of course, I was duly admonished by her, finishing up with the usual, 'I don't know what your father will think?' Which, however, did make a kind of sense, for it was of some consequence to me not just what my father would think but, more to the point, what he would do. So that, as the time drew near for him to return home from his office in Manchester, I began to feel progressively less joyful. Till, when he finally arrived home around 7 pm. and entered the dining room in his customary jaunty manner, he stopped dead as he saw our strained faces.

Fortunately, however, my father was never the sort of man whom one had to catch in the right mood to deliver bad news. So mother informed him immediately of my expulsion and my dear sister helped to fill out the account dramatically with eye-witness details.

When he had listened to the full story, I was relieved to see my father endeavouring to hide a flicker of a smile. But to calm mother's fears for her son's future, he promised that as soon as he'd eaten his evening meal he would go and see the old fellow.

Later that evening, to my intense disappointment, father returned to tell mother he'd persuaded Old Hoffy to have me back – again. He'd worked another of his little social miracles and I was duly sent back to 'mouldy old school', the short-lived experience of freedom behind me.

It must not be thought that I had anything against the Academy which I did not also have against any other school. Far from it. That anachronism of a private tuition establishment was the finest institution of its kind I ever attended. More importantly, I instinctively knew Old Hoffy was a true lover of learning, having taught himself music, mathematics, languages and, it seemed, every other subject as well. After Miss Cawthorne, Old Hoffy was the only other teacher who mattered to me. Perhaps he never achieved with me anything quite so specific as she had done, but he inspired in me a general love of learning which was to become increasingly important in the future.

(iii)   The School of Commerce

Following what I now see as my more fortunate days at Old Hoffy's private academy, I passed – regrettably – a scholarship to yet another eccentric educational establishment. This was called rather obscenely 'The School of Commerce'. And there, at fourteen, when most normal boys and girls were being taught mathematics, chemistry, physics, biology and so on, I was learning the dry intricacies of double-entry bookkeeping, shorthand, commercial arithmetic, as well as more about one or two other darker subjects still ... like human nature.

The School of Commerce, situated amongst the warehouses and business offices in the heart of money-making Manchester, was housed in a gloomy Victorian building with dim corridors, worn stone stairs, green civil-service walls, and classrooms full of shadows and dusty beams of light. And in the many corners of its sombre interior, made darker still by a forest of blackish woodwork and awful panelling, were huddled its co-educational pupils busily discovering that this peculiar teaching establishment was a jungle of commercial theory and sexual frustrations.

The Principal of the school was a pompous ass whom we had to suffer daily in school assembly when he foisted his miserable wisdom on us from the great height of a dusty stage. Then there was a crabbed old French teacher called Starkers, though no one had the least desire to see her other than fully clothed. She greatly enriched the life of at least one of her ungrateful pupils by taking us to the little village of Wilderswil situated where the Bernese Oberland is flush with flame-like flowers in summer and the Jungfraujoch weeps with edelweiss.

My worst personal crime was being hauled up before Piggy, the Principal, for having carved a superb Chinese Dragon on my rotten old desk. I recall the Principal's piggywigging perfectly, for his words outraged me at the time, treading as they did fair and square on my puritan sensibilities. He squealed, 'You're ... you're the sort of boy who writes on lavatory walls!'

More interesting were the periodic visits we received from successful businessmen whose presence was intended to inspire in us a like commercial acumen. There was one I definitely remember. He had come ostensibly to talk to us about trade with Latin America but what fired the imagination were his stories set in Mexico in the 1930s.

This company executive told us of how he had 'visited a bar in New Mexico in the early Thirties. I got talking with some of the locals, most of whom carried pistols. Somehow the subject of Western movies cropped up, and there was a heated discussion about cine cowboys who, with their two guns, are always shown shooting from the hip. The locals, many of whom were gringos, poo-pooed the idea saying that nobody could shoot a six-gun with any accuracy that way. But just then a stranger entered and walked up to the bar. For a while he listened to the argument that was going on, then he laughed at the idea that it was impossible to shoot accurately from the hip ... and he said they were all wrong. But nobody agreed with him. After all, most there were experienced gunslingers and they knew all about shooting, they said. But, without warning, the stranger turned to the barman and said loudly, "Your clock's wrong!" and he whipped out a gun and, firing directly from the hip, he put a bullet neatly through the centre of the wall clock, with the result that the glass shattered and both fingers fell off. Turning to the customers he observed calmly, "You see, amigos, it can be done?" Adding, "But you have to be very good, si?" And with that he swigged the rest of his tequila, dumped a handful of pesos on the bar to pay for the damage and left the place ...'

During the first term at that mercifully last school I attended, I had been a model pupil paying meticulous attention to each lesson, keeping my nose clean and my exercise books thoroughly neat. Yet despite all my efforts to be a good pupil, when the results of the first end-of-term exams had been announced, I'd found myself placed last in every subject and overall bottom of a class of thirty-odd pupils. It was disgusting considering how diligently I'd applied myself during classes. The result thoroughly annoyed me. So much so, that I paid no further attention to lessons throughout the following term, being often sent from class for gossiping or idling. But in secret I had taken home my text books and studied them furiously in the evenings. The upshot of which was that at the next end-of-term exams I took first place in the class in all subjects. Something which had so astounded the teacher that all the papers had to be marked again, though with the same result.

When I started at the School of Commerce I had achieved little academically save, of course, the passing of the necessary entrance examination to the school. When I left the place some two years later I still had no qualifications to my name, not even a single School Certificate or G.C.E.s as they were then called. And, in between, there had been nothing but the stubborn resistance of a romantic temperament: my refusal to conform to either the simple tastes of my fellow pupils for pop music and teenage sex, or to the less well-defined wishes of my teachers.

Yet I cannot deny that the school, built totally in the shadow of Mammon, was an apt preparation for my entry into the depressing world of commerce. And at the still tender age of sixteen, I went out into the 'real' world, crossing Manchester's own Phlegethon, the River Irwell, in an ominously reverse movement in mythological terms, and found myself in Salford. Not perhaps an auspicious start, but one of which at first I had some hopes.

(iv) Educating Myself

Miss Cawthorne had given me a love of poetry; Old Hoffy had inspired in me a love of learning; both had endeavoured to help me catch up on a lost education. But The School of Commerce showed up a serious flaw in my psychological make-up: I seemed incapable of being taught. Any learning which I acquired at that institution had been gained through self-tuition. I read the text books during the evening, in bed, on buses, anywhere but at school. And it was during these years, from early 1954 when I was not quite fifteen, that I also began my own strand of life and learning – also from books. But books not prescribed by my teachers.

One of my earliest poetic favourites was Roy Campbell. I first knew of his work through my father who was forever quoting lines such as 'The firing ceased and like a wounded foe/The day bled out in crimson' or:

> ... But as the turf divides
> I see in the slow progress of his strides
> Over the toppled clods and falling flowers,
> The timeless, surly patience of the serf.

or

> Theirs is no earthly breed
> Who only haunt the verges of the earth
> And only on the sea's salt herbage feed.

I became alive to the beauty of the lines and their rhythms, and also the verve of Campbell's poetry. I didn't know, then, that he was 'notorious' and much derided. All I knew was that the lines shone when I read them. They weren't bound up with the author, and I think this helped me, later in life, to learn to dissociate the poet from the poem. 'Poets are born, not made' my father believed. Though he did feel, as I do, that the reading of good poetry helps improve whatever gift or talent even the most naturally favoured possess.

Another poet whom my father was always quoting was Landor. Again it was the beauty of line which attracted me to him. Lines like:

> Soon shall oblivion's deepening veil
> Hide all the peopled hills you see,
> The gay, the proud, while lovers hail
> In distant ages you and me.

These early lyrical poets which I read, along with Keats, Gray, Masefield, some of Wordsworth, Shelley, Coleridge, formed the basis of my literary knowledge.

My father also introduced me to the plays of Shakespeare and then to Homer. I suppose I must have been around 15 or 16 when I read the *Iliad* and the *Odyssey* and both made a big impression on my mind. I'm not sure how mature an impression: I know the poetry was important, but I have a sneaking suspicion I also enjoyed the 'war' element of the *Iliad*; hadn't I told Miss Cawthorne that I was interested in war?

Sometime about then I first encountered in one form or another Milton's *Paradise Lost*. I know I had read it by my seventeenth birthday, yet I can remember asking mother for a copy for my nineteenth birthday as I didn't have one of my own. From the very first *Paradise Lost* represented for me a cosmic masterpiece. It had the variety, the philosophical insight and the grandiose vision that I wanted.

Yet despite all this reading of poetry and my instinctive feel for the beautiful, I was never tempted to put pen to paper myself. In an age when anyone interested in poetry feels they can write a stanza or two, this must seem peculiar. Yet my father's maxim (I didn't realise it was reputedly Horace's for some time after) about poets being born not made, made me less presumptuous than today when it is obvious that poets are made (in creative writing schools). In my teens I was a reader of poetry only. It was another ten years before I dared to put any thoughts down poetically.

Around this time, too, I became aware of philosophical and metaphysical thinking. I remember when I was sixteen getting involved in a discussion with two friends of mine, one of them just a little older than me and about to become a medical student. He was quite clearly nihilistic. I had never spoken on what I believed because up to then I'd had no 'beliefs' in that sense. It had all been inchoate feeling and instinct. But now I found I was disagreeing with my friend instinctively and openly and I suddenly became acutely aware of the philosophical side to the discussion.

Another primary seminal experience was probably around that time when I read Plato's 'Theory of Innate Ideas'. This notion that we have cognition of things before we have experience of them seemed to me so right. Though I would never, now, describe myself as a Platonist, I have always believed in his idea that there is a mind and a body and we can't explain the mind in purely mortal, finite terms. So Plato's *Republic* was a most important moment in my reading. When I was 16 or thereabouts, I also read John Locke's *Essay Concerning Human Understanding*. How I came to read this, I'm not sure, but it may have followed on from Plato – Locke was anti-platonic – or it might have been at the instigation of my father. I found it a very persuasive book. But I think it only persuaded me ultimately that Plato was probably right and Locke wrong. We do know certain things in advance of experiencing them.

My father was probably a great influence on my life at that time; but like many teenagers, I was more concerned in going my own way than in listening to his advice. Yet we must have talked much about politics and life in general – maybe literature. He, like myself, was mainly self-educated and had the added advantage of both age and being a free-thinker. I remember writing to him later in life and stating, 'I cannot understand how I passed so much of my teens at home arguing politics with you'. But I suppose I must have done.

Having left behind Captain W.E. Johns and his Biggles' books with puberty, I read few novels, but I did enjoy the works of Sir Walter Scott in my teens. I read many of his Waverley Novels, delighting in *Rob Roy, The Talisman, Ivanhoe, Quentin Durward* and others.

Years later, in a lecture given to English students at the University of Salzburg which I entitled 'Learning to Distinguish Poetry', I recalled the impact on me of modern poetry. I told of my love-hate relationship with Eliot and Pound: showing how it was Eliot's 'rhythm' and 'writing seriously of serious things' which had most influenced me, and expressing a preference for *The Four Quartets* over *The Waste Land*; how his 'grand and memorable phraseology', effortlessly combining concrete evocation with 'quasi-philosophical passages', greatly appealed. Similarly, I preferred Pound's *Mauberley* to his *Cantos*, admiring his technical virtuosity, but early perceiving that weakness which G.S. Fraser expressed as, 'A hatred of "abstraction"... implies a hatred for certain established Western processes of learning.'

While absorbing these two 'giants of modernism', I was also delighting in Rupert Brooke and Dylan Thomas; discovering Hopkins and Yeats; appreciating 'the cerebralist and skilful Auden' along with 'the plainer and more genuine Graves'. Another milestone on the contemporary road was the publication of the Penguin Modern Poets' series, although I did not begin to wade along this 'Nile of formless verse' – as one reviewer unkindly put it – until the late 60s. The series high-lighted for me just how far the formlessness of much contemporary poetry had drifted. I felt that not only had many poets abandoned exterior metricality, but in many cases the essential interior form was missing too. There were also writers who were more wits than poets and who, with their often amusing but merely clever cerebration, paved the way for the later Martian School. Last but not least, I learnt from Dannie Abse, (though in the Penguin series, I did not come to him through it) 'the virtue in difficulty' – a much needed lesson for a wayward and prolific talent like mine.

CHAPTER SIX
The Years that Threatened Paradise

With our departure from the Road for suburbia in 1954, paradise did not come to an abrupt end. The golden view of life, the ability to see clearly into the heart of things, did not immediately begin to distort. Shadows were to gather and crowd in, and that white horizon darken, but only gradually over a period of time. A period during which I was to experience not only despair but new and, in some ways, finer visions still. The paradox was that though impoverished by the move away from that illuminated and illuminating Road, I was, nevertheless, destined to be immeasurably enriched. But it was a spiritual enrichment – and not one to be had without a struggle.

The trouble began that day I paused to look down the long cobbled canyon of Hankinson Street, Salford. It was 1955. I was just sixteen and starting my first job. Father had got me employment with Samuel Handley & Co. Ltd., a firm of paper and twine merchants. I suppose, though I cannot precisely recall, I must have felt a mixture of excitement and apprehension on that first day. But one thing is certain, I did not immediately feel the full impact of the squalid and depressing environment – those acres of snarling chimneys and blackened, hopeless streets – into which I was drawn as into a brick-built bog.

Sid Williams, who took me on as office boy, was a nervous hatchet-faced individual like a set of electric wires in a neat blue suit. He was the full-time working director of Handleys.

As a young man Sid had been lifted out of poverty in Liverpool and 'groomed for stardom' by Old Man Handley, great grandson of the firm's founder. By the time I joined the firm, however, its owner would only turn up once a month to 'see everythin' wur doin' nice at works'. And it always seemed to me slightly absurd to see his white Rolls Royce parked in that ruler-straight slum street with a slow rain of soot like black snow peppering the car's beautiful bonnet.

For all practical purposes, Sid Williams was the boss. He was a kindly man at heart, but he never allowed that to interfere with his commercial acumen. I found him neither pleasant nor unpleasant to work for. Nor was his chief clerk, Noman Worthington, a difficult person to get on with. Norman had crispy fair hair, a fat angelic face, and a not entirely clean mind. He was, though, a lightly humorous man whose health was precarious. His nickname was 'One-Ball Worthington' from the fact – of which he was enormously proud – that, 'just like Hitler', having suffered from T.B. he'd had a testicle removed. To complete the picture of that backstreet office: it employed several typists in succession, always married women. Two only can I remember. One was a small thin woman called Beth who was married to a long distance lorry-driver whom she constantly described as a 'Tarzan of the Roads'. Because of my father's interest in boxing and keep fit, I've always been an admirer of physically-strong men, but Beth's description of 'Her Bert' somehow revolted me. Then Norman, who had seen this much publicised muscle man, described him as 'Under five feet five inches and rather fat!' So I ignored what Beth said about her husband after that. Where Beth was thin and mean-looking, Rosie was ample and Irish and jolly. With a little less insulation she would have been very attractive.

The complement of the office was completed by Ted Roberts. Ted was the firm's salesman. He was middle-aged, square-faced and handsome in a kind of leathery way. He reminded me vaguely of a rougher version of Nigel's old man. Ted loved three things: his work, football, and most women under eighty. Also, as was inevitable in his job, there was always a scent of the breweries about him. He had as large a fund of dirty jokes as had my father, which is saying a good deal for father was encyclopaedic in all branches of humour. Almost the first words of cocky Ted on entering the office each day were, 'Have you heard the one about the man who ...?'

From Ted Roberts I was to learn many things I did not know about the human animal, including just how animal it is capable of being. And in him I was to discover the precursor of a type to be endlessly repeated throughout my commercial life. The smut merchant.

Yet after only a few days with Handleys I began to experience the first symptoms of boredom that I'd had since my enforced stay in hospital in my first decade. Soon I became a typical 'clock watcher' and had begun to appreciate time in a way that one never does in the open air. The office wall was a pale green horizon of ennui; the white face of the clock stared back at me without expression; and even the lascivious calendar only added to the miserable sense of non-being. Though I did not know it then, I had joined the ranks of the living-dead.

Each day, as office boy, I would climb a flight of dark and narrow stairs to a small square room above our office. What served as an annex to the store room overlooking an endless prospect of mills, rooftops and backyards, was also the tea-room. It was my task to make the foul brew twice daily. For the umpteenth time I'd ascended to that room of filthy windows and filthier prospect, boiled an old tin kettle, and filled the bloated brown teapot. Then I'd put the blue cracked mugs onto a battered tray, cover the teapot with a verminous cosy, add a bottle of milk and sugar basin to the load, and carry it all down the dusty and rickety stairs.

It was a ceremony at which I became very adept. But practice never quite makes perfect, no matter what. And I had just begun the slow and careful descent of the stairs one mid-morning when the milk bottle began to wobble. Just as a jet of milk was starting to hose through the air, I calmly let go of the tray and brilliantly caught the bottle by its neck.

It really was a superb catch. There was even a moment's appreciative silence as I savoured the sense of triumph at having rescued the bottle and its contents. But the next moment there was the most appalling crash whose centrepiece, as it were, was the sight and sound of the great brown teapot exploding in the doorway at the foot of the stairs. Then, and only then, did I become aware of the full extent of my miscalculation as, in a snow of sugar, a monsoon of tea and tea leaves, and an avalanche of bouncing and slithering blue shards and broken cup handles, my colleagues in the office below received their morning 'cuppa'...

The early hopes that I would soon grow rich began to fade as I became enmeshed in the complexities of being tea boy, office firelighter and keeper of the petty cash book. With the declining of my ambitions, rather than despairing, I sought refuge in dreams and in snatching sneaky readings of Shakespeare in the half-open drawer of my desk.

There, each day, in the cramped front office with its tiny reception window at which hopeful commercial travellers would periodically knock, I would sit in delicious reverie. My mind would range over the whole dusty globe and visit places as far away as Canada and Argentina. I longed all of a sudden to travel.

But nothing came of my dreams of course. After all, on a wage of only £1.50 a week, it would have taken me a dozen years at least to have saved the fare to Canada. Besides which, now that I was a wage earner, I was obliged to give up some of my wages for my keep at home...

One day, however, in my frustration I conceived a more practical notion, had a more modest idea. It was the only really sensible bourgeois notion I ever had ... unless one is trendy and progressive enough to count marriage also as a bourgeois idea. Silently, I began to wonder about taking another job. And not just any other job, but one to which I might harness my passion for reading and study. For this was during time of self-education.

The result of my rather obvious thought was that, a few impulsive weeks later, I left that miserable office in Salford and, again with the help of my father, exchanged it for a slightly less insufferable place. In brief, I joined a firm of chartered accountants in Manchester after I had been at Samuel Handley's for a little over one dreary year. And as I walked up Hankinson Street, Salford to catch my homeward bus for the last time, my only thoughts were summed up in the phrase I had so often used as a child: 'Good riddance to bad rubbish!'

Willett, Son & Garner, Chartered Accountants, had their offices in the heart of Manchester close to that frowning extravaganza of black stone (probably grey now if it's been cleaned up) that is the city's Town Hall in Albert Square. By mutual agreement the partners of this firm said they would take me on for a trial period of six months at the princely sum of £3 per week. And if not found to be too wanting, as the phrase is, after I had been there for six months I would be allowed to stay and work towards the eventual taking up of what were termed 'articles' with the firm. It was the usual 'we can't promise anything but ...' arrangement.

There was, however, one small snag to all this. As mentioned earlier I had contrived to get through an era of enlightened education without acquiring any school qualifications, not even a single G.C.E. at the basic 'o' for ordinary level. So, naturally, such a near miracle of ingenuous carelessness was, for a start, a total and absolute barrier to admission to any profession, not least that of a chartered accountant. But it was not a problem beyond all possible rectification.

In my new and slightly less awful environment, I recovered some of my optimism. Besides which, as my first two terms at the School of Commerce had proved, I did have one useful personal quality: a strong will that had always proved to my advantage when I chose to apply it. Will-I-Am. Consequently, at my new employers, though by no means a model employee (I must be one of the few chartered accountants' articled clerks to have organized a strike ... though not a very successful one), during the six years I was with them, I sailed

easily through all examinations. In this I was helped by the fact that
in those days the entire exam-tuition for a trainee chartered accountant
was conducted by correspondence course. Which method of self-
tuition, as a natural book-worm, suited me best, though it was very
unpopular with the rest of my colleagues.

It was through Willetts that I met an unusual young man who was
to become one of my closest friends. Indeed, one of the only two or
three real friends I acquired throughout the lengthy, boring misfortune
that was my commercial career. One of the good things, perhaps the
only good thing, about working for a firm of accountants is that one
tends to get moved about a good deal. Even if such moves are only
from one cheesed-off counting house to another money-grubbing den,
at least it ensures some sort of variety in one's working life.

It was in the under-populated and over-spacious offices of his
father's import-export business that I first set eyes on Tom Jones.
There he sat, perched nonchalantly on the edge of an outsized steel
desk, calling to mind the image of a public school robin with his
brightly coloured waistcoat, his blazer and old school tie. A chirpy,
vibrant young man with a heart-shaped visage and big spectacles,
Tom had more natural laughter and *joie de vivre* in him than anyone
I've known over the age of ten, my father not excepted. Though of
less than average height Tom was Youth Incarnate. And as I got to
know him better, I discovered him to be alertly intelligent in an
enthusiastic-for-all-causes-however-humble manner. A liberal
idealist, Tom, while not exactly the archetypal public school
intellectual, had something of the well-bred radical about him. But
his serious streak tended to get smothered by his good humour and
his overwhelming sociableness.

Rarely, if ever, have I met a finer and more genuinely likeable
person; and he was a friend I soon grew to love. Despite our many
differences of outlook on politics and the rest, I always enjoyed his
company and never grew bored with it. Nor was I ever to meet anyone
else who did not share an equal enthusiasm for Tom's company; and
I have no recollection of him ever being the object of 'back-biting'.

'I'm Tom ... and this is Rosie, the old man's secretary. She's
preggers – aren't you, old girl?' thus Tom opened up our
acquaintanceship in his usual fashion: a manner half-polished, half
jestingly vulgar. He leapt off the shiny desk and shook hands with
my colleague and myself, as we both glanced automatically at Rosie
the typist who was ostentatiously knitting baby clothes. 'Rosie's

married to Alf who's a chef. So she knits instead of cooks. Isn't that right, Rosie?'

My colleague from Willetts had only dropped by to introduce me and to set me up with a pile of indigestible day books, journals, ledgers and such paraphernalia that it was an auditor's unexciting task to manually check in the days before computers. After which he departed with the words, 'Well, make a start – you've only got three days.' Or words to that effect.

Not much work, however, was destined to be done that day. For Tom and I, who'd taken an immediate liking to each other, began to talk ... and talk. And the substance of what we talked about was Tom. Tom Jones and his ideas on life. He was, then, mad on life.

Strangely, for so evidently happy a person, I soon discovered Tom to be hypercritical of many aspects of life and society. He was the first person I consciously recall to use the phrase 'the System': 'It's the System's to blame, old chap!' he'd exclaim at every turn. In this dissatisfaction with things he and I were not dissimilar. But in Tom's case it was a conflict that all too often tended to centre uncomfortably on himself and his relationships with the rest of Society.

Sometimes one sensed that Tom felt guilty of being a rich man's son, other times this merely became the launching pad that he, Tom, was determined to use for the betterment of humanity. Occasionally, too, I would detect a strong whiff of personal ambition, and would feel the pendulum in him swing in other, more nakedly power-seeking directions. But, mostly, one was the recipient of notion after notion from this highly impressionable public school Myshkin on how best to put the world to rights.

Early on, my most positive contribution was to suggest that if he was so dissatisfied with his present lot as a lackey of the family business – as he seemed to be – he should consider leaving his father's employment and cross the street to join myself at Willetts. After all, I argued, he already had the necessary school qualifications to enable him to become articled immediately and could embark straight away on a professional career. This would give him the desired independence. And, what was more, if I understood him aright, it was the 'useful career' that he appeared to be hankering after just then. I was much better at giving advice in those days than taking it!

Such was the mercurial nature of Tom that soon after our first meeting he followed up my suggestion to the letter. By agreement with the partners of Willetts, Tom moved into our office.

From then on our acquaintanceship matured into real friendship. A friendship that was to take a far more social than professional form as time went by. And one that was to become an incredibly active relationship because Tom was a supremely gregarious person.

It is difficult, without seeming to exaggerate, to convey the effect that this dynamo of youthful conviviality had on an ever-increasing circle of friends and acquaintances. No one who did not know Tom Jones in Manchester during the years 1958 to 1963 can truly appreciate the sort of person he was; nor, more pertinently, the effect he had on others. In my belief, Tom was a wonderful social being who did not lose his essential humanity by socialising. However, I will simply say that recently I asked a London friend of mine – a highly successful man of affairs with much experience of the famous and the rich – who he thought was the liveliest person he'd ever met. Without hesitation he answered, 'Tom Jones.'

Yes, from that moment a line of friendship was drawn for me that was to extend eventually all the way from Cooper Street, Manchester to South Kensington, to Kent and to Essex, with many interesting and varied twists and turns in between. A line that never frayed and was only destined to end tragically some fifteen years later on a lonely South Coast beach...

About the same time as I had first started work at that dismal little firm in the back streets of awful Salford, my father – perhaps intuiting my impending pain – also introduced me to a world that was to have a more profound, if less time-consuming, effect on me. The amateur theatre. And it was in the cafeteria of the Manchester Y.M.C.A. that I was first introduced to Dan Killip.

Like everyone else at that time, Dan seemed much older to me than he probably was. He had dark lanky hair and a used-up face with more lines and wrinkles on it than one felt he was entitled to. Circular rings made his eyes look like bruised pennies and he had a rigidly square jaw, a quantity of uneven teeth, and deep furrows emanating from the corner of his harshly thoughtful mouth and extending upwards past an angular nose to the corners of his faded chocolate-brown eyes. Dan was the producer and director of a small company of Shakespearian players; and he was the first man I had met who made a hobby seem like a full-time job. Also, as I was soon to learn, Dan was the name by which God was known to that drama group.

'So, you want to join us then?' began the desultory conversation.

'Yes,' I replied nervously, put off by his air of indifference.

He squinted at me with bored eyes, it was evident that the idea of having me thrust upon his highly incestuous little clique didn't appeal.

'But why do you want to act?'

How could I tell him that I didn't 'want to act'? After all, I knew next to nothing about acting. 'I, er, I ... don't want to act. I want to, er, take part in Shakespeare's plays.'

He had no answer to that, for his company was the only group of players that confined itself exclusively to the work of the Bard in all that damp dark city. So, after a few more trite and bored remarks Killip withdrew and left father and myself to poke our way through a mediocre meal in a loud canteen. But at least I was 'in' – admitted to the neo-Elizabethan world of the theatre.

For most of the year, Dan Killip's players would spend their time doing weekly rehearsals in an upstairs room of the smug ugly building that housed the Manchester Y.M.C.A. It was a curious red room of tinted mirrors, deep leather armchairs, and acrid-smelling ashtrays whose contents miraculously disappeared at the press of a button. And twice, or exceptionally three times, a year the group of Shakespearian Players would perform before paying audiences at one or other of the small theatres on the outskirts of Manchester or at the famous Library Theatre in the city centre.

It was in that weird red-lighted room, which seemed to beat like the very heart of the city itself, that I had my first introduction to theatre: to that repetitive but essential part of its ritual, the rehearsal. Stricken with a terrible shyness I remember walking into the room and sitting down in a corner. No one took a blind bit of notice of me.

But I did not then care about being neglected, for I was fascinated by what I saw before me. There were men and women, with something of the air of puppets about them, draped and positioned around the room. Some were smoking, some casually drinking cups of tea, some holding scripts ... but all from time to time getting to their feet, moving and *acting*. And from their mouths, just as if it was the most natural thing in the world, would float words and sentences of unearthly power, golden in their beauty: words of a poetry tinged with the glow of paradise. No sharper contrast have I ever witnessed than between the casual quotidian appearance of those people, and the world they successfully evoked.

That evening there began for me, amidst a plethora of verbalised imagery, a new spiritual experience. The décor of the place made it seem like the ante-room of some gilded brothel; but really it was the doorway to a new and fantastic world. That not altogether artificial Paradise which is the Theatre.

There I met Jim who played Orsino, Duke of Illyria. Then there was Fay who played Viola and was supposed to be in love with Big Jim Orsino, though the matter was far from clear. And Frank, already touched by age, who played Malvolio: 'Some are born great, some achieve greatness, and some have greatness thrust upon them!' – a part he played with all the passionate optimism of an insurance clerk. I recollect others too. Like Jean, whose large troubled eyes and anaemic appearance suggested a maturity that had only brought sadness. And tall thin Jeremy: one day to be a famous journalist but even then good for comic parts; Philip and Kenneth who always played either villains or buffoons because, despite their good natures, they looked the parts and that was enough for Dan the Director. There was, too, the almost-but-not-quite-beautiful Audrey whose white bosoms hinted delightfully in period costumes; and Bill who made an excellent frog-ish Macbeth before going on to make his name bigger in the even more tragic world of television. And, lastly, by way of footlight footnote, came such as Peter or Neville or myself – mostly habitués of crowd scenes and members of the Rhubarb Brigade.

But amateur actors though they then all were, they were plausible and skilful enough to be soon interchanging in my mind with Sir Toby Belch, Olivia, Sir Andrew Aguecheek, Rosalind, Prospero, Lady Macbeth, Falstaff and numerous other characters of Shakespeare's brilliant invention. Indeed, they played the parts so well at different times as to cease to be mere actors and almost become the characters themselves. A wonderful metamorphosis in the midst of dull reality.

Twelfth Night, As You Like It, The Tempest, Henry IV (part two), Julius Caesar, Macbeth and other plays I took part in over a period of about three years. 'So full of shapes and fancy, that it alone is high-fantastical', as Jim Smith used to boom in the first production I joined.

In fact it was how, from then on, I became two persons – through the power of imagination. By day the inmate of a cramped commercial cell situated on the edge of Hanky Park, Salford: that last misnamed place God municipally made, there being neither trees nor grass nor flowers nor any of the usual appurtenances of a park, but only sad miles of cobbled streets with houses whose chimneys grimly vomited the very firesmokes of Hell. But, by night, when not at home recovering from the remorseless visits to that office or trying to shake off strange cloudy fits of depression that had begun to assail me, I was losing myself in the sometimes comical, sometimes serious, always escapist world of rehearsals. It was a double-life that continued more easily still when, later, I moved to Willetts, whose offices were close to the Y.M.C.A. building.

'Okay, kids, let's have that scene again. And, if you don't mind, Sir Toby, I'd like to see you coming in a bit slower. You're not some bloody messenger hurrying news to the king but a ponderous old rake shambling about. Understand?'

Something of a decadent figure, a kind of decaying B.B.C. producer, Dan Killip was nonetheless excellent at bringing the best out of the cast, where there was any 'best' to be had. But never having met his type before I found him off-putting. Eventually, however, I got used to his effete prima donna act because, by and large, he ignored me.

Never more than a player of bit parts I was mostly happy enough. It is true that my ego suffered, but at least not having many lines to memorize and few cues to watch for, I was privileged to occupy what I now see as a useful position halfway between audience and player.

A spectator of both sides of the footlights, I was sufficiently uninvolved in each play to both penetrate and enjoy the magical tapestry of words and drama that was constantly building around me. That shimmering human and mystical landscape authored by Shakespeare and made flesh by my fellow actors did much to restore Paradise for me, and offset the sickening effects of the Black Hole of Salford with its huge poisoned River Irwell, its cavernous sooty railway arches, and its endless stylized streets, followed by the world of finance as a trainee accountant.

Young Oxley at play – (left) outside the summerhouse at 'Penrhyn' and (right) in 1952 with John, Bernard and Cecilia Wilson in their garden at 'Riversdale' further along 'The Road'. Below: 'The Road' as seen from 'Table Mountain' with 'The Dingle' in the left foreground.

64

The Manchester YMCA boxing team with Harry Oxley seated on the far right. Below: Patricia photographed with Catherine and Harry Oxley on a visit to London in 1964.

The Manchester Shakespearean players in 'Twelfth Night' in 1955, with William Oxley seated on the floor, second right. Below: the dress rehearsal of 'Little Women' with William and Patricia (right) as Meg.

66

Signing the register on April 13th 1963 "in a dark and drab northern church that Patricia's presence alone made radiant."

CHAPTER SEVEN
Once having been in Ecstasy

Exhausted, Philip and I lay down in a warm-as-orange sun on the boundary of the cricket field – drawn by the delicious green scene. Soon I had forgotten my companion who was, in any case, intent on the game, and I began to drift into that calm state of superconsciousness which follows bouts of ecstasy and out of which poetry is made.

The whole flat earth, from my grass-touched chin to the truthfully blue horizon, was a carpet of endless summer dotted with trees like a few subtle brushstrokes. When I turned my head I could see the many-mirrors river, breaking like luminous thought against the medieval arches of Clopton Bridge. Nearby was the plain modern stateliness of the Shakespeare Memorial Theatre, while straight in front of me lay eternal-seeming parkland with quietened strings of parked cars, coloured clusters of picnic-happy people, and marquees tall as sailing ships. I was become the lens of some flashy camera, opening to record the impress of a subtle-toned landscape taped across with paths and decorated with painted drips of coloured flowers under the immense sky.

Yet I was more than a mere camera, for a camera is mostly a passive and mechanical device. I was bringing together, whilst my eyes reposed on that beautiful scene, a three-day story in which little seemed to happen, *yet everything was experienced ...*

In much-thatched Shottery lived a woman, an ancient hag who wore a patch over one eye and had a black cat that sat on her shoulder. She said to me: 'Don't worry, dearie, everyone, but *everyone*, thinks I'm a witch! 'Specially when they know what Puss's name is.'

Not able to fully appreciate the antique cottage smelling of centuries of damp stone that we'd just entered, nor able to believe that the weird old crone was other than a witch, I merely stammered, 'What, what *is* your cat's name?'

The old dame cackled knowingly at Philip who had stayed in the cottage before. 'Why it's Satan ... isn't it, my love?' she replied stroking the cat on her left shoulder.

Using an old stick like a gnarled third leg, Julia – for such was the old dame's name – led my friend and me up creaking stairs to the room beneath a hayloft warmth of rafters and thatch.

'There's your beds,' said the ancient brusquely, then added, pointing to the one I was to sleep in, 'That's the one my first lodger had. He was Richard Burton.' Leaving us with that piece of theatrical information to digest, she again became a shaky part of the shaky stairs and disappeared.

'Crazy old dame!' expostulated Philip polishing his specs before starting to unpack. 'You'd never guess she was once a famous actress. Found out when I stayed here last year. Dan always books those he loves least in here! Or new people like you.'

I poked my cranium out of the small window and surveyed the beautiful but overcrowded garden. It was filled from wall to wall with roses and lupins, with lavender and unbloomed hollyhock and a hundred other flowers. I was totally absorbed by the only annual pilgrimage, in which I participated, of our Shakespearean company to Stratford-Upon-Avon, made out of homage to the Bard; and it was proving once more that an even better world than this existed if only one could find it.

The third bed in our room belonged to a permanent lodger: a small-time actor and budding playwright from the Memorial Theatre. He had dark hair and glasses and was a bit Jewish-looking. He is probably famous now if I but knew it. But I'll just call him Harold as I seem to recall that was his name. At night Harold would lie in his bed talking without respite – as little children do after a particularly exciting day.

Harold was the first real intellectual – if one excludes my father with his somewhat backwoodsman's erudition – whom I had encountered. We discussed Sir Walter Scott's novels which I liked very much at that time but which Harold loathed. We also contrasted the playwrights of the past with those of the modern theatre. And as I lay in the dark listening to this 'university wit' – this type so well portrayed in Kingsley Amis's *Lucky Jim* – I formed an impression of the effeteness afflicting the English intelligentsia: the sort I was later to come to think of as 'colour supplement intellectuals'. An impression that was to grow as the years went by and which, in part, had its origin in that mysterious insomniac's preference for the vacuous social realism of the 'kitchen sink theatre' as against the universal truth of the likes of Shakespeare, Marlowe, et al. Rightly or wrongly, and with all the presumption of youth, I was convinced Harold was a victim of the crass fashions of his time. But despite our fundamental disagreements we three got on like a cottage on fire ...

From that cottage with its white-washed walls, its brass bellows, its bed-warmers, its horse trappings, and the bird-twittering straw above our warm beds, Philip and I would set out for the evening productions at the Shakespeare Memorial Theatre. And what a galaxy of stars brought the Bard alive there! We were to witness the almost consumptive tenderness of Dorothy Tutin's Juliet; the lesbian shrillness of Peggy Ashcroft's Rosalind in the Forest of Arden; above all – though never again shall it be seen – to witness the severity of Wolfitt's performance as the storm-wrecked and passion-wracked Lear! Yes, such were indisputably powerful experiences in my young life. It was art – or culture if it is preferred – giving fresh substance and greater meaning to life.

Another memory, equally vivid, is of the interval in the very first performance I attended at the Memorial Theatre in Stratford-on-Avon. Our group had drifted out from the drinks' bar through swirls of beer and sherry on to the balcony of the theatre. The magic of Shakespeare's writings, so vitalized by the actors, clung to me like a smell on the clothes. I was so 'full of shapes and high fantastical' myself. The scene on the balcony was made for Renoir. Beautiful girls in painted dresses – they still wore them in those days! Men in striped blazers or evening dress. All was a blending of colours and flesh, of words and motion against a romantic backdrop – the painted flat green miles beyond the silver scimitar of the River Avon. When I looked hard beyond into the sun-honeyed longing landscape of that summer evening, I knew I was alive and in love and *certain* – though of what I was certain remained a mystery. I was barely out of school and still only a freshman in the University of Life.

That same evening after the theatre Old Julia threw a party for our drama group at her cottage among the roses of Ann Hathaway's Shottery. All the windows were open and, as the night scents wafted gently in, a babble of voices floated out into the subtle Shakespearian twilight. Dan Killip and his austere wife presided as usual. Jean Starkey looked more than ever our diminutive neurotic answer to Dorothy Tutin. A man, nicknamed appropriately 'Ham' carried crates of Bass about and bellowed a lot to no purpose. Frank 'Malvolio' Edey was, as ever, full of quotes and wheezy anecdotes; and it became harder than ever to believe him an insurance clerk. Frank had the manners of a faded actor and something of the air of Goldsmith's village schoolmaster about him.

By contrast, those on the periphery of that small coterie – the outsiders, as it were, such as myself – had little to say: certainly nothing 'brilliant' or witty. Though spotty and horse-faced Philip who was, in fact, a teacher, mixed well. Oddly, I recall that when Paul Rogers the actor arrived, I was pulled out of a dark inglenook by Dan and promptly introduced to him. He was the first 'famous' person I'd met, if one excluded certain cricketers. He drank long and maturely for the whole flushed evening seated in a chintz-covered armchair being lionized by our little group of theatrical amateurs. Unfortunately, my mother having instilled a dislike of heavy drinking into me, I sat for much of the evening disappearing into a vortex of priggish disapproval as I listened to various boasting tales of boozing exploits.

On the whole I found I detested actors. I hated the gooey affectation of even our own little provincial troop. Only Frank Edey with his unique blend of Augustan wit and clerkly ordinariness; and Jean who was a fragile creature and sad in a mature way like a divorced woman: all painted and powdered nervousness with large lugubrious eyes; and the brotherly Philip Hornbrook, did I really take to. But I'm bound to admit that even the superior university wits in the company, who were the most drily affected of all, were above-average in sensitivity.

... Sensitivity? My waking dream as I lay on the warm grass beside that cricket ground on the banks of the Avon was full of sensitive images. None brighter nor more tender than that of Patricia whom I had recently met. A quiet introspective girl yet one who was earnestly romantic underneath. One deeply young and more deeply shy. One moment she had seemed not to exist; the next there she was, standing in the corner of my heart like a cool, chaste statue. A creature of sun-warmed marble amidst flowers who had come from I knew not where to release all the feeling of which I was capable. To colour my sky with a romantic hue and sensitise it with love. Yet she was only there, in spirit, at that moment in Stratford by the Avon ...

Warwickshire I found a rich and beautiful county; a place that gathered all England's best freedoms into the bosom of Nature. Nor was it surprising that it was there, among those thatched cottages, those warbling streams and glowing fields, that a simple country lad had turned into the greatest poet the world had ever seen.

Frank and Philip and I spent many luminous hours wandering that blended tapestry of a county, enjoying its country sentiment of sun-dried lanes and pollen-powdered fields, its pretty villages and deep green rivers beside which cheerful fishermen sat, long-rodded, under curling willows. I recall how we three strolling players rested for lunch beneath an oak with the sun's light like a curtain of gold draped round us. Stripped to the waist we ate sandwiches and chatted and pulled on a bottle of cider. Everything was so fertile-seeming, friendly, and so frenziedly lovely! Felicitous. With the thought of one girl in my mind, the feeling of her in my heart, there seemed hope for the whole human race. Hope for Frank stuffing bread into his frog-like mouth, hope for short-sighted, sleepy Philip, and hope for everyone, if only...?

A path, an ordinary path, a path of the quotidian ran from Shottery to Stratford. I daresay Shakespeare himself knew it. One went down a lane near Ann Hathaway's cottage and Old Julia's cottage, crossed over a little wooden bridge that spanned a gleaming stream, and joined this path where it began its modest journey and mild progress across yellow fields towards Elizabethan Stratford.

... As I lay half-watching the cricket match on our last afternoon in Stratford, I thought of *that path* – my first loved lane. It had been the insignificant scene of a most extraordinary moment for me. An intensely personal moment in which I'd known Paradise again. Had known that other world: had seen this one returned to its pristine state.

Frank Edey, Philip Hornbrook and I – the three most important of the Stratford Pilgrims as we thought – had set out on our first morning to re-join the rest of the company who were staying in town. It was a stunningly beautiful early summer's day, all golden and gladsome. I think it was Frank who'd said he knew of the footpath across the fields, 'Away from all the traffic'. So Philip and I had automatically followed him.

It was then that something, which even now I cannot explain, came over me. Just as we had crossed the tiny stream with its green and white lily-boats, I began to sing. What I sang is gone forever. But I recall beginning to walk faster and faster. Soon I was in the grip of a strange and powerful rhythm that carried me some yards physically ahead of my friends, and an impossible-to- measure spiritual distance in front of them. I entered a field of whitegold corn interspersed with red-eyed poppies and, ridiculous as it may seem, I began to dance as well as sing. To dance for sheer joy. And I quite forgot my companions, never more than twenty yards behind me.

Abruptly, I sensed I had stepped into the mouth of a great cone: its glass apex resting on the far horizon. Above was a crystalline sky whose free-floating clouds were feathers from angels' wings, with a shining sun that spoke to all creation and that breathed and murmured its yellow syllables. I was in a living sea, an ocean of bright surging corn. Most of all I was conscious of the mirage of this world. Birds paused beside me in the air, insects became hesitant and slow, with bees and butterflies suddenly sinking in unison among flowers and poppies – speedwell, stitchwort, buttercups and o-so-red poppies – whose colours all glowed in *thoughtful silence*.

Then I seemed to see figures everywhere and nowhere. People, angels ... and the blue-eyed girl I loved. She was there, yet far away in her rapture of pretty dresses. She was a presence and an absence of feeling; a coming and going as in drunkenness. A life-focus. I found life at once more crowded and deserted than in any city street as, once more, I experienced the eternal presence in everything. A fine eternity glowing. I danced and moved in fountains of joyous feeling, the spray dry on my face. And I felt I owned everything, save God and my far away love. My absent beloved, Patricia, had become the gateway of feeling to the eternal. This I now know, years on, is the function of woman: the mediatrix betwixt the One and the Many. The trance was only partly shattered by our arrival in the ageless streets of Stratford and the gentle ridicule of my companions. Frank Malvolio declared, 'Ah, what t'is to be young and in love eh, Philip?'

For the rest of that day I was disturbed, neurotic with happiness. The passionate undertones of infinity continued to echo in me. And the next day I went back alone among the arcadian cornstalks of that same field. I walked by the cream-blossomed hawthorn hedges and looked down and down into the dark stream that flowed tenderly under the wooden bridge. Drunk and bemused on nature's essence, I wanted to devolve again into that fine cone of imagination. But, in the end, all I could find were traces of gossamer by the field's edge where insects and bluebottles resembled magical beads on the leaves of thoughtful hedges. That day I wrote my love a letter in which I said I had seen her face in a flower ...

*   *   *   *   *

Although I have described these years of my life as 'the years that threatened Paradise', this was true in all respects save one: my courtship, if I may be permitted a somewhat outmoded term. No man, I'm sure, ever entered on so troubled a period of his life and yet, at the same time, experienced a more thrilling and purely good companionship as I did then. Falling in love is the most effective counterblast to such stultifying and corrosive times that can be imagined. True, I also had a father whose conversation was to prove a great help in clarifying my frequently muddied and muddled thoughts. But nothing was so good or effective a solution to my problems as that immensely complexifying, greatly simplifying, and soul uplifting experience of love.

On April 13th 1963, a somewhat dull day weatherwise, I married Patricia, my earthly Muse, in a dark and drab northern church that her presence alone made radiant. She was a girl whose temperament perfectly complemented mine ... after the usual few thousand traumatic little love-soul adjustments that all unique and loving human beings have to go through. The days of our honeymoon were spent in Jersey, beside a mystical and luminous sea that forever circled a high cairn of moonrocks on top of which, like the white finger of love and truth, stands the Corbiere lighthouse. There we wandered together an island whose:

> Sun-burned lanes
> Hot beneath the hawthorn and the elderberry
> Run through earthwarm
> Fields stretching down to sand ...

A happy story whose better part lies beyond words; or, at least, is confined to images of poetry. But suffice it to say that I rediscovered Paradise there on that island of love in all its glory and eliminated, had things been otherwise, any doubts that might have grown as to its very existence. For she whom I wed held out moments of intense vision once again for me that were like glimpses of seablue pools in her white hands. Gave such loving light that all the doubts which a lying society might well have implanted in me were dispelled.

Such were the facts, behind which lies the mostly inexpressible. We had married shortly before I qualified as a chartered accountant. My two best friends, Tom Jones and John Wilson, had both gone to live in London by the time Patricia and I married. And in less than a year we, too, had done the same.

CHAPTER EIGHT
Other Edens

The crazy variety of a great city disoriented Patricia and me for a while. But we soon got to work on it. The first fortnight – after our arrival at St. Pancras' Station one pigeon-coloured evening of lights, excitement and an overloaded taxi – was spent with John, the sole survivor among my friends from the days of the Road. In the street outside his flat that first evening we arrived, I experienced a small moment of ecstasy: the dark night pullulated above me, above the great city; the yellow street lamplight flowed like amber blood into my heart; the house walls shone welcomingly; a million threads of smell were in the air, a tapestry of air woven by the city's long history; and my mind absorbed all the details in a humming night. The low plastered wall of the compressed garden, the small hedge, the knocker on the front door, the red doorstep, the square front window, the milk bottle empties ... all the shapes and colours had spoken in the aura of lamplight. Nor in daylight was the scene to disappoint me. I loved London from the first moment I lived there. Inside John's tiny flat, with its faint odour of vegetable cooking oils and generations of men's socks, the three of us lived together. His the only life properly unpacked.

For a while Patricia and I experienced a vague anxiety as we searched for somewhere of our own to live. But it was a dreamy quest really, one that was made up of hesitations and shoulder-shruggings each time we heard of a place that 'might do'. Until, all at once, John's landlady – a dumpy little woman in love with a huge dog that she had paralysed with comfort – found us a spacious flat in a house of genteel lugubriousness only a few streets away from where we were already. Soon we were settled into a pair of lofty, old fashioned rooms, plus a tiny kitchen, in a house that echoed with memories of servants and more gracious times. Our rooms were on the second floor up a flight of wide and creaking stairs. The hallway had a mirror that was large enough to step through and there was much truculent plumbing in the shared bathroom. Also we acquired a strict English landlady who was probably just about the last of her breed in a street where Asians, Cypriots and West Indians lived in explosive harmony.

Dartmouth Park Road was but a short walk from Spencer Rise where John lived; whilst not far away was Highgate Hill with its ghostly old cemetery where the poet Coleridge was reputedly buried, and its newer burial ground that sports the ridiculous decapitated bronze head of Karl Marx on top of a slab of marble. But more attractive than the nostalgic streets of houses were the weaving green acres of Hampstead Heath. Lost numbers of hours were spent by Patricia and me just wandering that undulating and brilliant parkland with its three glories of Kenwood House, a white lakeside piece of Regency elegance built above a mirroring lake on the banks of which orchestras played on summer evenings; Parliament Hill which justly boasts the finest view of London's ever-mobile skyline; and the deep grove of the Vale of Health to traverse which is like walking through a Constable painting. The Heath became our green labyrinth of Spring; we drowsed there side by side on listless days of Summer; knew its eglantine woods and misty ponds in Autumn; and scrunched its iced-over paths and frozen grass in Winter.

Most mornings I would walk the Heath whilst Patricia made breakfast in the flat. And, once, we both arose at 5 am. to discover the sheer joy of a golden and green summer with mist exuding from all the minted vales and glassy lakes, and we saw a sudden fox flash across the grass like a bronze brush through cottonwool air. And of a Saturday morning it was often our habit to walk over the Heath, go up Keats' Grove with its memories of lyrical nightingales, and into hilly Hampstead itself, where we'd bury ourselves first in some bookshop and, after, in conversation and cream cakes at the Hungarian cafe, or have lunch at The King of Bohemia: game pie, salad and a pint – all for 7/6d!

In those days Paradise was regained. And my romanticized vision – call it what you will – began to perceive tracts of Paradise, that beautiful shadowy dimension, even behind the veils of huge brickwork that otherwise so confuse the simple gaze within a great city.

At first we had few friends in London except for John and Tom, so Patricia and I spent a great deal of time exploring extensive areas of the Metropolis on foot. We were a young provincial couple, fresh-eyed in the great Metropolis. But it was not long before we could draw a line from Tower Hill to Notting Hill Gate and boast we knew everywhere in between. A couple thirsting for the new and unexpected, anxious to examine a great city's coat of many colours, we would set out and walk from Dartmouth Park Road, NW5 to St.

James's Park, or to the Mansion House, or to Hyde Park and Marble Arch, or to lowly Southwark. Sometimes, too, we'd take a windy riverboat up the Thames to Kew and Richmond; or a stuffy tube train out to the melting countryside around High Barnet, or in that other direction which we were to grow so much to love: Epping and Ongar.

At the same time as we assimilated the vast and bony structure of greater London, we also sought to fill the quiet leisure hours of evenings after work. They were evenings spent in the comfort of the flat, overlooking a street periodically loud with sudden cars and disturbed dustbins. Domestic evenings whose timeless quality matched our carefree dispositions, and which were only punctuated by the arrival of our friend John. John who was tall, thin and bespectacled – a novice in humour as well as life – and like ourselves just beginning to find his feet in London. A generous and interesting friend to have around, if one not so questing in spiritual matters as we were.

A typical day usually began with Patricia slipping off to catch the 8 o'clock bus on Highgate Road for she had to be at work a full hour before me when I was only working in the City. Consequently, after washing up the breakfast dishes I had plenty of time to gather my wits and briefcase, don a suit, and amble round the corner to Spencer Rise and John's flat. There I would enjoy a smoke and another breakfast of some excellent coffee plus either toast or a bacon sandwich.

John had always been bad at getting up in the morning, as well as being rather indifferent company so early in the day. The arrangement was that my arrival would – like a latter-day knocker-upper – ensure his getting up in good time for work. In return for which I was rewarded with a second breakfast, while he'd make head-scratching and yawning efforts to be pleasant company. On the whole the arrangement worked well, and for both of us the day would begin as a gentle surfacing to reality through an atmosphere of tobacco, coffee and frying bacon. Then, thoroughly prepared to meet the world, we'd both head down to the tube station where, like two blood corpuscles, we'd soon be sucked swiftly through the rattling veins of the Metropolis.

In those days I was still quite pleased to have risen from office boy to chartered accountant against what many people – including my boss in Manchester who admitted he thought me 'backward' – regarded as formidable educational disadvantages. Consequently I was, for a time, prepared to go along with the usual notions of 'success'. And as I found life in the capital congenial I was tolerably content with my location. What was more, I was being paid a high salary and my extra-mural literary activities seemed to fit nicely into the spare time available at the flat. Nor did I feel any particular tensions, or seem to have any particular problems of a personal nature. Though this was, I am sure, entirely due to being blessed with a sensible and loving wife.

Early in 1966 we moved to a small and then still beautiful town called Epping. A town just kept out of the clutches of the Metropolis's suburban tentacles by the considerable barrier of Epping Forest which lies athwart the town on its west side. Although motor cars were plentiful enough even then, it seemed few had yet discovered the many by-ways between Epping and Ongar.

I well remember the undisturbed ease with which John, Patricia and I could walk to the pub at Fiddler's Hamlet; stroll down a dry lane confused only by the scents of a spring dusk. In the day time one could idle equally freely sunshot lanes where pink campion blushed at the roadside. For, at that time, the M11 motorway and its spaghetti interchange with the M25 were only some planner's sick dream. But what a change in ten years! What madness and what beauty eaten up!

Our house in Brook Road, of which Patricia and I were very proud, was one of only half a dozen semi's facing a landscape of breezy wheat fields, tall trees, a rattling stream and a hill with a farmhouse at its dreaming summit. No more perfect a setting could be imagined for an ordinary couple expecting their first baby. To that house, which even had roses round its front door, we brought our daughter Elizabeth, born in University College Hospital, off Gower Street; and, later, our second child Katie, was to be born in that house.

In the same year as Elizabeth laughed and cried her way into our lives, like Thomas Traherne I began in earnest to seek Paradise again. I found it first in fragments in a surrounding countryside of small lapboard houses and pubs with rose-crimsoned gardens; or glade-deep in Epping Forest; or along the innumerable footpaths and lanes strung across that county. Here in the twilight, midges turned to specks of gold:

> By the unbreakable peace of a pool's surface
> Where clouds, not time, pass over its face ...

Redolent, too, with a supernatural green was the walkway meadow between the Anglo-Saxon church of Greenstead and delightfully shoddy Ongar itself. All was an area instinct with paradise, beauty and poetry, whether in winter when:

> The misted porcelain of a morning sky,
> This mild damp winter moves in me.
> Like a dark sea the chopped earth glisteningly
> Waits its inevitable new birth,
> Each rigid furrow a ripple of hope.

Or summer when:

> The yellow path burns at the field's fringe
> The wild flowers colourfully nod
> Bird songs crack in the scented heat
> And butterflies crazily glide in the airy sweat.

On moving South, I'd had a greater void to fill than Patricia, for I had been used to studying most evenings for the previous six years, and study is a habit which, once acquired, dies hard. So now that was over, I had much time on my hands. Soon, however, and despite a head buzzing from a day spent in the booming City, I returned gratefully to the world of 'proper' books after a too long lay-off.

It was during this period that I read further long poems and began to read more twentieth century poets, Eliot and Pound in particular. Patricia bought me Neville Coghill's update of *The Canterbury Tales* and I also read *The Faerie Queene* and some David Jones. Robert Graves swam into view, as did Dylan Thomas and the Argentinian poet Borges. I became a voracious reader, buying new and second hand books at every bookshop I visited. It's almost impossible to list what I bought and read in those years. Nothing seemingly was too heavy or too light: I read the whole of John Buchan, and Arthur Conan Doyle, along with treatises on philosophy by Hegel and Schopenhauer. I read plays by the Irish writers Synge and O'Casey, as well as other psychological dramas by Ibsen and Chekhov. Patricia and I read Palgrave's *Golden Treasury* together, as well as several Shakespeare plays. I delved into the Romantics, the Renaissance writers, the Augustans; in fact, the only books I remember resisting were the novels of Jane Austin which Patricia tried to persuade me (and still does!) to read. But I did read the Brontë sisters and agreed with her on their excellence.

Firstly in the flat's silence, then in our new house at Epping, a million doors began to open for me and I saw almost immediately a new way to satisfy my soul. As I started to work my way through the classics of both poetry and prose, I discovered for myself the glorious treadmill of Literature. Everywhere I came across written proof, encountered hints and glimpses of that wonderful landscape I'd kept seeing all my days. And for the first time I found myself viewing the same Paradise through the eyes of others – through writers.

Sometimes, it is true, it was a sad and bitter vision I beheld. Not a romantic view at all, but one that was volcanic, blood red and larvaed with suffering. But other times I saw the same milkwhite rivers, greeny meadows and the cornfields and dingles of my dreaming boyhood. Never fixed, this 'land unknown' was and is always changing, like human nature. For Paradise is no world of boring contentment, but a place of action excited by beauty. A place of flux yet one that is absolute: changeful yet changeless like human nature. From the first I noticed a balance there that was forever maintained; and my initial perplexities at the dark and light contours of pain and joy soon passed away.

Then, one day, I wrote a poem. An insignificant poem and a small enough event perhaps. Yet had I known it, I had taken the first step towards weaving my life into a seamless whole where before it had been so many scattered threads of consciousness.

CHAPTER NINE
Literary Beginnings

I also began to rediscover Paradise through proximity to London. Epping was only at the end of the Central Line and I could be anywhere in the Metropolis within the hour. Which brought the literary life of the capital within easy reach.

But most of all, Paradise was the flowering of any talent I might possess as a poet. I felt I was reclaiming Eden, that other world, in words. Phrases, stanzas and paragraphs – all disclosed a not-always-coherent map in time of that world which is 'nowhere and yet everywhere'.

I had always been an active person and it seemed not enough to confine myself to an ivory tower built of pencil and paper. As Robert Graves wrote to me, 'Poetry is not an art but a way of life'. And although I was to be a long time coming to a full appreciation of what he meant, I found I needed to carry my poetry beyond the printed page ... into life itself. So though I continued to go daily to the City, I changed my job from that of ubiquitous auditor to a position in the humdrum ambience of a bank in order that, by being more settled, I might facilitate my literary activities. And from late 1966 the literary side of my life assumed an increasing importance.

I quickly discovered that Epping itself had a host of literary connections and historical associations. The forest had once been royal hunting ground, hence Queen Elizabeth's hunting lodge near Chigwell. Many literary persons had lived in its environs: Tennyson at High Beach; William Morris; John Clare who was for two years at Dr Allen's lunatic asylum in the forest; T.E. Lawrence; Sir Thomas More; and Daniel Defoe, who wrote the *Journal of the Plague Year* from imagination in retreat near Wanstead. Ben Jonson was a frequent visitor to the ruined mansion of Copt Hall that had been gutted by fire around a hundred years ago, and must have enjoyed the same seemingly unending view of arcadian countryside that one still gets from the burned shell.

If the social whirl of my friend Tom's parties had, at times, seemed slightly decadent; or my life as an actor one of dusty affectation; both quickly came to seem quite normal by the standards of the exciting, if at time suffocating, literary market place of which I gradually became a part.

My first actual encounter with literary society came in the shape of something called *Manifold.* This odd organisation was run by a mother and daughter team named Elizabeth Ann Harvey and Vera Rich – two ladies who were often at primadonnerish variance with each other. The group also published a magazine of the same name.

Manifold was international in scope, parochial in outlook and, as might have been expected, had a heavy feminine flavour. But, unlike many later feminist publications with their obsessive menstrual conditioning and shrill Women's Lib manifestoes, *Manifold's* chief weakness was a tendency to trivial tittle tattle. On the other hand, by much of the Sixties' low standards, the editors had a certain taste and catholicity that looked positively refreshing when set beside the blown husk of so much repetitive experimental meaningless modernism that still loudly greeted the Age.

One constant feature of all *Manifold's* gatherings – whether it was a simple *soirée,* a chatty cocktail party, a rum recitation or a bumptious banquet for over two hundred subscribers – was the way-out cuisine (or so it appeared then), always prepared by Vera and her mother and conveyed in giant enamelled bowls all the way from Highgate to Fetter Lane or wherever the event was to be held. Great litre bottles of home-brewed liquor, tasting like a mixture of elderberry wine and vinegar, were also humped along together with masses of crockery and cutlery – all of which in an after-party atmosphere of feminine bitchery one was expected to help wash-up.

This association with *Manifold* was the beginning of a whirl of literary activity that was to take me all over the country and abroad. Whether this activity was low key, as in the early years of our later 'exile' in Devon, or carried out with feverish rapidity as often seems the case now, it still affords those glimpses of Paradise for which I search, and will go on searching until ...

A name that frequently cropped up at those *Manifold* gatherings was that of Norman Hidden, chairman of the Poetry Society. In those days the Society was looked upon as the centre of the poetry world; it was a far more respected and lively body then than the rather depressing place it later became. And with the authority of the Society behind him Norman, too, was a respected figure. He was, also, a most energetic man who found time, apart from his official duties, to run a free-for-all poetry forum and workshop at the Lamb & Flag pub, Covent Garden. The meetings of 'Workshop Two' as it was known were held once a month in the upstairs Dryden Room, named after the famous poet. It was an antique, L-shaped room with a creaking floor and stained ceiling liberally varnished with beer and poetry. Norman would sit like a retired, silver-bearded Don Quixote in the Chairman's leather-padded throne – nothing so simple as an ordinary chair for Norman – and preside genially over the meetings.

Because of their regular occurrence, as well as the predictable shape of the evening, it is now almost impossible to remember any particular occasion – they all run into one. First a well-known poet like George Barker or John Heath-Stubbs would read their poems, then there would be a long interval for beer-swilling and shouted conversation, followed by a second half in which members of the audience read poems they had brought.

Even those evenings when I acted as chairman in Norman's absence, or when I read my own work, do not individually stand out. But the problem lay as much with me as with the nature of those meetings. I expected, and still expect, serious standards in poetry and the trouble was at Workshop Two a kind of literary Gresham's Law operated in that the bad inevitably drove out the good. Of course, it was a sign of the times; an era when a sort of shoddy funfair mentality prevailed, and publication of the second rate was an easier and more frequent occurrence than that of the best work. But that seedy crowded room, that pseudo-literary setting, was a microcosm of an important idea taking hold of the Sixties at all levels: the democratisation of Bohemia. Poetry readings had, somehow, become performance, a mere act. *But was it poetry*? No, certainly it wasn't! And ten years previously no one would have taken such a performance as anything but poor quality music hall, certainly not poetry. But when I tentatively suggested to Norman that there might be more to poetry than whimsical social realism or no-content-at-all technical gamesmanship, he turned his sophisticated gaze on me and said dismissively, 'Oh, you mean we should all write religious stuff like Kathleen Raine?' Which was not what I meant at all. I was merely making a quiet plea for a poetry that celebrated more than the surface of things. Such a general and philosophically shallow outlook was all too much for me and I began to take less and less interest in *Workshop*.

Yet the total experience of *Workshop* undoubtedly burned into me like paint on the soul. It was messy. It was lively. It was even phoney. It was often depressing, but rarely dull.

Neither was my correspondence with my father. Being able to communicate easily with a parent, to be able to discuss freely the most exalted as well as the most trivial topics, is a great gift. Though I had left home in 1963, my father and I had been determined to continue our 'discussions'. At first, we corresponded fitfully, but when we moved to Epping, I received as many as four or five letters a week. A vital correspondence which shows, perhaps better than anything else, my slow conversion from accountant to poet, and my growing rift with the poetic society of that time.

I'd written to tell him all about Norman Hidden's *Workshop*, of course, and when I heard some aspect of it was to be broadcast on the radio, I told my father to listen in. His response was swift – the next morning I received the following letter:

'I have just listened into, or had my ears assailed with, dull monotonous mediocrity masquerading as poetry. Prose surely? Apart from the reminiscences of intimacy of a bespectacled spinster, a librarian's wistful yearning for the confidences of love, and the empty imagery of a tawdry passionate evocation – there was nothing that a second rate journalist could not have bettered.

'The attempted chorus speaking blank pathetic prose was as damp as a rain-soaked Nov. 5th bonfire. Surely these are not the inheritors of Shakespeare, Milton, Homer, Virgil, Keats, Coleridge, Wordsworth and Shelley? T.S. Eliot would have turned in his grave could he have heard such adolescent denigration of a glorious language. The standard was very little higher than that "pop-art" type-written effort I read at Epping. Surely these are not the arbiters of poetic taste and culture: "hen shit and testicles" and "a child's toy dream" are hardly the props to elevate the language to sublime infinity.'

I tried to encourage his letter writing after he was taken ill with a form of muscular sclerosis and rushed into hospital in 1966. Due to his hyperchondriacal tendencies, I became perturbed about a possible lack of will-to-live developing in what was, basically, a pessimistic nature. This became pronounced when the firm to which he'd dedicated all his working life – over 50 years – threatened to make him redundant in a very underhand manner. I remember writing, 'When you finally retire [in the summer of 1967] we can *live a whole literary lifetime* in the next six months!' After his retirement our correspondence took on a hard literary edge and I tried out my many theories and hypotheses concerning literature and poetry on him. The times I'd been working away from home had been periods of intense mental ferment. I was always thinking, searching, almost desperately trying to expand mentally. I was almost choking with ambition to *know* and all this was poured out in letters to a sympathetic listener: my father. He was not just sympathetic, he was critical; he read my immature ideas and, drawing on his own vast reading and erudition, tempered them with practical thoughts and suggestions. For, as he himself put it, he was 'determined to go the distance'. He was no mere listener, but engaged actively with me in the search for what I called 'truth', and encouraged, with his letters and enthusiasm, my rapidly expanding mental processes. It was a complete two-way correspondence, with myself the young apprentice, he the wise and kindly master. He wrote widely on beauty and music in poetry and his ideas influenced me both consciously and subconsciously: I still believe that a poem *per se* should have elements of beauty, celebration and rhythm, even if the subject matter is anything but beautiful. In one of his early letters, he wrote, 'All we can do is to keep trying with every faculty we possess to find that something worthwhile – that "yea" as against the "nay" in life.' To 'Icon' (as he always signed himself), that something worthwhile was always beauty or truth.

To me, just starting out, my father's reading seemed to be encyclopaedic. Yet despite this, and the honest, sincerely-felt opinions which flowed from his pen, he was a man beset with doubts. He would often quote other authorities when he felt they expressed exactly what he wanted to say, trusting their words rather than his own. The possession of a 'magpie mind' and an almost near-perfect memory enabled him to acquire the habit: 'where I have (as I often do) found the writer's words more expressive and clearer than my own, I have let the author speak'.

I, too, have been accused many times of this habit, and looking back through these letters I see, perhaps, from where I acquired the tendency. My father was also a stickler for intellectual honesty and would never try to pass-off such quotes as his own. Again, when I use others' words, I put quote marks around them. This has led to many reviewers accusing me of merely stringing together quotes in my writings – an accusation they do not make against less-honest writers!

But all-in-all, these letters were an ingenuous voyage of self-discovery; we both thought with pens in our hands, contradicting ourselves and each other in the hope that we were moving forward to a greater understanding of literature. I remember beginning to read for the first time Coleridge's *Biographia Literaria* and the enthusiasm with which I urged father to order it from the library as it 'will EXPLAIN the POETIC VISION as nothing else will'.

There were very few literary and philosophical questions we didn't touch on from the momentous 'What is poetry?', 'Who or what is God?', 'The exact nature of poetic creativity' to the nature of the divine experience, to trivial discussion on individual poems in current magazines. We would often preface our letters with 'titles' such as 'A Short Note Concerning Critics' or 'A Success or a Failure?' which was all about The Poetry Society (even then it was a topic of conversation!).

The letters were frank and completely uninhibited, especially when reporting the contemporary literary scene in which I was becoming more and more involved. In those days, the Poetry Society used to run 'Summer Schools', a kind of poetical gathering where poets, editors, publishers and other interested parties would all come together on a university campus and talk and argue away a weekend. I went to three of these, at York, Oxford and Bristol, with a long-time friend David Beugger. I wrote copious reports to my father, as can be seen from one of his replies which begins: 'Icarus (my father's name for me in these letters). This is an acknowledgement of the fulsome 33 pages of good graphic narrative received...' These narratives contained both serious and amusing incidents. For example I wrote after going to York (1969):

'Many people think Seamus Heaney the best new poet to come along for some time. As yet, I think it is far too early to say anything. However – business man that I am – I took the precaution of stopping off at Foyles and picking up a copy of his book ... Heaney's language is very skilful and there is some content in it. It is Larkinesque-derived poetry ... which believes if the 'feel' of objects is conveyed then you have a poetic language. In its deep touch-colouring it is remotely Dylan Thomas. None of this makes for a *certain* poetic future, but Heaney is well-read and well-informed so he may give us something worthwhile...

'I submitted two questions to the Brains' Trust on the Sunday morning: 1. Literary history shows that there have been fewer good critics than good poets. If the panel agrees, does this make the role of the critic more important in literature than that of the poet? and 2. Does the panel agree that the logical extension or conclusion of all "movements" in poetry is the establishment of a *literary tyranny*?

'They debated the first question. I clashed with Gael Turnbull who thought all critics a waste of time. I said his attitude was ridiculous because critics were essential as long as art remained a suspect phenomenon ...'

Needless to say, my father and I thrashed out answers to these questions along with many more. I also wrote from Oxford (1970) to tell him about the Saturday night reading:

'The readers were William Plomer, Brian Patten, Alan Brownjohn and Jeff Nuttall. ...

'Next there was Jeff Nuttall, uncouth, crude and highly intelligent author of *Bomb Culture.* Nuttall was repellently effective. In me he aroused anger; but the effect on David was most entertaining. Bad language etc. (foul or sexual) are utterly taboo for David and – to the great consternation of a completely silent audience – throughout Nuttall's reading he sat holding his head as if about to vomit, groaning audibly and saying, quite loud enough for several rows to hear, such things as "Shut up!", "No more for Christ's sake!", "O I wish he'd finish!", "This is not poetry!". In addition he made all kinds of noises with his mouth: never have I heard so many variations of "Tut, Tut!" In front of me was the most enormous, hairy giant of a man, clearly a supporter of Nuttall, and I thought any minute he would turn round and let fly ...'

I'm often asked why 'Icon' and 'Icarus'? I can only surmise at the answer. 'Icon', short for Iconoclast, suited Father's subversive temperament; for while mild and gentle in relationships with the rest of the world, with me he would argue out every point of every argument. He insisted on addressing me as 'Icarus' because, to quote, 'I like the name'. Yet he flatly repudiated any connection between himself and Daedalus, the mythical builder of the Cretan Labyrinth. Patricia, who has edited a book of our letters (*On Poets and Poetry*, Salzburg, 1988), suggests that deep within Icon was a primaeval notion that poets fly too near the sun of creativity and run the risk of the long fall to spiritual death. On more than one occasion in his letters he exhorted me to be careful of my talent, to rest, to take things easy, not to burn myself out, etc. Especially before I'd had my first book published.

By a fluke – having had hardly any poems published in magazines – *The Dark Structures and Other Poems* was published in the autumn of 1967. This came about through the first poetry magazine to which I ever subscribed: *The Poetry Review.* The Mitre Press often advertised poetry books in its pages. Frequently seeing these notices, plus the occasional review of one of its books, I assembled a collection of about 40 poems and sent it off. In due course, a letter came back from a Mr. Shaw saying 'we like the unusual lyrical quality of your work' and, as I lived in Epping, they invited me to their premises in Lincoln's Inn Fields for further discussion.

Their 'premises' consisted of a remarkably bright but dusty basement in Sardinia House, just off Kingsway. Mr Shaw proved to be a neatly dressed clerkly young man of around my own age; but the true embodiment of the Mitre Press was a small Pickwickian figure straight out of Dickens who went by the remarkable name of Mr Fudge. Mr Fudge was well into his eighties and to this day I cannot understand how or why either he or Mr Shaw had any interest in poetry. The only comments I can ever recall either making of a critical or literary nature was that Mr Fudge once held up a book and said, 'Boy, they do publish some rude books these days!' The book in question – which he held well away from me – was Alex Comfort's *The Joys of Sex*. (It was to be years before I discovered that Alex Comfort had once been a well-known poet, but had found more lucrative employment for his pen.) As for Mr. Shaw – apart from what he kindly wrote about my poetry in the letter inviting me to meet them – the sole thing he ever said about poetry was, 'One day you could be as well known as Dannie Abse or Jean Kenward.' An observation which I feel does not call for any comment from me!

Today, the firm would be in danger of being classed as a vanity press, if only because it required a small contribution from its authors towards publication costs. The books they published were all hardbacks and letterpress, and even I could see that the contribution asked for was very nominal – just over a hundred pounds. The books were very well produced by the standards of the time (often better than those of the biggest publishers) and they were well advertised and quite often reviewed. But I still think there was an element of the vanity press about them; though in today's small press world, the Mitre Press's arrangements with their poets would be regarded as unrealistically fair ... they even paid royalties quarterly and gave the author a dozen free copies on publication. But as people always advised 'Never pay for publication' I never went back to them, even though they continued to publish books for many years afterwards.

I was, however, most anxious that my father would see that first book, *The Dark Structures and Other Poems*, in print, even though it gained me no niche in literary history and very few reviews, being totally overshadowed by another Mitre Press book published the same day, which was an immediate sensation in all the papers. Anne Lewis-Smith's *Flesh and Flowers* – a selection of erotic poems – became front page news in both the tabloids and broadsheets, though why I cannot now recall. Patricia thinks it was because of the explicit erotica in the poems; and by a woman! She remembers the author being on *Woman's Hour* talking about sex and poetry.

My father had seen and commented on many of the poems in manuscript, offering advice and encouragement and was delighted with the book. He wrote, 'I must confess that to have seen this collection in print so early surpasses my wildest hopes and expectations'. All I'd pompously replied was, 'This publication will solve nothing. For me the road will be long and hard ... History tells me that the road for the believer and true poet is always long ...'

Yet the publication of my first book did signal a change. Gradually, my father learned all about my discontent and my grandiose plans to change things. The late Sixties had seen the beginnings in me of what was nothing less than a full-blown reaction against most of the things that era stood for. It was a most spiritually significant phase for me and, in reality, became more an actual part of my life in the Seventies. Outwardly, small time publishing was the chief manifestation of this crisis; inwardly all was intellectual and emotional turmoil. We thought of many different schemes then –

Change. September 1970. With a weak autumnal sunlight playing on the trees that skirted the lake behind my parents' house in Manchester, I had sat in the back garden and discussed with my father the possibility of starting a literary magazine. I also showed him some notes I had made towards the project. That same month, but a year later, Patricia and I left the Hiddens' flat for the last time, parting amicably with Norman, after having assisted him with his magazine for two years. In my quest to find myself as a poet, it had become apparent that I needed to go my own way; which was, in Norman's eyes, 'élitist and solitary'.

CHAPTER TEN
Publish and be Damned

I had left Norman Hidden's flat boiling over with a passion at so many false aspects of a false decade. I was on the verge of exploding, of being galvanised into a frenzy of literary activity, for I'd grown increasingly anti-political, and my early childhood experiences of what, for want of a better term, I called 'the divinity in things', had left so indelible a mark on me that I could no longer go along with the shallow materialistic ideals of the middle-class into which I had been born, nor abide the liberal socialistic nihilism of Sixties' thinkers like Normal Hidden. Above all, I was seething with plans to start my own magazine – an incarnation of the anger which had, like a suppressed geyser, been bubbling up and fermenting within me for at least the previous three years. It was my almost inevitable reaction to the Literary Sixties. I called it *Littack* – 'literary-attack', the name coming entirely spontaneously – and was damned for it ever-after.

For most of my life I have been anti-political, my principal concern being with poetry – something which is generally far less controversial to the majority of people – so how is it that I still meet people, even after all these years, who exclaim, 'Oh, you're the person who published *Littack*, aren't you?' And you can tell from their tone it is one of those leper-moments, a moment of prejudice when you know that you've met someone who has heard bad things about you.

What was *Littack*? And what did it, and I as its editor, do so remarkably wrong that I became the living proof of Saintsbury's observation that the English literary establishment is 'slow to forget and even slower to forgive.'?

Littack was a small magazine, one of hundreds that litter the literary landscape, devoted to the printing of poems and related articles: a magazine intended to give a critical survey of the state of poetry and poetry publishing at that time. Its circulation, as is the case with most such periodicals, never exceeded about eight hundred copies. By current standards of desk-top publishing, it was not particularly well-produced: though for its time it was better than many of its competitors. It was first published with the help of Patricia and our friend David Beugger. He put up half the capital to help found The Ember Press, a small publishing firm named after Ember Lane, Esher, where he lived, and the project began. With the second issue we moved the base of operations to Epping. By the time we reached our third issue we had acquired an overseas' editor, the expatriate poet Peter Russell who lived at that time in Venice. But throughout the whole life of the periodical I was the controlling editor who decided what did, and what did not, go into the magazine.

My father had admired Nietzsche, Wyndham Lewis, Jonathan Swift and Roy Campbell, and, by way of contrast, Montaigne. This was an explosive cocktail of writers to expose any young man to, and I felt the explosion! I also read that 'arch-fascist' Ezra Pound, at the same time as I was helping Norman Hidden with his monthly *Workshop* events at the Lamb & Flag. The result of all this was that I conceived a strong feeling of dichotomy between the anything-goes liberalism represented by the world of a poetry impresario like Norman Hidden, and the more dynamic and confident approach of the likes of Pound and Wyndham Lewis.

Eventually, when I began to plan my own magazine platform and creative 'movement', I had in mind Cyril Connolly's distinction between the programmatic or dynamic magazine which sought to push a manifesto of ideas about poetry, and the more passive miscellany which simply publishes what is available at the time of publication. Opting for the dynamic approach, the first issue of *Littack* mounted a whole series of critical articles, which were often savagely satirical as well as rationally argued. As I was the only writer involved, I wrote the whole of the first issue myself, using my own name and various pseudonyms in order to give the impression of several fellow contributors. If I'm asked why I didn't advertise for contributions, I can't be sure of an answer. I know I felt very isolated in my antipathy towards the prevailing intellectual climate, but I also think that I wanted the whole concept to burst upon the literary world fully grown. An unexpected time-bomb – influenced by Wyndham Lewis's *Blast*? I can't say after all this time. But I felt that I couldn't put out a magazine with only one contributor. Yet despite the bad impression which most of the contents of *Littack* 1 made, I was soon receiving more than enough offers of poetry and prose to guarantee that I would never be short of contributors again.

Looking back at that first issue of *Littack* I am struck by both the level of spleen that motivated it and the sheer comprehensiveness of its attack. I wrote in a promotional handout that poetry had become 'intolerably obscured by the propaganda for false values at all levels of thought'; and 'until the whole of English poetry is out of the Pound Rut, and the Academic Rut, and the Rut Rut, nothing much will improve for any of us'. I invented Jason Hardy, a sort of 'brutal backwoodsman of the Poetry World who would react violently against the rotted liberal *zeitgeist* that pervaded the English and American Literary Scenes'. People were left in no doubt what *Littack* stood for. The first editorial spelt it out with staggering comprehensiveness:

1. To provide a venue for all those poets and writers who have long been oppressed by the deliberate grinding poverty of exclusion from 'established' magazines ... for no better reason than that they had something to say ...
2. To publish all work that has literary merit AS HEREIN DEFINED BY EXAMPLE OF THIS MAGAZINE ...
3. To give greater preference to poetry in future issues ...
4. This magazine is committed to the individual ... rejection of the idea that meaning = message ... and also rejects, specifically, the following notions as being ultimately dangerous to the freedom of the artist ... :
    a) that all men are equal (if equal means the 'same').
    b) that the State is something men serve, rather than vice versa.
    c) love thy neighbour (even if he's a rogue).
    d) for the Common Good (if some of the common good is clearly the common bad).
5. This magazine commits itself to:
    THE DEFENCE OF THE CRITICAL INTELLIGENCE...
    THE DEFENCE OF STANDARDS IN LITERATURE
    THE DEFENCE OF FREE SPEECH AND THE PROMOTION OF ITS USAGE
    THE OFFENCE OF POETRY
6. There is an absolute sense of values which writer after writer, poet after poet, affirms but which the mass of people either deny, or are in ignorance of.

To be positive it is often necessary to be, at first, negative. It was clear to me that the Sixties' radicalism had set going a creeping tide of censorship, despite all its loud claims to the contrary. I believed, and still believe, in the right and exercise of free speech. The true poet and artist must be free to think the unthinkable, and to communicate it. Such is the heart of creativity. But the 1960s, having thrown the bone of pornography and so-called sexual freedom to people, promptly threw out the baby with the bath-water and instituted the gradual censorship which has led, thirty years on, to political correctness. In opposing a prescriptive ethic for poetry and what I saw as a proscriptive programme for universal brainwashing, I went against the current, rowing vigorously with *Littack*.

So what were the sort of things that upset people so terribly? Well, for starters, the magazine said outright that the majority of contemporary poetry was mediocre if not downright bad. Not only was this a too sweeping generalisation, for there were good poets around, but it was a statement which immediately lost me the sympathy of my only natural allies, namely, my fellow poets. Then publishing satirical squibs such as the one entitled 'British Intellectual' obviously lost the magazine the intellectual vote. There was also more satire, especially of the Juvenilian sort written by Jason Hardy, in *Littack* than in any comparable magazine since the Second World War and it lost me a great deal of sympathy. Of course, the Alternative Establishment also rebelled *en masse* against *Littack*!

Following this swingeingly negative start, the second issue began by publishing the more positive 'Vitalist Memorandum'. Written in a staccato short-hand style – similar to Pound's 'A Few Don'ts for Imagists' – it suggested the need for a new poetic approach which it called 'vitalism', and defined it for poetry as: ' a firm statement of feeling, ideas, in a strong language'; adding the need for 'more statement and less image than Pound advocated'. In several places it attempted to define or suggest the real significance of words like 'Littack' and 'vitalism'. Thus, '*Littack*, the attitude of mind (negative mainly) which will lead to vitalism (positive)'; and '*Littack One* laid a new attitude of mind. A new circuit was established – it is now necessary to run a current through. This is vitalism – the philosophy of the new release. A new poetry of ideas, of feeling.' In the following issues, this First Vitalist Memorandum was subjected to critiques by others, principally Peter Russell and Anthony Johnson who both took a positive view of what was being proposed and went into lengthy analyses of its ideas.

But, as Anthony Johnson perceived, it was not so much a new poetry *à la* Pound, as a *renewed* poetry that was called for. Hence his phrase 'a new vitalist poetry', used not to distinguish the poetry we wanted from all poetry that had gone before, so much as to indicate that our poetry would represent a continuation of the great tradition of real or vital poetry: the old vitalist poetry of Shakespeare, Milton, Donne, Wordsworth, Keats and Tennyson at their best. We wanted a non-academic verse and one not characterised by Alvarez' 'unity of flatness' but one that 'absorbed a given reality' and came alive with it. A poetry that danced to the tune of spirit, thought, idea and feeling; and which avoided either that malady of flatness which characterized the Movement Poets, or the sickness of hysteria which one found in Ginsberg's *Howl*. In his 'A Program for Vitalism', Anthony Johnson perceived this and expressed it brilliantly. In issue 6, the Second Vitalist Memorandum took on board some of the feedback from Russell and Johnson and other poets who, for a while, were close to the magazine like Anthony Rudolf, Richard Burns and Walter Perrie.

For the most part the magazine was ignored by the national dailies and the periodicals most associated with the literary establishment; it was ignored in the quarters that are supposed to count. Nowhere in the Establishment was it openly opposed with sound arguments. With the exception of some short (usually hostile) reviews in the small magazines, the whole venture was met with 'the censorship of silence'. For example, *Platform* (now *Pennine Platform*): 'What *Littack* calls its "dynamic neutrality" is, in fact, no more than a peevish elitism reminiscent of Lewis and "Old Ezra" at their worst'; *Second Aeon*: 'sometimes it's funny, sometimes it's stupid, it's certainly different!'; while *Oasis* contained a line which has almost come to represent *Littack*: 'An odd beast this ... goes in for shouting from the rooftops in capitals ...'. In *Encounter* Douglas Dunn referred to 'the preposterous *Littack*' and the *Sunday Times*, in a short review obviously used as a filler, called it a magazine firing 'star-shells and bombs at the literary establishment in the name of "vitalism" ...' but added, 'the standard of poetry is high.'

Very few others thought the standard of poetry high, even those individuals who were more responsive to *Littack*. Peter Russell had written from Venice, 'Let me say at once that while the ideas you have are excellent, I don't think the poetry is too hot ... some spelling lessons might come in handy too.' Michael Horovitz summed up with, 'If you were seriously concerned with improving the state of poetry you wldn't waste yr own & yr readers' time pointing so emphatically at what you consider bad or petty'; while Sean Haldane wrote from Quebec, 'The poetry you publish in your review is spastic, constipated and strangely timid, as if anything more than the hard (not always so hard either) description of objects would blast your little digestive systems apart.'

However, a few individuals did enjoy all the fuss; Harry Chambers wrote that he had 'enjoyed all the ballyhoo about *Littack*'; and Lawrence Durrell, 'Bravo ... your paper has zip...!'. And Tom Scott wrote from Edinburgh, 'The first number certainly has vitality and more imagination than I have ever seen in a poetry magazine this century... I feel rather as if, having been making a last stand with my back to the wall, suddenly I am overwhelmed by relief troops after years of siege!'

After the magazine had settled to a less attacking stance more people became interested. For instance Hugh MacDiarmid wrote after the first four issues, 'I like *Littack*. It has started well.', while Peter Redgrove responded to the attack on academics with, 'I know of no university man in this country who is aware that in cultures other than our fag-end Protestant one, poetry permeates all actions, everyday and uniquely, like a secular liturgy of joy and sorrow available to all.'

But it was its attack on Arts Councils and the grant system which raised many passions. Ian Hamilton Finlay, himself involved in a dispute with the Arts Council, was 'extremely interested in your comments on Arts Councils and Censorship. I think your perception as to the nature of the age is absolutely right. The wonder is so few people see it.' Peter Abbs was 'glad to see you are not supported by the Arts Council, and that you are opening your pages up to poetry and imaginative prose... I agree wholeheartedly with your emphasis on imagination.' Mike Shields, who now runs *Orbis*, wasn't in agreement, 'Arts Council grants *do* help people, you know – our magazine [*Here Now*] wouldn't exist without them', though subsequently he changed his mind.

But I shall let the critic Geoffrey Grigson have the last word on *Littack* 1. '...my monsters of F-art wouldn't all be yours, but I am for dissent. You might go over dissent with a wire brush; and it will seem stronger and be easier to read if you narrow the page from 17 or so words per line to 12 or 13. And no more phoney knights apparently about to pee (or having pee'd) on the cover.'

But it would be misleading to suggest that *Littack* was a carefully planned venture. Had it been so, it might have been a far more successful venture than it was. In fact, despite the notes I made for my father, *Littack* was more the product of an inspirational brainstorm, than a carefully thought-out scheme. I conceived the First Vitalist

Memorandum while out walking in a field near Epping, and when I returned home I wrote it down in about ten minutes without any subsequent revision that I can remember. All the faults and flaws of expression, all the spelling mistakes, the flights of fancy, the good and bad insights came this way. As, indeed, did the bite and abundance of satire which adorns – or disfigures – the first two *Littacks*.

Finally, philosophy and philosophical ideas have always been important to me. This interest received a great boost when I'd read Coleridge's *Biographia Literaria*. Consequently, as *Littack* proceeded, more philosophical and metaphysical articles found their way into its pages, culminating in my 'Neo-Vitalism: A Post-Existential Philosophy of Fact' in *Littack 8*. This was the culmination of my ideas for a new poetry, for the Poetry of Vitalism. And even if there never really was a group of Vitalist Poets, and certainly no school as such, no one could argue by then there was not a sufficiency of data and blue-printing to have nourished several schools of poetry. But I guess this is England where ideas do not take hold easily. As far as poetry is concerned, fashion and other ultimately irrelevant factors have more to do with the making of movements and trends than ever do serious ideas. I exaggerate? Where would 'The Mersey Poets' have been without the pop musical phenomenon of the The Beatles? Or where would the 'Northern Irish School' have been without 'The Troubles'?

The magazine ran for twelve issues between 1972 and 1976, but in trying to answer the question as to what I hoped to achieve by it, I realise some of the issues were more important than others. As a provincial whose deepest intuitive knowledge was of Paradise and the cosmic intelligence underlying all things in nature, it came as a rude shock to encounter a metropolitan world governed by an establishment of nihilists which not only flatly denied the reality of those things I had experienced as a child, and in some degree had continued to experience as an adult, but which also positively discouraged mention of such matters. This meant that I found a whole area of metaphysical awareness being actively proscribed. So the most positive thing I sought to do with *Littack* was to hammer out a new aesthetic for poetry to counteract the prevailing dominance, among the more fashionable mainstream poets, of this nihilistic social realism. A new aesthetic which would equally counter the effects of the growing revival of avant gardism that was coming out of America (and which has led to what is now loosely termed 'post-modernism').

No Accounting for Paradise

Neither the Establishment-backed traditionalists, such as the Movement Poets, nor the American hippy imports which made up what I termed 'the Alternative Establishment', appealed to me.

Peter Russell's words – 'Of course, you'll be ostracised...made an outsider' – seem to have rung more and more true. Yet we're all 'outsiders' as poets. It's not just for the likes of a *Littack*; it's for our insistence that man (or woman) does get glimpses of Paradise – can know beauty, can know truth. And when I have made a mistake or done wrong I regret it. I am often asked was *Littack* a huge mistake? And if so, do I regret it? In 'career terms', certainly it was a mistake. What should have been a crowning achievement proved my albatross and I have worn it round my neck ever since. But as I have never seen poetry in terms of a career, but rather as a vocation, I can't honestly say I've lost much sleep over it. If it really has impeded recognition of what few poems of mine really deserve it, then I do regret that; and when Patricia was excluded from a place at two out of three London University colleges when she applied to do her mature student's degree, when she was turned down because she was married 'to the man who edited *Littack*', I did regret that. But how can I really regret what Tony Rudolf called 'Oxley's self-education in public'? Or that the scales partially fell from my eyes in the process and I was able to discover that, after all, there were some good poets about? Or simply that I got a lot of fun out of the whole venture? Indeed, as one review put it, '*Littack*'s targets were chosen for their size rather than for any effect a bull's eye might have'. But that it did hit a few 'bulls' eyes' has been seen over the ensuing years. For instance, Anthony Thwaite once told me to my face, years afterwards, that *Littack* had made him 'very, very angry indeed'. And if further proof is needed that its attacks hit home, by the Eighties, it was forming the subject of a thesis in at least one university!

Very close to the time of *Littack*, Gerald England turned up at Epping. Over a meal I asked him the usual questions about the future of his magazine *Headland*, but he replied that it was near-bankrupt and couldn't afford to continue. So I said, impulsively, 'Don't let it fold, I'll take it over.' He accepted so I took it over, changing its name to *New Headland*. During the years I ran the magazine (1971– 74), it was a miscellany: I didn't try to run two programmatic magazines at once. But I was able to use it to give poets a second chance if *Littack* was full. Despite *Littack*'s reputation, most people wanted to be in it, around 5% only wanted to be in *New Headland*!

I also started *Laissez Faire* (a critical broadsheet which ran for six issues between 1972–75). I was fed up with the you-scratch-my-back-I'll-scratch-yours' attitude in many little magazines, I passionately believing criticism should be more than merely elucidatory. I felt the magazine scene was very exciting and that a bit of evaluation by studying a few magazines in each issue would be useful. I wanted to encourage criticism because at that time, many magazines dismissed criticism as of no value. Poets were gods, above criticism! Criticism was not necessary for their kind of poetry which was so supremely perfect that criticism had no function! *Laissez Faire* was a reaction against the prevailing attitude that all writing was of equal value. I believed then, and I believe now, that a really good critic is much rarer than a good poet and in the broadsheet I said so.

I also helped co-edit *The Village Review* with Quenten Lane; was overseas editor of *Lapis Lazuli*, an American magazine; as well as having a short-lived advisory status with the early *Chapman*. Robin Gregory invited me to become a member of the eccentrically huge editorial board of *Orbis*. No one seems to know why this was done, except perhaps that it enabled Gregory to print the names of well-known poets (or in my case, notorious) on the masthead. I was asked to state whether I would review books, select poems, give talks etc. but none of these things happened.

I suppose during this period, around 1970 to 1976, I was involved in one way or another with six magazines. Though I had a full time job and a young family, I was so interested in what I was doing that when I had no domestic duties I would simply carry on where I had left off in this tremendous, wonderful task. Patricia was a great supporter, making time available for me.

And though as dismayed with the London literary scene as I was, I felt that, on the personal level, things were better. I was happily married with two lovely daughters, and still had my vision of Paradise – that essential feeling of joy and oneness with all creation. Also I had poetry, not just my own verses, which I was still struggling to write, but the poetry of the ever-present, ever-living poets of the past, as well as the work of the new friends and acquaintances I'd made through the magazines. In short, I felt I had few real problems personally. But I was becoming too smug.

CHAPTER ELEVEN
The Politics of Living

By the time I had reached my thirtieth year it was no longer true that I had 'few problems'. What had seemed true during the years Patricia and I had lived in North London, and for a long while after we moved out among the forest and fields of Epping, was becoming less so. And it ceased to be true one stark evening that we received a phone call to tell us Tom was dead.

No death, not even that of my father, affected me as much as did the death of my friend Tom Jones. In father's case, the fact that he had constantly re-iterated his belief in Man's 'three score years and ten' – plus the fact that he had lived a 'reasonable span' – helped to soften the blow. When I received my sister's message to tell me father had died suddenly – though my heart stood still and I was terribly shocked – I felt at least able to decently grieve. Felt it was 'in the nature of things'. I wept tears; felt sad and lonely at the departure of so vital an elder, such a loved parent; and poem after poem was jerked out of me in sorrowful pæan. Yet, for all that, my reason and my heart assured me it was a ripe death.

Not so in the case of Tom. Tom was drowned early one morning off a South Coast beach. He was supposed to have gone to work the previous day but hadn't. Instead, he had left his home in Weald in Kent, said goodbye to his wife and child, and for reasons we shall never know had gone off in exactly the opposite direction to normal. Then, early on the evening of that same day, his wife – who thought him at first still at work – had been surprised to get a telephone call from a hotel in Bognor Regis. He told her he was unsure as to how he had come to be there, but said he was now feeling fine and not to bother to come over and collect him by car (in any case, she had their baby son to look after) as he'd just stay the night at the hotel and be home for breakfast.

In fact, it was the police who turned up the next day. For Tom's body had been found shortly after dawn on a deserted beach not far from the hotel where he had gone so inexplicably to stay. As to whether his death was suicide or accident was never determined. And, in due course, an open verdict was returned on my friend.

I will not easily forget that funeral cortége of maybe a hundred or more young men that wound its way out of the lovely greystone church one bright January day in the village of Weald. All that vast social web of friend and acquaintance that Tom had so amazingly and blithely spun for so many years was, for a moment, centred on that pretty little church and its graveyard. It was Tom's last and biggest party and everyone was there. I saw faces I'd not seen in years, and it was as if there was being created, for a brief instant, all that life he and I had shared in Manchester and London. All that life *he* had created for so many, many people in the Sixties. It seemed like a 'requiem for the Sixties', if I may borrow my friend Brian Pearce's phrase.

In the second of receiving that telephone call to tell me Tom was gone, I was pierced through and through, as if by an arrow of ice in the heart. All my joy and energy was suddenly dried up. From a raging torrent of vitality, I became, in seconds, a dried up river bed of feeling. And for months afterwards I had a secret nightmare fight against an almost overwhelming awareness of mortality in myself and in those around me. Everything and everyone suddenly seemed so fragile. I felt in Rilke's words: 'The greyish draughts of emptiness come drifting from the stage'.

It was whilst suffering that rude and brutal awakening to the harsh fact of mortality – for which my childhood contact with death and suffering in hospital had proved no preparation at all – and whilst the consequent *tedium vitae* was upon me, that I also became aware of the precarious balance of my way of life. I knew then that I had many problems, and that I had been kidding myself in thinking that I had few, if any.

Yet whichever way I looked at these new-found difficulties I realized, in truth, they were but emanations from a single source. Were so many electrons, protons and neutrons, so to speak, clustering painfully around the golden node of that intangible vision of Paradise which had always haunted me. The truth was that with Tom's death I had been dealt a major blow: the experience that ages, the grief that matures. Even so, I still felt I had no good reason to surrender to the pessimism of normal adulthood. By the strength of the vision I carried within me, I was driven instinctively to resist the force and effect of death. Death was a chain of supreme slavery that I did not welcome or want. I had no desire to 'go gently into that good night'. But with the death of someone we love, we all die a little ourselves. And such an 'unjust' death as Tom's caused a scarring of the very tissues of my being.

I had long resisted growing-up – 'maturing' as my elders had always blithely termed it – if it meant, as it usually did, abandoning the vision of Paradise first discovered in childhood. If it meant giving up something which I knew was true and taking in its place that shoddy and blinkered adult habit of viewing the world as so many flat, coarse surfaces. But I felt, and still feel, that memory is *more* truthful and accurate than any present experience, because it is only when experience has passed through the sieve of memory and been sifted of all confusing inessentials, passion and distraction, that we can come to see things as they really are.

In other words 'maturity', which adulthood wanted to force upon me and which Tom's death seemed the ultimate blow of a material world designed to re-inforce and assist in compelling my submission, I saw but as surrender. Even so, 'You can't resist the facts of life!' – or so my own reason loudly exclaimed. But I did resist. I was driven to it. And now I know why. It was because I would not give up the true City of the Imagination for the false Suburb of Reason with all its dismal 'facts'.

I remember sitting in Crawfords' famous tea rooms in Edinburgh discussing metaphysics with Walter Perrie and Joy Hendry and not knowing that it was the very day Tom was dying. I remember, too, walking up Bridge Hill, Epping with my two children, the sheer will-power of so simple a task cutting my soul as a despairing depression descended upon me the like of which I had not known since my days in the hell hole of Salford. Lastly, and most acutely, I recall breakfasting at my friend John's house in the heart of the beautiful Oxford countryside. John, my sole surviving friend from the days of the Road – that first paradise of all – was now a successful businessman, one who was rich in many of the material things of life. I was still inwardly numb from Tom's funeral. Numb, too, at the thought of how all those glittering traces left in every corner of my being by that early, contemplative snail of Paradise, seemed now but black trails of congealed blood on the tarnished surface of existence.

That weekend, in a cold and frosty Oxford countryside, I spent rounding off a long and miserable poem that Tom's death had intruded upon. It contained lines like:

> I could not stare at any picture
> Without I felt all slip away;
> And yellow petals were butterflies of pain
> That fluttered within again, again ...

> We took a night walk as it were to prepare
> For my descent into awful being –
> For the pain, the harrowing, the journey
> I knew not where.

Gradually, however, I passed this unsought watershed and found I began to attack all problems with a new self-awareness. Most of all I took a fresh look altogether at my way of life. I observed that I was a young man living a semi-suburban existence on a comfortable salary of around £6,000 a year (one could be comfortable then on £6,000 a year!). One who had a helpful and intelligent wife, two lovely daughters, and a beautifully situated house with only the smallest of mortgages on it. A young man of more than average energy who, in addition to possessing a highly respected 'paper' qualification that opened all possible doors in the commercial world, filled his spare time with every kind of pursuit from gardening, parties and travel, to the voracious consumption of good literature, as well as doing a great deal of writing and editing. Nor was I without a wide circle of friends and acquaintances.

Yet, for all that, I had become a young man who, despite such advantages and assets, was like so many people – thoroughly dissatisfied with his way of life.

For the present however, there seemed no solution in sight. Tom was gone it was true, but I had many other friends, and innumerable responsibilities. So I soldiered on at my job in the City and continued to pursue my literary interests. Those literary interests, and a wonderful wife, were a positive help at this difficult period in the early 1970s ... and, occasionally, the solace of travel.

CHAPTER TWELVE
The Solace of Travel

(1) En Deya

During the autumn of 1972 we visited Majorca, primarily for a holiday but also to visit Robert Graves who lived just up the coast from where we stayed at Puerto de Soller. I must have been twelve or thirteen when I'd read Graves' biography of Lawrence of Arabia and was much excited by it. My next conscious thought about him had occurred late in 1964 when Patricia and I had listened to Graves reading his own poetry on the radio. We'd thought him an appalling reader! During the later years I had increasingly come into contact with his poetry, but it was not until 1966 when our friend David Beugger gave me a copy of *No More Ghosts* that my interest in him as a poet was irreversibly quickened; and his affect on me as a poet began to be cumulative as I read more of his work. Sometime in 1969 I'd read his *The White Goddess* and this had proved to be one of the great events of my poetic life. Two things had captivated me.

First was the thrilling 'chase' through an eternal mythic landscape. The book was and is, of course, a rag-bag of eclectic scholarship and obscure mythic lore: but that was its attraction for me. The book had the effect of driving me back to many of Graves' Celtic and Græco-Roman sources and, in addition, I found myself directed to many another work on myth and anthropology. It was all a heady experience, like with Coleridge's *Biographia Literaria.*

The second and even more important lesson of *The White Goddess* was that the book seemed shot through with an understanding of the poetic process itself. When Graves spoke of poems having their own 'poetic logic', I had felt instinctively he was right. And when he spoke of 'poetic unreason', I felt straightaway that here was a man who understood that the rational logic of prose and scientific thought was not the all. Only the poetic impulse, he'd written, forms a consciousness that is at all adequate to the encompassing of the subconscious mind.

Reading *The White Goddess* induced in me a revolution of thought, a creative excitement which had gone on for months. Also, and inevitably, I had written to Graves giving my responses to the book. He'd replied that, 'The White Goddess came to me unexpectedly (not in a "frenzy" just an enlightenment) in wartime, when I had no recourse to libraries and knew no Welsh or Irish. It came piece by piece not in an organised mass. I wrote the book in six weeks and it took me years to revise the facts. It is one of the inexplicable things that happen to poets, if they don't join a gang ...' That letter sank straight into both my conscious and subconscious minds like a creative acid into water.

Many people have often assumed that because of my poetic theorisings and interest in philosophy, that the only poetry I appreciate must necessarily be either overtly visionary or philosophical. But I could early appreciate Robert Graves' poetry which is not 'overtly' anything but poetic.

Graves and I had corresponded intermittently for the next few years. He it was who made the single most influential remark ever communicated directly to me, 'Poetry is not an art, but a way of life.' This altered the whole course of my thinking, and contributed, ultimately to a considerable change in my life-style. I'd sensed, too, that both Graves' poetry and the occasional remark on personal love in his letters had taught me about that other great mystery in life: woman. I well remember he'd written that, 'I hope you will find your own poems suddenly coming to surprise you: if you love the right woman and remain free, they should.' 'Freedom' and 'the right woman' – these, not uxory and the wrong woman, nor the poisonous influence of the casual relationship, are the essentials of true love and poetry. These were things I also believed in so it's really no wonder I looked upon him as one of my early mentors. And when it was suggested that we went to Majorca for our holidays, I readily agreed. But it just wasn't for the holiday ...

The story of our first attempt to find his house doesn't bare thinking about; of how we wandered all day over the 'high sierras' only to end with near sun-stroke and sore feet. The following day Patricia and I went to seek Graves by boat, and eventually found the house, tucked away up a steep valley redolent with wild thyme and rosemary. Paradise on earth. He was so friendly to both of us, especially to me, a young writer, finally inviting us and anyone else to an open-air poetry reading the following day. But Patricia felt she couldn't leave the children with David and her mother for two days running, so it fell to David and me to go alone.

9.45 am found us aboard the *Peña Brava* bound for Deya. The official sailing time was ten o'clock, but a bit of excitement occurred on the quay before we left. A fisherman had caught a *pulpa* or small squid. There was much 'ugh-ing' from squeamish tourists – especially when it wrapped itself round the fisherman's naked foot.

At ten we set sail and eventually docked at the stone cove, from there to ascend the perfumed gorge full of thyme, pine and jasmine. Everywhere was grey and thick olive-green, and streaked with yellow flowers. The rough, stony path was strewn with short, brown, shrivelled pods: a kind of bean that 'St. John the Baptist ate in the wilderness', or so Graves told me later. Streamwater ran singing through this rocky gulch and flashed like bits of lemon-silver ribbon whenever it emerged from behind bush or sheltering stone into the sunlight.

There being no sign of life at Casa Graves, or *Canelluñ* as it was called, we wandered along the road towards Deya, wondering where was the 'theatre' of which Graves had spoken, the one at which the reading was to be given. I remembered he had gestured vaguely across the road, and muttered something about it being 'a hundred yards away'. Yet we reached Deya village before finding any building on the right of the road. And a *posada* was clearly no theatre.

Just as Beugger was beginning to do his favourite head-scratching bit, and I the excessive frowning, we spotted paintings stacked against an outside wall and a notice which said *Art Exhibición*. We looked in through the door, saw more paintings and some books and then spotted a notice which said 'Dorothy Bradbury'. Cleverly I deduced that 'this' was no Majorcan! 'This' proved to be an American lady bearing all the marks of an emigré artist. So I repeated my question about the theatre and Robert Graves to her: a rather serious-looking figure bent over a scroll of white paper. She answered sharply and simply: 'He probably means the sort of Greek the-ater he has on the terrace jest below his house.' This was a sufficient enough clue; and the two of us backtracked in the direction of Graves' house; walking along the terraces which ran below the level of the road.

It was the usual rough going that one soon grew familiar with in those parts, and it promised to yield nothing. Only empty semi-circular terraces ringed by stone walls. Eventually, however, we came back to the road near the poet's house and discovered a gate dead opposite his drive with a clear path leading down the terraced valley up which we had just scrambled, but at a different angle. Suddenly, a figure appeared a few yards away, dancing about among the rocks and trees overhanging one of the terraces. He was waving a zoom-lens' camera and gesturing into some trees. So we headed for him. As we did so, we saw a group of people, including Robert Graves leaning against some rocks beside a short steep, stone flight of steps. He stood with his feet wedged in the steps and his back propped against the rocky slope. On his head was a battered sombrero; and he was, along with others, apparently waiting for something to happen. Facing him was a 'nymph' in a low-cut sari, with thick coils of black hair and golden-brown flesh. Squatting next to him was a young silent girl. A few yards away was a larger group speaking in American accents. I went and greeted him.

'You're going to give a poetry reading, aren't you?' I asked stupidly, for sake of conversation.

'S'posed to be ...' he said, half apologetically. 'When *they* tell me the equipment is ready,' he added, gesturing towards two rather hairy young men.

A few minutes passed during which we sat down with Graves. Little of interest passed between us. Then we were all suddenly ushered, at someone's suggestion, down through trees to a little stone theatre under an outcrop of red rock. It was a 'classic' setting surrounded by trees, 'On some near olive-terrace, in the heat'.

The audience sat on stone tiers with Graves and a sheaf of papers facing us. It was all casual, chaotic and dominated by the incompetent arranging of the amateur camera team. Then, yet another American, with a monkey named Chico, arrived and released the creature. Naturally it ran up the trees overhanging the theatre like any monkey would. Nor could it be persuaded down. So, throughout the short reading, it crashed about in the trees showering leaves and bean pods upon the audience. And, not satisfied with this achievement, it contrived to urinate directly on the head of one member of the audience!

Graves first gave a short introduction, discussing the 'inner and outer ear' in poetry. He talked of the 'public and private' poem; and he asserted interestingly that '... the inner ear is more selective than the outer'; adding that the outer ear was really a confused and crude instrument when compared to the inner – 'Especially that of urban man, being as it is, so continuously subjected to a bombardment of confused sound.'

'All the poems I shall now read are recent pieces, some written in the last few days, except for one that I wrote in 1963.' He started to read then stopped abruptly. 'Who is making that noise? A child? I'm sorry, I can't go on with children here.' And he petulantly sat down.

The offending child was quickly removed. But the monkey was permitted to continue its antics. As if to emphasise the predicament caused by the noise and interruption, the poem he next read was entitled 'Poet's Curse' and there was laughter in the audience led by his wife. Every poem from then on was interrupted by something; including re-positioning of the camera man, the recording equipment, etc. Apart from Graves' outburst against the child, he was immoderately patient throughout the disorganised proceedings.

A longer interval came because the cameraman suddenly felt ill. I thought there looked nothing wrong with him – apart from his rather unprofessional handling of the equipment. Someone sarcastically offered him a throat lozenge *for his camera.* When, at last, the poet opened his mouth to continue, Graves dropped all his papers on the semi-circular stone stage and, simultaneously, the tape of the recording equipment escaped from its spool like a long, black snake from a box.

I talked to Graves in this further enforced interval about some of the sources of his *The White Goddess*, a book I had just read. I also introduced him to David, who recalled a recent famous reading by Graves at the Mermaid Theatre. Graves had fond memories of the occasion and said, 'See that girl there ...' referring to the one with much breast on view. 'She it was who suggested that chairs be brought on the stage to accommodate the overspill audience'. Beugger, brilliantly I thought, replied, 'Yes. I remember you signed a copy of your book for me; and Sir Bernard Miles gave me a biscuit!' Graves looked at him open-eyed, wondering if the sun was proving too much for this Englishman.

Eventually, the recording equipment mended, Graves proceeded to read a couple more poems, finishing up with one entitled 'Touch my shut lips'. Everyone applauded it, especially its last two lines:

> There falls a silence stranger far than speech,
> A silence from which tears flow.

Lines which called Wordsworth to my mind. But such thoughts I kept to myself.

Graves scrabbled his papers together in a heap by his feet. He looked benignly at his small, crouching audience. His wild, spiky grey hair in tufts beneath dappled shadow from the overhanging leaves – where the monkey still played; his cultured but craggy features; his quick-to-muse eyes; all added up to – a poet.

'I can never remember any of my poems off by heart. There is only one I know... I'll try and say it for you.' He proceeded to recite a four line poem that began something like: 'I die for you and you die for me ...'!

In the green hillside glade that wrapped the garden theatre, the small audience began to break up. Graves went around picking up the shrivelled black pods of 'St. John the Baptist beans' and filled his sombrero with them. The monkey, by this time having come down the tree and set about the poet's manuscripts like a hungry scholar, was carried away in someone's basket happily devouring paper.

Slowly, reluctantly, we made our way up the terraced valley with the 77 year old poet moving like a mountain goat over the treacherous, flaky stones; a feat which caused me to remember how he had once climbed with George Mallory of Everest fame, and had been noted in his youth for his 'sense of balance' – a quality which still persists strongly in his verse. An impressive elderly figure, with a certain prize-fighter manner about him, and what Beugger termed 'presence'. But was it 'presence'? That seemed a cheap journalistic term. It was more like the slight distancing of the poet: that of being a spectator in, but not of, the crowd.

We left him at the entrance to his gravelled drive, surrounded by an entourage of Americans. He half-turned towards us, slightly bemused by all the people, and waving goodbye, said, 'Yes, do go to Jaime's ... they do a good meal there'...

(II)   The Sage of Venice

Among our travelling companions on the *Orient Express* from Calais, was an Italian who spoke English with a Welsh accent. He was a retired coal-miner with a large, solemn-faced wife, returning from twenty-two years of Welsh life to retirement in Italy. A little old man with a bald head and a bad leg that had been crushed by a coal-face fall. Between them, he and his wife had a dozen suitcases full, I feel sure, of coal. They insisted on bringing them all into the suffocatingly narrow sleeping compartment which already contained the suitcases of four others!

The train wound through France and then on into the Alps, and once, when halted inexplicably, I lifted up the blinds to find we were stopped in a dim blue and white wilderness. I confess, though, I found travelling on the *Orient Express* less of a romantic adventure *à la* Graham Greene and more of a sheer struggle – especially at night, with all the bone-shaking and the snoring ... but Patricia had got a taste for travel after our visit to Graves and we now planned to spend our tenth wedding anniversary in Venice, with another exiled poet, Peter Russell. Hence the 'romantic' notion of travelling on the Orient Express!

After twenty-four hours we did finally arrive in Venice. From the station I phoned Russell and, shortly afterwards, we found ourselves on the Grand Canal in teeming rain and heading for the Lido.

Il maestro, the Sage of Venice, Peter Russell – addressed everywhere in the city as the 'Professore' – was waiting for us in the beating rain at the landing stage. He wore a grey jacket over a white roll-necked jersey with grey trousers and black shoes. His hair – white streaked with soot and nicotine colours – ran round his face giving him the appearance of an elderly, faded lion. In height around five foot nine or ten, he was built like a sprightly dynamo: square and wiry. The predominant aspect of this very serious man's expressive face was laughter ... many generations of smiles were imprinted upon its pink-skinned, beard-encrusted surface. Patricia and I had barely set foot off the gang-plank when he whisked us into the nearest bar for *vino bianco*. This visit to our first bar was important because a pattern was immediately established.

Tre bicchiere di vino bianco per favore!' the *Professore* would exclaim. And time would be allowed to slip by to a constant refrain of 'Just one more little glass ...'

His home at Corte dell'Arco was a small, stone flagged and run-down courtyard next to the church of San Nicolo at one end of the Lido. Russell rented a dwelling which he called his 'cottage' in one corner of the quaint, tumbledown courtyard. The focus of the house was a small kitchen where he cooked and wrote looking directly onto the side wall of a monastery behind the church. There were two tables covered with oil-cloth: one under the window was piled high with papers and books; the other against another wall was dotted with eating utensils of a fairly gruesome order, and a forest of green wine-bottles. On a ceiling-high rack built of orange metal that occupied the whole length of one wall were stacked more papers, books and files plus innumerable records and a gramophone. In a small cramped alcove was a cooker, a dangerous-looking cylinder of gas and a double stone sink. It was an odd-shaped room with, of all things, an I.B.M. typesetter on a table. A useful but surprising possession this £3,000 machine for a penniless poet!

I've described this domestic den in such detail not only because it was the focus of the house, but because Corte dell'Arco was where Patricia and I had chosen to spend our tenth wedding anniversary! In a bed barely big enough for a thin gnome, Patricia and I retired for the night. But such was the hour and condition in which we went to bed each night, we never had the least difficulty getting off to sleep.

At this stage in our stay – there being plenty of funds available (namely, ours) – Russell did not consider there was 'Anywhere on the Lido where civilized people can get a decent meal'. So on that first evening we took a boat back to the Arsenale.

Our first meal in Venice was at a *ristorante* tucked away in the more swish shopping area near St. Mark's Square. I forget it's name, but according to Patricia it had 'pink wash over rough plaster walls; amber glass in mullioned windows; yellow cloths over red tablecloths; yellow serviettes; and each table was isolated from its neighbour by wooden partitions'.

In this setting we were treated to the first of many Russellian monologues that nothing, save a good idea, could interrupt. Russell the polymath talked on all subjects that came up; science, music, painting, literature ... all appeared abiding passions with him. Then there were 'tall stories' – many certainly true; literary anecdotes in abundance; and fantastic details of his personal life – all of which boiled pleasantly to the surface through a wine-wet sea. And however sinful – and many were certainly that! – the stories never offended against the Muse ... even if, sometimes, they stood fair and square against taste.

Peter and I were up early the next day, as most days, immediately continuing our dialogue of the night before: a long flow of ideas *de rerum naturae*. But around noon we took the *accelerato* to the Arsenale again. There we began the first of many tours of the streets and waterways of Venice. And mini-triumphs they were too, for the *Professore* was incredibly well-known among all the shop-keepers, cobblers, carpenters and patrons of many bars.

At six o'clock we knocked at Olga Rudge's front door and were admitted into the house where Ezra Pound had spent six months of his life every year since he'd been released from St. Elizabeth's Hospital in Washington, and from where he had departed this life less than a year previously. Immediately, on entering, one saw the famous Gaudier-Brzeska statue which had once adorned Pound's front garden in Paris. The living room, dominated by a big open fireplace, was simply furnished with two bookcases mainly containing books by or about Ezra. We had come to listen to a tape-recording of the recent tribute paid to Pound at the University of Dublin. The whole performance, even on tape, was of a much higher standard than the similar occasion at the Mermaid Theatre in London. Then Olga searched out some tapes of Ezra reading poetry and we had the rare experience of hearing the old master read a Shakespeare sonnet.

Afterwards we went to dine at Montins' *ristorante*, a long, low series of rooms opening out onto a covered garden at the rear. Its walls were covered with an excellent collection of paintings, many of them left behind by struggling artists who came and ate too much and couldn't pay the bill. The food was 'good and cheap'; or, to modify Russell's extravagance at our expense, 'good and expensive'. It had beautifully laid tables and efficient waiters in white jackets ... an ideal place to eat out on one's tenth wedding anniversary.

The following day began as a serious 'cultural' sightseeing tour of Venice. We went to see the beautiful fifteenth century church of Santa Maria dei Miracoli whose inside is entirely marble. It has a delicate, feminine feel, and a wonderful painting of the 'Miraculous Virgin' behind the high altar. Next, at my insistence, we went to see the famous equestrian statue of Bartolomeo Colleoni by Verrucchio which stands defiantly on top of a high stone tomb outside the church of Santi Giovanni e Paolo. Enormous power radiates from this triumphant piece of sculpture and I had been particularly anxious to see it after reading an appreciation of it by Wallace Stevens.

Coming out of the church we bumped into one Aldo, a carpenter, who insisted we accompanied him to a bar with a low wooden ceiling which sagged noticeably towards the middle. Wine was poured for us all at a fast rate by the middle-aged wife of the proprietor, while the latter promptly began to paint the place in our honour! After a few glasses of wine Aldo started to recite a long rambling poem. According to Peter, it was a popular nineteenth century political ballad with bawdy overtones. Poetry in Venice appeared to be still very much a thing of the people, for when Aldo stumbled over a line, it was promptly corrected by the woman behind the bar.

We were a long time in this overheated and very friendly place – after which Aldo insisted we went to dine at his brother's *ristorante*. Here again we were made welcome, a table being cleared for us – that is, a tablefull of locals were unceremoniously slung out into the street. Wine was immediately produced, followed by heavy cut-glass beakers, followed by seafood on heaped plates: everything to be eaten Venetian fashion, with fingers and bread.

This was the moment of truth, as they say. I had said to Peter over the telephone before coming to Venice: 'Don't worry, Patricia and I are very adaptable'. Now we had to prove it by tucking into huge scaly shrimps on sticks, other molluscs and stuffed octopi, tentacles, suckers and all – which we managed with a lively sophistication. I look back now on our gastronomic courage with amazement, and can only think we must have been very full of wine before we'd even started!

Finally, Peter decided it was time for us to depart. But it took all of twenty minutes' back-slapping and handshakes before we got out of the *ristorante*. Patricia and I were closely questioned about our ten years of marriage. Photographs of our daughters Elizabeth and Katie were passed round. Then I was both reprimanded, and commiserated with, for not having sons and made to swear I would try harder next time!

Once, Patricia and I went alone for a long stroll on the Lido. It turned out to be miles of colourless beach and green changing huts belonging to huge soulless hotels. It was impossible to actually get onto the beach for most of the way because of high, concentration-camp-style wire fencing. So on a dismal concrete spur jutting out into the placid water, we wrote our postcards to friends in England – in complete ignorance that a postal strike had begun the previous day.

One evening when our funds were getting low we ate on the Lido at a restaurant Russell desired to visit because he had once 'punched the proprietor on the nose', and wished to determine whether or not he was still unwelcome there. As we were not thrown out, we dined on the Venetian speciality of *spaghetti alle vongole* and Peter told us many details of his life, including his ill-fated marriage to the wife of an admiral whom he'd met at her husband's funeral. We heard, too, how he'd gone into business as an antiquarian bookseller – a business which had grown very wealthy and then declined as he'd started diverting its funds and his energies to literary ends. He culminated with the spectacular affair of his having nine African wives when living in Soho. He met the first wife at a dance in a Soho night club, 'At first there was nothing doing, but I was so fascinated by her that I won her over. We lived together for a while, and I was more than happy with the arrangement. But she wasn't. Right from the start she insisted that "in her country" it was not considered good for a man to have only one wife. I told her I was perfectly happy with just her. Besides, I couldn't afford any more wives. But she would have none of it, saying "in her country" it was not the custom for the man to keep the wives, but the other way round. So she undertook, out of her love for me, to find me more wives. In the end, I had nine in all. And she was as good as her country's word, for they really did keep me ... and honestly as far as I know.'

It was a cool but vibrant evening with some evidence of stars as we left the restaurant and strolled back along the waterside corniche to Russell's house. I postulated the definition that 'Beauty is the heart of light' as I looked across the bay towards the lights of Venice. This caused animated discussion, Russell being immediately taken with the idea. Together we subjected my inspired little definition to the closest critical scrutiny all the way back to Corte Dell'Arco.

These discussions did much to help me place on a more rational plane a great deal of what I knew of 'the other world', that spiritual place not bound by physical laws which I call Paradise. Another day came and still the talk flowed on. Then Patricia and I left the *maestro* to his own devices and took the *accelerato* across the lagoon. We had decided to spend a day touring Venice. Also, it was necessary to refurbish our depleted funds. After visiting the American Express office, we went to San Marco in order to view the church at leisure. Then we visited the Accademia. This must be one of the great art galleries of the world – stuffed with masterpieces of Titian, Tintoretto, Giorgione, Carpaccio, Parma Veccio and Bellini.

On leaving the Accademia, Patricia and I took a long walk beginning at the Dogana Steps, immortalised in *The Cantos* of Ezra Pound. Like Pound back in 1908, we sat on the steps for literary sentiment's sake and mused over the waters of the Grand Canal.

At around one o'clock in the morning, Anthony Johnson arrived – a tall, sallow complexioned figure wearing a small Italian beret and a long black raincoat. He looked an almost priestly figure and so much more the foreigner than when we'd seen him at his family home in St. John's Wood.

Though it was very late, Russell insisted talking far into the night about Anthony's poems and finally plunging into an original Sanskrit text from which he read aloud, translating as he went along. Finally, we got a camp bed out of a cupboard and set it up for Anthony in Peter's unused office upstairs. Then we all retired, just as dawn was fingering the shutters of the house.

Johnson, Russell and myself spent the following morning in further debate. A discourse which hardly seemed interrupted by our short night's sleep. Patricia went off by herself to do some shopping, perhaps wisely for the atmosphere in the kitchen had become increasingly rarefied. Shortly we'd all be needing oxygen – or so it seemed.

That evening, at the end of the heaviest intellectual stint since we'd come to Venice, the four of us crossed the Lagoon in a violent thunderstorm. The *vaporetto* was tossed about almost unmercifully in thudding luminous waves, and great streaks of lightning forked across the domes and towers of the city. This was our last evening in Venice so we splashed out in more ways than one, returning again to Montins ... what with water running erratically over the pavements and cobblestones outside, and wine running over our palates inside, everything seemed to flow perfectly, including Russell's talk. We heard about his childhood in Gloucester, his years at Malvern Public School and holidays on Lundy Island. I have a bright picture of that last meal, all being well away in *vino*, with me pumping question after question at the *Professore*. Anthony, very attentive to everything Russell said, was fascinated into silence by the unending spate of words. And Patricia, slightly flushed at the cheeks, obviously enjoying herself, with Venice drifting round and round in her mind, and details of it floating in and out of her eyes.

To take the story further and recount the innumerable little incidents that befell us on our way back to England would need a separate chapter. To tell of our boat journey in which we were called upon to help fill in a custom's form for a Turk and his wife; or to recount how our train and all our luggage vanished temporarily while in Paris; or to speak of the strange family from Hull who knew more about Italian painting than most experts ... all would fill many more pages so I will leave us here, dreaming about Venice as the wine flowed over us in Montins...

Epilogue

Our visit to Graves helped make the Majorcan holiday into a success, despite much of the time being filled with customary tourist-oriented things: sea, sangria, sun and conviviality. But what is more important is the effect the holiday had on my attitude to life; and to the vision of Paradise...

On the morning of our last day on the island to which I had come primarily as a literary tourist, I viewed the Sierras de Alfabia for the umpteenth time from the balcony of our bedroom. The sun was thinned to a far silver disc by a grey haze of clouds which lay banked along the mountain ridge like a snowdrift. A cool breeze blew down the valley and I guessed winter was not so far away.

The evening of the same day I took my final look up that fruitful valley. It was so peacefully and purply dark save for the lights of a single, ship-like hotel at the mountain's foot over to my right. A warm and evocative night with a scented breeze; and on that breeze I heard faint music. Then, as I closed the shutters regretfully, I turned and looked at my sleeping children. They really had no need of holidays to find Paradise. For them, Paradise was not just in odd picturesque corners of particular parts of the world called 'beauty spots'. It was everywhere. But at midnight, on the summit of the Sierras' winding road, in the coach heading for Palma airport, I gazed back at Soller for the last time and saw it lying like a cluster of white stars on the dark plain, like Paradise.

Similarly, after I left Venice, which had proved a paradise of ideas, I concluded that English literary life had become almost a tourist affair, was fragmented. Whether this is a good thing or a bad thing, I couldn't decide. And it made me ask, of what possible use are such literary traipsings? What does it matter whether you read poems in a council house in Jarrow or talk with Robert Graves up a mountain in Majorca? Whether you read poems in the Home Counties or walk with Russell along the Venice Lido? Good questions – for I felt I could truthfully say that literary life had little or no value at all. Yet, on the other hand, from contact with certain minds I cannot deny but that I have benefited. To have known such people as Robert Graves and Peter Russell – only a fool would count it not a privilege, let alone not beneficial. And, to be even more specific, have I not already suggested that from Russell I learned that the laws which govern this world are not necessarily identical with those of Paradise?

Even so, I suddenly realised Paradise had become, for me, reduced to just such a few metaphysical lights in the dim world of adulthood. The thought made me both sad and angry, and so much so that I resolved from that moment onwards the darkness of the world would not be allowed to advance more upon at least one man's soul, if he could help it.

CHAPTER THIRTEEN
Thoughts leading to Exile

Epping as a locality, and as my home for ten years, meant a great deal more than these few pages might seem to indicate. It was, firstly, the place where my daughters lived out half of their infancy; and it was where *Littack* – as distinct from the more modest *Littack Supplement* – was published. Above all, it was the place where Patricia and I owned our first home. The place where our marriage became identified with nature itself: the splendour of cornfields and rose gardens, green hills and glowing streams, white-laced hawthorn hedges and intimate woodland glades. Most of all, it was the place where we first learned that love might not, after all, be the transient thing many of our friends said it was. For there, for us, it became a feeling which, like the beauty of nature itself – that beauty which teaches wisdom and understanding – is as immortal as the corn of Thomas Traherne.

Diffidence, as well as space, prevents my fully documenting the tremendous part Patricia played in keeping alive my vision at this juncture, but:

> When that fire seemed almost out
> She upon its embers blew.

To her, in large measure, is owed the solution to the problem that so troubled me. For all the accuracy of my vision, for all my theories of 'how to live', and for all the insights provided me by Fate, *she* it was, with her practical determination and forceful understanding, who translated the theory into practice.

When we'd first moved to London in 1964, I'd worked for a large firm of accountants. Four years later, after working for lengthy spells in the City as well as travelling to various parts of the U.K., I accepted a post with the merchant bank, Lazard Brothers. There I worked for the next eight years. Throughout this period when I was a full time chartered accountant there had been a steady – though at first not by me admitted – intellectual drift away from all that accountancy stood for. And even in a firm distinguished for its tolerance of eccentricity among its employees, no one actually understood what it meant to be a poet. It was Wyndham Lewis who said, 'I have no wish to dominate others, but neither do I myself wish to be dominated.' Working in an office, whether one is top-or-bottom dog or, like myself, somewhere in the middle ranks, I found the roles of master and servant, boss and bossed, increasingly ridiculous ones. I felt that this hierarchical system – the City's pecking order – tended to de-humanize all who participated in it for any length of time, and unless people were prepared to believe in their own individuality, and that of their fellow human beings, there was no way out of the 'system'. Even with individualists, there will inevitably still be the leaders and the led, but at least there would be no more bosses – 'bosses' being quite a different species from 'leaders'. All these thoughts and ideas I owed to my years in the stultifying atmosphere of dry offices and streets filled with car fumes, in the famous one square mile of monumental beauty and ugliness that surrounds the Bank of England.

Many times during this period I'd lamented to Patricia the causes of the loss of Paradise, and of why people of an urban, material-seeking and status-craving set-up become spiritually starved. I had told her why the pursuits of physical comforts to excess and the resultant ever-increasing need for money and security lead to a wide-spread bluntedness of feeling towards the finer and subtler and more beautiful things of the spirit. I had angrily decried insurance policies, pensions, mortgages, high salaries, and all the other suburban badges of respectability. I had cursed the small-talk, the rat-race, the car worship, the adulation of pets, the continental holidays, the dull marriages, the hatred of learning, the double-standards, the love of money for its own sake ... everything in fact that was normal, suburban and philistine. I had pointed out, too, that through fear and insecurity both young and old were accepting with ever-increasing ease ever deeper ruts and greater conformism.

Lastly, and most loudly of all, I had informed her that the price of all this social folly was a life lived at a mediocre level in a world devoid of spiritual values, a place without hope or knowledge of Paradise, and one in which people were neither happy or sad but just plain dull.

Yet, despite all my talk, my own way of life in much of its details conformed exactly to that which I denounced! Until, that is, one day when, in her quiet but firm manner, Patricia said to me, 'It's time we did something about it then!' And she did.

*   *   *   *   *

To give up a secure job and throw oneself on the mercy of Fortune is not many people's idea of good sense at the best of times. But to do this when clouds of economic uncertainty were gathering over the nation and nearly two million people were already out of work would be, to most people, plain madness. Of course, in the Sixties it was fashionable to do this sort of thing – and also easier because in that Age of Affluence jobs were ten a penny – especially if the drop-out was young and with plenty of time to grow out of 'such nonsense'. But I was not that young, being well on the wrong side of thirty already. Nor was my timing right, the Seventies being quite different from the Sixties in so many ways. Even so, it was the course of action Patricia and I had finally determined on: and in May 1976 we 'gave it all up' as they say.

Actually, it was comparatively easy to give up my City job, despite its lucrative salary, its pleasant working conditions and excellent fringe benefits which included a cheap mortgage, good insurance cover and a huge pension to look forward to in my dotage.

Rather more difficult was the thought of leaving our many friends in the Home Counties. Risky, too, for a budding man of letters who had yet to establish himself, was the prospect of getting out of touch with the literary world. But hardest of all was the thought of leaving all those wonderful little nooks and crannies of Epping. Those shining summer fields and that great pensive forest which seemed such integral parts of that Paradise in which I loved so much to dwell. There were bound to be wrenchings and heart-searchings about the move for many reasons.

Again, and still dealing with the economic ogre: although I had always spent money within my means since we'd moved south, I had, nevertheless, spent right up to those means. Consequently, I had no capital or savings with which to buttress this 'foolish venture'. All Patricia and I had was a house which, because of the inflated values of property since 1966 when we bought it, we knew we could sell, pay off the mortgage, and buy a cheaper dwelling in a more remote part of the country. But at least it would be a house entirely of our own and not one rented from some Building Society. So that was a start.

In the end we decided to ignore the economic consequences of our actions. And we determined we should not, if we could help it, live off the State. Instead, we would put our trust in the Muse in every way, as our friend Kathleen Raine had advised us we should. Lastly, and most importantly, we also knew we had to do our level best to ensure that no one else was made to suffer for our 'selfish' actions. Primarily, this meant our children; but it also included anyone else who might conceivably be affected.

Once we had announced our decision both to ourselves and our friends, we immediately encountered two not unrelated difficulties. Firstly, we had to contend with a multitude of well-meant but useless questions that were pressed upon us at every turn by everyone we knew. And, secondly, we had to be prepared to make the maximum effort to combat in ourselves that anxiety complex or habit of 'worry' which is so inevitably a part of the suburban syndrome.

Fortunately, with regard to worrying, Patricia and I had mostly smashed the habit: probably because our thoughts were too often preoccupied with considerations which left little time for inwardly groaning. We were never self-pitying people. But I did regret the fact that I might get out of touch with all the petty and partisan excitements and happenings of the London literary world. I felt I needed to meet people of stimulating intellect from time to time. But at least, I was aware of this problem from the beginning of our exile, and that was something.

The endless probings about our decision to quit the rat race were truly amazing. I had not known, for example, that one simple question, 'How are you going to live?' could have so many variants: How will you manage? What will you live on? Where will the money come from? Who's going to provide for the wife and kids? Will you be able to get by all right? Have you got capital? Have you another job lined up? Where's the bread and butter coming from? Can you make enough money as a poet? ... and so on, *da de da de da*! Not, of course, that I didn't understand the questions or the anxieties of everyone from my own mother to the most casual of my acquaintances. But the difficulty arose through the sheer monotony of the question, and also because few seemed to really understand when I replied to all these queries: 'I am going to write poetry, so the Muse will provide!' Or, more facetiously, 'Paradise flows with milk and honey, and there's no charge for it.' More sensibly, Patricia tended to refer all questions to the biblical parable of the Lilies of the Field and leave it at that.

*   *   *   *   *

The day Harold Wilson resigned as prime minister the sky went black over the City of London. Lightning flashed and branched in electric veins through the bulbous and rain-bloated clouds above Moorfields' half-built Barbican flats. Michael Whitehead and I stared up at the gloomy and ominous sky from our fourth-floor office next to Moorgate Station in a fertile silence ... very fertile for me.

Michael and I were both in the employment of Lazards. Though we had been friends for more than a decade, he was technically my superior. A modest, shy Christian, but highly competent accountant, Michael was a paradigm of cautious respectability with whom I have always had a most harmonious working relationship. He had shown a remarkable tolerance of my heretical and often extreme viewpoints, frequently and forcibly expressed over the years. If I have been witness and judge of the compromises he has had to make between Christianity and the World, equally he has been a spectator of like adjustments that I, in my turn, had to make to survive in a world of implacable reality which, though it may still love lovers, does not love poets. Yet not once, for all the mutual provocation, did either of us accuse the other of hypocrisy. And because he was more friend than boss, I had been quite unable to broach a particularly ticklish matter with him. If it hadn't been for this totally unexpected resignation of the British prime minister, plus the oddly cataclysmic weather which had seemed so symbolic, I wonder to this day how on earth I should ever have got round to making my own announcement? But, as things turned out, the conversation, brief as it was, went something like this.

'Harold is going to resign!'

In those days everyone knew who 'Harold' was; just as, a decade later the whole world knew who 'Maggie' was. Michael had just put the phone down, a look of mixed dumbfoundedness and delight (he was a Tory) on his pale, angular face.

'Harold is resigning,' he ejaculated again.

After a brief, nervous pause, I said: 'And so am I!'

Perhaps because the timing was just too apposite; or because of the strangely violent and unreal storm that raged outside the office building, it was to take me quite a time to persuade my friend that I was genuinely in earnest. He thought I was joking.

*   *   *   *   *

Walking in the long field adjacent to the brook of Brook Road in Epping, Essex, where I then lived, that green field which summer always turned to a quivering gold of shining ranks of corn (that 'liberty and equality of gold', as I described it once in a poem), I had first conceived of what the Sixties crudely called 'dropping out'.

Opposite our house a great hedgeless field – what had once been several fields – sloped to a gentle, horizon-filling hill with a white farm at its summit. A wide track wound to the farmhouse. To the west the silver Central Line snaked Londonwards, disappearing along the shady edge of Epping Forest. While slightly to the east a thin, grass-trodden path followed the line of a former hedge between two fields, up and over the farm hill to a tree-shaded lane next to a grand house called Coopersale Hall. It was a lane where primroses, cowslips, forget-me-nots and campion once massed to celebrate nature's gentle seasons. A paradisial way now visibly wilting and retreating before the twin evils of pesticide and a huge coming motorway. The London Orbital, symbol of the Rat Race, the M25, was then being built.

Our house overlooked a paradise of blooming nature. There Patricia and I walked and talked; and in those pollen-counted environs brought into the world our two daughters. But, as I say, it was a threatened paradise where birds would vomit forth more than song, and butterflies shrivel and die. Those dreaded words 'commuter', 'suburb', and 'progress' (which have long replaced 'peasant', 'poverty' and 'peace') were increasingly in the failing rural air. Words inimical to paradise. Therefore, it behoved us to find another paradise. If not for ourselves, at least for two small girls half way through their golden infancy. For us, too, in a way, who felt we had been *forced* to grow disenchanted with Epping by its declining delights. But where, and how, to find such a new place? A place where the imagination could thrive as it had done at first in Epping?

'Trust in the Muse, always!' repeated Kathleen Raine, that wise sibyl of Chelsea, with whom we had talked it over at her house one day in 1974 or 5. Advice we finally followed.

Another friend, Dannie Abse has always maintained that the best rhyme for 'Heaven' is 'Devon', so in the end Patricia and I settled on moving to Torbay in the south of that beautiful county. She had always loved the countryside, and I the sea. So we looked for a place in sight of both. Then sold our house at Epping, filled two removal vans with our books and furniture and, together with Elizabeth and Katie, and Patricia's mother who'd come to live with us in 1970, set out to a new home and a new life. And the result was Brixham.

*   *   *   *   *

Brixham is in the soft spot of England, South Devon. Brixham in blue Torbay where the sea is smoothest in the British Isles for most of the year. Brixham the fishing port of Torbay, where the airs of Dartmoor and the English Channel meet to gentle balmy effect. A small port crowded with lusty trawlers, rusty crab boats and, because of its new marina, with yachts of every conceivable type from the simple to the flashy. A harbour squeezed between two hind legs of land, with houses drawn tightly over those legs like chequered stockings. Around the harbour are rows of 'grock shops': souvenir places for summer tourists. A fishy place (sometimes in several senses), it is, mostly, busy noisy with the mixed indrift of tourists, the shouts of fishermen, and the crash of hammers on steel plating as boats are repaired. Often, too, there is the smell of painting and the blue bouquet of acetylene torches cutting metal.

Apart from the fishing community – who are of all ages – Brixham has a large retired population. So that, together with Paignton and Torquay, it is sometimes referred to as 'the Costa Geriatrica'. To service these communities, plus the seasonal influx of tourists, there is a large sprinkling of shopkeepers, estate agents, solicitors, accountants, the usual banks, and a body of hoteliers and boarding house keepers. Finally, to complete the demographic picture, there are some arty-crafty types (often more crafty than arty!), the odd local writer or two, and one poet ... me.

How Patricia and myself came to alight upon Brixham was largely accidental. We went for a holiday, liked it, and stayed: metropolitan and suburban disenchantment having set in. A 'respectable career' no longer appealed; besides, I had always been inexplicably fascinated by the seaside world. Sun, sand, souvenir shops, and that murmuring, changingly-changeless glamour of the sea, seemed always to add up to a special freedom – a healthy freedom, not mere licence. Everything about it was, and is, magical to me. The sea in its ceaseless ebb and flow is a mirror of human nature in its every mood. I have always felt that to be on a seashore, especially one that is not too crowded, is like standing at the very frontier of being: there where the finite meets the infinite. I expect Bedouins feel something like this in desert lands; and mountain people with their high mountains. But I, an Englishman and maritime, feel it most beside the sea.

I had also known that this infinite radiation of the sea, plus the happy anonymity of a tourist place, an anonymity less purely alienating than that found in a big city – was especially congenial to my reflective-creative temperament. I had discovered this first on our honeymoon in Jersey; then at Lyme Regis and Guernsey on other holidays. On the latter island, for example, in a few days only I had written a whole chunk of my longest poem, *A Map of Time*. Also, I knew that Brixham – or, rather, its neighbouring village of Galmpton, some years before, had proved creatively congenial to no less a poet than Robert Graves whose work I greatly admired. His book *The White Goddess*, a most influential study of poetry and myth in our century, had largely been written at Galmpton, together with some of his best poems, so this I regarded as rather a good omen for my own work, and a plus point for the area.

Again, having loved the countryside so much around Epping, especially in our early days there, Patricia and I wanted any new place to offer a similar rural environment. But, not being car drivers, our scope for house-hunting and exploration was somewhat limited. Despite the fact that much of Torbay is fairly built up, it nevertheless offers easy access to a wide variety of attractive, even idyllic, countryside. It did not take us long to establish the existence of a network of delightful walks far exceeding anything Epping had ever offered. So that we quickly perceived that we had stumbled upon as ideal a mix of landscape (mountains alone excepted) as England could offer, especially if one added the near river valley of the Dart, and the not-too-far away wilderness of Dartmoor itself. To have a climate where palm trees and cacti flourish outdoors all the year round, was an added attraction. So, like many another writer and artist before me, I fell in love with the West Country.

Yet what were the disadvantages? For the nonce (if one disregarded the great prevalence of dog dirt on Brixham pavements and grass verges) there was only one disadvantage; though I confess it was more in other people's eyes than mine or Patricia's. It was, of course, the money question. I had given up a highly paid job in the City. And because I had spent all surplus moneys over the previous half dozen years in subsidising loss-making publishing ventures of one sort or another, I had no savings, any more than did Patricia.

However, our house in the Home Counties fetched more when sold than the cost of the new one in Brixham. With the result that, after all expenses of moving had been deducted, we showed a profit of around £1,300. With that sum of money – the equivalent of perhaps £5,000 today – we allowed our hitherto conventional life to go west.

CHAPTER FOURTEEN
Living in Brixham

The house we bought is white, looks razor-sharp in sunlight and is the end one furthest from the road in a terraced row of six cottages. It is pushed up the far end of an unpaved lane in Furzeham, a district situated above Brixham harbour. I learned that the man who had built this row of individual dwellings some forty years previously had hailed from St. Michael's Mount in Cornwall. Hence the name of our little lane: The Mount.

We have a small, often unruly garden on three sides of the house. A garden full of flowers and shrubs, a plum tree, and an elderberry tree. And there are both purple and white lilac bushes in the Mount, while the rude stone wall that separates the lane from some allotments is everywhere draped with lurid pink, and sometimes red, valerian, as well as with herb robert, ivy and creeping toadflax. Devon walls are always remarkable for the free flower show they afford, and this is what makes them amongst the most attractive walls in Britain. Nowhere else is it truer than in Devon to say that the walls literally blossom.

My study was on the sunny south side of the house. For several weeks after we moved to The Mount, I busied myself with turning it into a highly personal den of books, posters and assorted bric-a-brac: some oddments of the latter which I collected from the seashore. Indeed, my study was to be eventually shelved with bleached driftwood rescued from the languid waves or pulled from crevices in the giant rocks of the Brixham Breakwater. My friend Quenten Lane from Essex and I, skilfully supervised by Patricia, created a rude library of shelves and books.

Naturally, every writer requires a base; and his or her study is just that. And it must be arranged just-so if it is to serve as a secure centre of creativity. Likewise, every writer, and especially a poet, is at the centre of a network of largely postal relationships. For a poet writes innumerable letters to fellow poets, to editors and publishers and, if he is fortunate, to patrons and readers of his work as well. If, like myself at that time, he also happens to edit a magazine or an anthology, he has even more – often hundreds more – letters to write and receive.

Such activity – like the writing of poems, reviews, manifestoes, etc. – even for the most famous poets is a largely unremunerative task. Which is, of course, why the uninitiated regard the writing of poems as a hobby rather than a profession. To a poet, however, such activity constitutes the truest and most exciting, the most spiritually rewarding of all activities.

Getting my study up-and-running, as the phrase is, was both exhausting and exhilarating. A labour of love second only to that of making poems themselves, and actively communicating with one's readers and fellow poets. For to live the imaginative life is best of all because least dull of all. And, as I suggest, healthiest of all.

Still, life is about people, not about ivory towers. Without people who, in an harmonious world (which this is not always, or often) are the *consciousness of nature* – without people there would be no experience. And without experience there would be no poetry. For poetry is 'the off-scouring of life', as my fellow poet Charles Sisson has insisted.

Consequently, I had to get to know the people of Brixham; or at least some of them. And one of the earliest persons in Brixham with whom I became acquainted was an artist called Cyril Bennett.

*   *   *   *   *

In good weather Cyril painted on the old Fish Quay. A tall, handsome, silver-haired man who attracted my attention for two reasons. Firstly the novelty of watching a man paint in the open air amongst the colourful (and not always so colourful) crowd that milled around the harbourside. And then, because he would sometimes rise gracefully from his canvas stool and amble about the Fish Quay. He had a *hauteur* not unlike that of Robert Graves.

His paintings had a delicately expressive line and an ability to capture well the variety and richness of Torbay's colourful summers, so Patricia and I decided to commission one from him. A bright harbour scene in oils.

It was a warm evening when we called at his 'studio', a rather un-artistic semi', though sufficiently unkempt to give the impression that it was the abode of an artist. Cyril and his wife welcomed us hospitably. Cyril was especially pleased to receive a request for a painting. He assured us, 'I always rise to the occasion for someone who is really interested in painting, and not just a bloody grock buying it as if it were a glorified picture postcard!'

Patricia outlined her fascination with skies of character, and I emphasised a liking for colour. All of which comments increased our local Constable's enthusiasm for the project. Then we learned that Cyril had once been a different sort of 'constable' in his younger days. We also discovered that Cyril had travelled a bit in his youth and he regarded this as a sort of litmus test of enlightenment. When the talk tacked again, it was to painters of the past. I happened to mention the work of William Blake. But Cyril aggressively dismissed Blake as 'old fashioned and full of religious images'. It soon became obvious Cyril was a local painter to the point of being a limited painter, though he had the instinct to express himself well in landscape or seascape.

Having always been drawn to people by something other than their masks and prejudices, I accepted Cyril's invitation to attend the monthly meeting of the local arts' society. It seemed a good way to test the waters of local intellectual society. It met in a drab church hall at the top of a very steep street overlooking the harbour. In its genteel way the arts' society proved hilarious, crowded with self-important middle-aged men and women, all of them Sunday painters. The only two present who made any real impression were Cyril and the local optician. The latter clearly had a theory about light and was busily, if vainly, trying to convince himself and others that artistic truth is only a matter of finding the right scientific formula. It was to prove my sole incursion into Brixham cultural life. For the next few years what culture I encountered was either in my study or during occasional trips back to London.

* * * * *

A short stroll from our house brings one to Fishcombe and Churston Coves: rocky, delightful and impressive inlets overhung by wooded cliffs of red sandstone. One ambles down to Fishcombe through the pine trees and shrubbery of the Battery Gardens, formerly a chunk of the estate of Lord Churston. During the Second World War it was heavily fortified – hence the name. A little further away is Churston Cove, at the mouth of a deep rocky chine.

In winter the sea in this shared lagoon of Churston and Fishcombe is a luminous greeny-grey; but for most of the year it is a crystalline blue. As the beaches are mostly pebble and sand-free, the water tends to be glass-clear with seaweed beds and the rocky seabed easily visible. *Mostly the sea is calm the year round. For Fishcombe and Churston coves are the most recessed inlets in all Lyme Bay, of which Torbay itself is but a bay-within-a-bay: a bite out of the smooth curved coast which runs from Start Point to Portland Bill. In bad weather many ships shelter in Torbay.*

During our first summer in Brixham Patricia, myself and the children spent many golden days at one or other of these coves. We sunbathed, read books, fished, we explored the flower-fissured rocks and, most of all, swam. Because 1976 was such an exceptionally hot summer that shaded only gradually into the mildest of winters, Patricia and I managed to keep up a daily swim for the first couple of years even in winter. In that near-tropical summer we became the youngest members of a quasi-geriatric group of all-weather swimmers who gathered every day at high tide for their ritual ablution. Easily the most likeable member of this group was Norman. He had a round moonface with large twinkling eyes; was tall and brown-bodied. One of those rare men who, like Hans Christian Anderson and my own father, exerted a great fascination over children. So it was a great loss when we heard, the following year, that Norman had died suddenly on a winter holiday in Spain. No more would he shout his jolly greetings to passers-by from the allotments overlooking the Battery Gardens. No more would the children hear him call out as they trailed off down to Fishcombe: 'I'll be down myself soon. Just hafta water mi runner beans first!'

'Tarzan' was a very different character, an unpopular self-fancier. This hunkily-built fellow, whose real name was Jeff, was in his sixties when we first moved to Brixham. He was generously girthed, solid and strong with it, a true 'Tarzan' – only partly gone to seed! Throughout the warm season, when not actively engaged in improving his tan on the beaches, insulting visitors or troubling teenage bathing beauties, Tarzan would wander about attired in only a pair of belted shorts and trainers. One overcast and chilly day Patricia encountered him, she on one side of the street, he on the other. Unusually, Tarzan was wearing an anorak and hood, though still in his shorts. Seeing Patricia, he greeted her by bellowing, 'Mornin' love! I see ye don't recognize me with mi clothes on!' At which, a hundred shopping heads turned in Patricia's direction as she fled into the nearest shop. Oddly, this 'character' died suddenly as well. And in winter. Unlike Norman, Tarzan was mentioned in the local paper.

*   *   *   *   *

Sea swimming has played an important part in the life of Patricia and myself. To many it is a foolish pursuit. 'What's it like today then, eh?' or 'Better you than me, mate!' To us, though, it is an experience of sensual clarification and refreshment, a subconscious lustration. Something elemental.

Rocks. Ribbed, jagged, rifted, skin-smooth or barnacle-rough rocks. Rocks sharp, tactile, sensuous and having an ageless, mysterious thissness and thatness. Rocks of the sea. Sea-water, the pure malleability of incarnated light. Moonwater, sunwater. Water that mirrors clouds, water that leads into clarity, and water that distorts. Water which is 90% of us: thinking water. Water that can exaggerate. Water that embodies a sense of harmony. Water that bespeaks moods in hues and sound. The perpetual music of water. Our beaches are, as I have said, predominantly stony. Sometimes broken glass, driftwood, seaweed, battered plastic bottles and plastic fish crates, rags, dead dogfish, limbs of busted crabs: detritus washed in by the surf. But only after storms are there really messy beaches; or when criminal tanker captains wash-out their boats far out at sea.

A blue lagoon of a bay. Golden sunfall days. Hues and moods governed by long fingers of breeze on hands of sunlight. High green headlands and colour-carded cliffs, beach huts and cafes. Around Brixham coastal place names: Elbury Cove, Oyster Cove, Churston Quay, Fishcombe, Freshwater Quarry, Ladybeach, Breakwater Beach, Shoalstone and Berry Head. Brixham: as good a place as any, you might say, to live. Perhaps better than most for health and healthy reflection? Well, for a poet and loved wife and children at any rate.

* * * * *

During the early years in Brixham, I eventually got myself two part-time jobs: one was as a gardener at an Old Peoples' Home – with Patricia as 'head gardener', myself useful for digging, sweeping patios and mowing lawns – the other book-keeping. But there was always three or four days a week which were still wholly my own: poets' days when I wrote, answered correspondence, went for walks or swam or generally 'indulged' myself – as people put it!

I also had plenty of time for my children. Though after 1982, they had less time for me: wishing, as children increasingly do, to go their own ways. Fortunately for Katie and Elizabeth – and for their parents too – Brixham was, and still is to a certain extent, a place of remarkably little crime: even if, morally, it is less sound than its numerous very active churches might suggest. But there was time for the children. For a number of years what they most wanted from me, and from Patricia to a lesser extent, was to organize and umpire innumerable games of rounders on Furzeham Green. As a result, we had many magical evenings, evenings when I would simply set off carrying a rounders' bat, soon to be followed by crowds of kids who appeared from seemingly nowhere, so that I came to feel like the Pied Piper of Rounders, with a bat in place of a flute.

*   *   *   *   *

Furzeham Green is an emerald slope overlooking Brixham's outer harbour. It has a fine view of all of Torbay. Just to walk that way is to draw spiritual sustenance from a scene that, on a clear day, extends all the way to Sidmouth and Lyme Regis, and sometimes even as far as Portland Bill. On bright summer days the rich sun glistens on waves, such moody waters, and often pools of gold develop like beaten foil at dawn or dusk. At night a silver liquid road opens up past the breakwater leading to a full shining moon. It is peaceful, tranquil. It is tranquil – except every mid-August! From time out of memory, the fair then comes to Furzeham Green; an event greeted with ecstasy by all the local kids.

When our children were still young – as they were in that glorious summer of 1976 and for several summers after – I found myself drawn into the fairground experience. Nay, nagged into it. One day there was an open space called Furzeham Green, the next, a whole town of canvas and stalls and caravans will have blossomed overnight. Then, just as miraculously, one week later, it would be gone – again overnight – leaving nothing of its presence save yellowed circles and squares on the green grass.

Traditionally, Friday night has a firework display on the lower green, and it is Friday night 1976 that I remember best. I left the family to watch the fireworks and went off in search of the boxing booth. My father once boxed in one of these fairground booths and I had a deep curiosity to see one in action. As I listened to the manager outside, surrounded by his aggressive acolytes, I was easily seduced into the marquee. An elevated boxing ring stood in the middle from where the manager eventually began issuing challenges on behalf of his warriors – a small but rather murderous-looking middle-weight with a broken-nose; a tall, slender masked figure known unoriginally as

'The Mask'; and a podgy, out-of-condition British Sumo wrestler with an unkempt beard!

The first bout was nothing more than a brawl between the broken-nosed pugilist and a tattooed ex-sailor from Devonport who was quickly overcome. The second challenger was, however a local. As with his predecessor he had no great boxing skills. He merely rushed about the ring waving his arms like an out-of-control windmill, managing to survive all three rounds. Though the manager did not feel he had earned his £3 prize money, the crowd did and joined in a heated debate which resulted in the contender being given a couple of quid in compensation.

The two bouts of wrestling proved a farce. The Mask was not really built for wrestling at all, having the figure of a middle-distance runner. It was soon obvious that whatever prowess he possessed was being severely tested by a boy from the local secondary school. At the conclusion it was highly doubtful as to whether The Mask or the schoolboy had won; a point vociferously argued by more than one member of the audience in that sweaty tent under a dark Devon sky. Finally, The Mask stood with arms folded, smirking as the promoter, who also doubled as referee, awarded him total victory.

$$* \quad * \quad * \quad * \quad *$$

Imagine me boarding a steam train on the Paignton/Kingswear line. The engine is shiny green, the coaches G.W.R. humbug-brown-and-yellow; and as the Lydham Manor 4-6-0 *class locomotive puffs out of Paignton Station I settle myself in the observation coach. I observe: like Larkin, I see a bowler begin his run; I catch a fraction of blue sea between backs of boarding houses; I see flowers everywhere, large pink valerian alongside the track, yellow toadflax, late campions.*

The train arrives abruptly at Goodrington Sands and there, in all its silken fullness, is the sea. Between the railway and the sea is a long row of beach huts and I recall the odd fact that, for years, one of those huts was used by the Irish playwright Sean O'Casey and his family; the author of Shadow of a Gunman *and* Juno and the Paycock *decamped from the slums of Dublin to spend the greater part of his life in Tory South Devon – and him a lifelong communist.!*

The line curves up from Goodrington to Broadsands in a gradual, gracious arc over two of Brunel's elegant viaducts. Below are the fullest vistas of Torbay, a soft and colourful seascape: beaches and coastal woodlands; cornfields beside the sea; short green hills that come right down onto the beach; Broadsands and finally stony Elbury Cove, a raised pebble beach surrounded by thick woods of pine and oak and ash. I am aware of how important beauty is to life.

Hooting its whistle, the Lydham Manor *turns abruptly inland and soon the engine is hauling its cream and brown coaches into Churston Junction. This was Robert Graves's local station and where Agatha Christie, who also lived nearby, used to alight to be collected by chauffeur-driven limousine. Leaving the station the line runs straight through magnificent rural prospects. The beautiful countryside around the Creek cannot have altered much in fifty years – one moment high banks of flowers and trees, next a tunnel, then from latticed trees and deep woods, a glimpse of Dittisham, a cluster of white cottages across the River Dart. As the rivermouth comes into view, Dartmouth can be seen across the river, while in front of the train is the small village of Kingswear. The whole ambience, for all its riverboat life of yachts, trawlers, ferries, pleasure boats, has something of a dream's claustrophobia about it which seems appropriate as the vintage GWR locomotive hauls its carriages into the anachronistic station. But then those things are not unreal, they merely participate in a greater, more poetic reality of the imagination that we are, perhaps, most aware of when relaxed.*

As I am now relaxed: remembering what a friend's wife said to me once, as we sat in their car at Kingswear waiting for the ferry to transport us across the river. We were discussing poetry and the beauty of the Dart. She said, 'A poet always carries his beauties in his head wherever he is.' 'But doesn't everyone?' I replied.

*　*　*　*　*

It was a beautiful spring day the day I discovered Old Hallsands. The sea shone with that incomparable calm luminosity one finds in South Devon. It was like a kingfisher caught in sunlight. The clifftops covered in yellow gorse; and gnarled bushes leaned away from the memory of winter winds. Yet, as Patricia, myself and two local friends ambled down a lane in the direction of the sea, we already knew that it led to nowhere. Its only ending now was in the sea ... and memory.

Once there had been a place called Hallsands: a thriving fishing village built on a raised beach beneath cliffs. It had had a single cobbled main street, on one side of which the houses had backed onto the ocean; on the other more cottages and houses had nestled under high cliffs. Fishermen's cottages, a pub called 'The London

Inn', a piggery, a brewery that made old-fashioned white beer, and a general store – these I had read of in an old book. But not any more is there Hallsands.

The sea in this area, the South Hams, is schizoid. In summer nowhere is the sea gentler or bluer. Nowhere can it change more rapidly, or with such devastating results. Remember the devastation of Torcross which appalled the nation in the winter of 1978 – 79? It's the same bit of coast, just a few miles from Hallsands. This inexpressibly gentle sea is paranoic beneath its timeless surface because of currents deep in the English Channel that thrust up past the Lizard from the bad-tempered Atlantic.

Even so, Hallsands' remarkable raised beach was always protected from the worst this capricious sea could do by a hidden sandbank, The Skerries, out in the bay. A bulwark of shale and sand, formed by the interplay of tide and hidden current, had built up over the centuries and formed an unseen protection for the village, so that even in great hurricanes that blew up every quarter of a century or so, the mighty anger of the sea was always finally frustrated. Frustrated, that is, until towards the end of the last century when it was decided to extend Plymouth dockyards. The Board of Trade, disregarding local knowledge and the pleas of the South Hams' fishing community, granted a licence to a contractor to dredge undersea shale from the Skerries Bank. This action irreversibly altered the direction of the powerful undersea currents; and with its natural defences impaired, Hallsands was doomed. On one bad winter's night in the 1890s, the first great onslaught occurred. It damaged a number of houses on the seaward side; and it breached the crude seawall that had been built in anticipation of such an event. Rapid erosion of the beach then began, and it shrunk year by year. Then the main street collapsed, undermined by the tide, and had to be shored up. Finally, in three nights of storm in January 1917, the sea came in all its mad fury and devastated Hallsands, leaving but a single dwelling in the whole village.

Ghost villages haunt the mind with great immediacy. It seemed to me, as I sat among the ruins of Hallsands village, that disaster was the perfect paradigm for the consequences of man's thoughtlessness and misguided interference with nature. I was a small microcosm of awareness. A part of that sense which has been growing over the past few decades of the disastrous, and perhaps irreversible, damage humanity has done to this planet. Hallsands epitomised not only man's destruction of his environment, not only his blind non-cooperation with nature, but his capacity to destroy absolutely a way of life as well.

Just as man and nature are interconnected bodies or organisms; so, too, ways of life are organic growths. The one depends upon the other. Whether it be the Brazilian rain forests, the ozone layer, or a simple raised beach like the one which had sustained the Hallsands' community, all are essential and necessary. In a moment of vision, that was no more than a distant metaphysical image of great wonder, I perceived among the ruins of Hallsands the inchoate and essentially spiritual *memoria* which are the beginning of a poem. Many months later I began to write the sequence which became *The Hallsands' Tragedy*. It was all I, as a poet, could do to pluck back into life some remembrance of a lost way of life so that, perhaps, Hallsands may live again. Eventually it was published in 1993 by Westwords Publications, almost ten years after my first visit there.

During my years in Devon, I have written many poems which stem from places I know and have visited. But some have taken on more significance than others. This has often happened because not only did a particular place stir my imagination, but there was a metaphysical dimension involved: a sense of the numinous which coloured the vision. As I've tried to say already, my visit to Hallsands was one such occasion. And for once, I did some 'research'. What happened was that around a year later I still had the vague metaphysical image at the back of my mind and I was finding it hard to describe. I asked Peter and Lorna Hunt, the friends who'd initially introduced me to Hallsands, for more information about it. They leant me a book of local history, I read it and all of a sudden, I felt I'd got some basic historical information, enough to enable me to write the poem. After that, it flowed quickly, and within a few days I had the first draft.

This was the second poem these particular friends had helped into being. One of the first excursions with them was to a place called Pudcombe. It was a beautiful spring day and we walked part of the Coastal Footpath – that 500 mile route from Minehead in North Somerset which meanders round the peninsular to Poole in Dorset. It's an up-and-down footpath visiting coves and headlands in turn and that day we must have walked some of the more spectacular parts. I was very taken with the harmonious beauty of the area: sea, sky, trees, flowers, even seeing a fox, all coalesced into one perfect whole. Yet when I tried to reproduce it in words, it never came right. It must be one of my most revised poems; I still refer to it as my grandest failure. I wanted to record paradise – but found myself unable. It has become significant as the title poem for the collection Patricia published when she started Acumen Publications in 1992. She was taking a desk-top publishing course at college and had to do a project. So she produced a book of my South Devon poems and called it *The Patient Reconstruction of Paradise*. All of the poems, save the title poem, had been written in response to two long walks, each lasting several days, which she and I alone took along the Coastal Footpath. I felt many other poems were much better than the title poem, but Patricia was insistent that this was the most poetic title. Perhaps she was right.

The other important Devon-inspired sequence I wrote was *The Mansands' Trilogy*. Situated much closer to Brixham, Mansands is a stony beach at the mouth of a graceful valley backing up to Hillhead. A wide-open chine of sweeping fields, largely treeless, and time-gnawed-off high cliffs containing an abundance of slate, Mansands beach sucks in and out its wild swirling mouthfuls of stone and blue-grey tide. It always seems an empty sea there, unlike in nearby boat-bustled Torbay; and, even at the height of the tourist season, the not-easily-accessible Mansands remains peaceful. Its long trailing vale, its tiny climbing path leading away from the shore in a blaze of campion, valerian, stitchwort and other flowers which fill the heated months of spring and summer; or the climbing away sweeping immensity of green land towards blue sky and distant Dartmouth, all conspired to produce lines like:

> Mansands, stunning landscape
> of beach and bay and mighty hills behind,
> your lonely immensity
> curves in a single wave to sky
> and then shrinks back silently
> into the still blind stone heart
> that feels the lost spray
> of so much lost joy.

The walk taken so often in the years since 1976 to this place became a kind of pilgrimage into the beauty and heart of nature: sea nature, land nature – the two inseparable. And when I came to write this poem, which is, in effect, an extended meditation in three parts, all the features of the walk to Mansands surfaced in it. As did my thoughts of 'the great escape' which I had made from 'the uncreative emptiness of cities'. Far more than anything in *The Hallsands' Tragedy*, more even than the title poem of my collection *The Patient Reconstruction of Paradise*, *The Mansands' Trilogy* deserves the name 'metaphysical', for it blends philosophical discursiveness and statement of a metaphysical order, with a revealing lyricism:

> natural yearning
> nature gives
> like tucking sunlight in our hearts

Once more, in this poem my preoccupation with paradise surfaces most especially in feeling:

> the joy of paradise
> collected in a shell
> where on Mansands I praise
> a heaven after hell.

That is how the poem finishes and it is a clear testament to the fact that I felt I had not merely patiently reconstructed paradise but actually rediscovered it.

But what is this Paradise? And where does one find it? Paradise is this world: but this world seen aright. That is, it is the natural world of earth and mankind, the non-humanly created world seen in all its glory. It has no specific location. It is everywhere and it is nowhere. Though we often get our own keenest glimpses in some places more than others, and we remember those places. My places have been various: the Road, Shottery, Epping and South Devon especially.

But how is this seeing possible? Perhaps only the truly 'pure in heart', as the Bible says, are capable of seeing it whole and seeing it steadily. Children, possessed of a pre-pubic and uncomplicated sense of wonder, see the world as it really is, as paradisial. Great poets like Shakespeare or Dante, in spite of their too fleshly mortality, clearly describe it in their most inspired writings. The rest of us – who are creatures too much of finitude and the mundane, unable to concentrate for more than a few seconds wholly on anything with minds that flit about like butterflies of angst – get but few glimpses of Paradise. And often, even then, those 'glimpses' are but lost sparks blown about the back of our minds from the almost quenched fires of childhood.

CHAPTER FIFTEEN

Eccentrics and other Literary Visitors

Over the years we've had many visitors to The Mount, despite its remoteness from the Metropolis. And none more interesting than the literary visitors. Nor ever a more remarkable one than our first in the August of that long hot summer of '76.

One evening a burly and hirsute young man, like a last incarnation of a Sixties' hippy, arrived at the house. He enquired for me and was shown into my study by a puzzled Patricia. Soon, I learned that this serious specimen of youth rejoiced in the rather grand name of Conrad Ryder-Large and had hitch-hiked all the way from Edinburgh where he had bought a back issue of *Littack*, plus a book of my poems. As a result of reading them, he had been possessed of an overwhelming desire to make my acquaintance! That, however, was as far as I got for the time being. Another knock at the door and this time Patricia ushered in a uniformed policeman! I shall always remember the look of alarm in her eyes. After the briefest of conversations our visitor was escorted from the premises to a waiting police car. An event that occurred in full view of all our neighbours' windows, from which can be seen all the comings and goings from our home.

It seemed, as we discovered later, that our visitor, having struggled up from the town centre with a large backpack, had disencumbered himself of his luggage on Furzeham Green. He had sat next to a total stranger on a bench, then enquired the way to 'the poet's house at The Mount?' The man knew nothing of any poet, but he was able to direct Conrad to The Mount. Because of its sheer weight and bulk, Conrad had left his backpack with the man and said he would come back for it shortly. After a while the stranger had grown tired of waiting and phoned the police. They, on the information which the man had been able to give them, soon followed Conrad up to the house. Conrad admitted to them that he had quite forgotten all about his worldly possessions in his enthusiasm for conversing with me, the poet! Why this should be *I* couldn't quite see, but it is what Conrad had told the police. Also, I couldn't grasp why the police had first taken the backpack to the local nick some miles away before searching for its owner? But, to parody the Bard, there are more things in

Devon, and especially in Brixham, than are dreamed of in any reasonable philosophy.

By the time Conrad and his mislaid gear returned to us – on foot – night had fallen. As a result, of course, none of our neighbours could have witnessed his return. Consequently, there was no need, as Patricia somewhat ironically observed, to enquire 'what the neighbours would think?' They would think only what they had seen: a man being taken away by the police from the Oxleys' house – a man they did not, because of the dark – see returning. I bet they wondered what sort of company poets kept!

As to what conclusions I came to eventually concerning this disciple out of the dark, I shall keep to myself. But I owe Conrad one thing at least: another glimpse of Paradise. It occurred as I was returning across the oval field on Churston Common, having escorted this strange young man as far as the main road where he intended to hitch-hike back to Scotland. In a state of deep concentration, I was strolling along the dusty lane towards the sea at Fishcombe Point. The sun above my head seemed a golden dish fastened onto summer's seamlessly blue dome. The lane, a mere cart track, ran through an oval cornfield which was utterly still in the heat haze. The drooping green wall of trees in Churston Wood leaned over the landscape, and there was no birdsong, only the hum of insects in hedges. I was walking and walking as in a dream: but a dream which seemed to lead into some greater-than-normal reality. During that walk I suddenly found I had experience of the world as Paradise again. It was like the experiences I had had as a child when I dwelt in the Road. A clear perception of the unity and the immortality of all being in a few moments of time.

Later that day I wrote a poem which, alas, is an all-too-inadequate recreation of that walk into wonder. As a record of one marvellous moment early in our Devon life, it is worth recalling:

THE LANE

When I left him and walked the mile-long lane
I realised I had talked my way to Paradise;
Just where the last of summer's full sun fell
Towards the first wither of autumn's undeceiving leaves
The sentiment, the country sentiment, smiled warm and still
On me and hung in green and flung gold
Across the old dust of the delightful lane

That led through my mind to the far-off peeping sea
Beyond the bulging wood of Churston Common.
Stillness, too, hung among the chaff the reapers left
In the oval field that slept beside the wood
Where the fires of June were wont to light neat poppies
Among the glowing stalks of corn;
And huge banks of trees a green contentment wore
While the long hedges kept their incredible life
Of fly, spider, butterfly, wasp and bee
Working the honeyed wonder of late blossom and wildflower.
There was untouched freedom in that untouched scene:
A sense of eternity in that seaside country lane,
And every argument that I had ever known
Dissolved, was resolved, became needless there
Where late summer and autumn casually met
To present in a fused truth of afternoon light
To the innocence of my foolish middle years
A suspended ecstasy, a sentiment that all might share
Who cared to walk that sun-wrapped lane, that day.

Maybe, here and there, in that poem some glimpse of Paradise is
afforded: some echo of its immortal music, its airs?

*   *   *   *   *

Between 1976 and 1980 I edited six issues of The Littack Supplement
*from Brixham. 'The best thing to come out of Brixham since "Abide
With Me",' wrote Sir John Betjeman in a letter. In some ways it was
a continuation of* Littack, *but without the satire. It was more a
broadsheet than a magazine, containing poems and reviews. It kept
me in touch with the literary world, for editors and publishers still
sent me books to review. Indeed, up to this day, all the books from
Penguin for review in my wife's magazine* Acumen *come addressed
to* The Littack Supplement! *As well as editing, I was consolidating
my reading. All the books that had been important to me and which
I had read in a fervour of adolescent excitement, I now re-read in the
more settled atmosphere of my new study. Through having time
available I went back to Homer, Virgil, Shakespeare, Milton, Dante,
Coleridge (prose and poetry), Wordsworth, Blake and many another.
I was also writing furiously and Patricia always maintained that she
could tell when I'd read any particular poet because the style was*

reflected in my own writing! But eventually, I grew tired of educating
myself in public and 1980 found me writing the following Epilogue:

> Every poet undergoes a personal revolution ... my way was *Littack*
> [which] took the form of a polemical argument with any of the
> world which cared to listen or contest. Though not personally a
> loud individual, in my writings I was very noisy... in order that I
> got certain intellectual matters sorted out. I think I was right in
> warning against collective pressures on the poet, intellectual
> conformism and state control of the arts. I know I was right in
> opposing the spirit of cancerous doubt eating the modern soul
> and causing the de-spiritualisation and de-vitalisation of poetry;
> but I was also wrong and perpetuated much injustice against many
> contemporary poets who, in their quieter way, kept the flame alive
> and who could write better poetry than me. So the time has now
> come for me to foreclose on a number of activities which have
> become redundant to my central aim of writing good poetry, and
> one of these is *The Littack Supplement*. There is also, at this time,
> the personal question of shortage of cash...

*   *   *   *   *

Correspondence to and from The Mount consisted for the most part
of letters, poems, the occasional book for review and, least welcome
of all, the return of one's own work rejected by various publishers
and publications. Especially was my poetry unwelcome in quarters
heavily subsidised by arts councils because of *Littack*, where I had
been very critical of state patronage of the arts.

Now and again, though, an acceptance came through, or a
publication was received with a poem of mine in it: all occasions for
joy for I was far from being the most successful of writers! But, at
least, I was writing what I pleased. Though when a writer writes
what he or she wants, it is usually not what anyone else wants them to
write!

To most people such an inward correspondence as I was receiving
would seem more of an avalanche than a flow of communication.
But at least one is famous, if only to the Post Office. And that can
have advantages: one's mail rarely goes astray. For example, the
playwright Christopher Fry once wrote to me a hopelessly mis-
addressed letter to a street in a suburb of Exeter which is nearly forty
miles away from Brixham. I may not be famed for my poetry, yet to

the Post Office, even as far away as Exeter, I was evidently well-known – from the quantity of my inward mail. So with no more delay than a second class stamp might have induced, I received Christopher Fry's missive at The Mount.

If the correspondence was large, visitors, in those early days, were no more than a trickle which only tended to increase a little in the summer season. Most were welcome in our Devon 'exile'; and hardly any proved tiresome. Our visitors came from places as far away as Osaka in Japan or Salzburg in Austria; or from as near as Salcombe or Exeter. In only one case did we ever discourage a proposed visitor, a pal of mine from the old days in Essex, Melville Hardiment.

Mel was a wild man. A Beat Poet who had reached the age when it was no longer decent to be such things – apart from the fact that the Beats were no longer fashionable. When I first knew Mel, he was 'getting on in years' in everybody's eyes save his own. He'd gained some local notoriety, too, when, in a clapped-out old Ford, he'd contrived to run into a funeral procession in broad daylight in Epping High Street. Apparently, just as the hearse was turning at the traffic lights by the church, Mel had managed to stage a spectacular head-on collision with the lead vehicle.

Personally, I didn't mind Mel at all. He was interesting in his eccentric way. But Patricia was discouraging of any attempt to encourage him to follow us down to Brixham. She thought him irresponsible, not only in his car driving but in other facets of his life as well. This had never worried me, for Mel was very friendly towards us both, and only now and then would borrow small sums of money. I never cared that he didn't repay me because, in those days, I could afford the sort of amounts he needed, though like many people with no money, Mel had the sort of tastes that prove costly to his friends. Then there was the additional problem in that he had a young family. Patricia, proud of her new house, didn't like the way he let his children write all over indoor walls and was worried they might do the same if they came to Brixham, a bad example to Elizabeth and Katie. So, in the absence of invitations coming thick and fast from Brixham, Mel decided to encourage himself to visit. This he did by writing me long letters outlining his plans for bringing himself and his household to reside with us for unspecified periods of time.

After a while, however, on Mel's receiving no active endorsement of his holiday plans from myself (and much active discouragement to me from my wife), he turned somewhat unsympathetic. From time to time over the next dozen years, he was to write increasingly reproachful epistles implying deep disappointment in my character. However, as each year went by, the letters became more and more infrequent; and I consoled myself with the thought that no man in this life can hope to please everyone, even every one of his friends.

But enough of letters. Life is more important. On the other hand, is there that much difference?

*   *   *   *   *

When I first came to Brixham I couldn't really swim. My strokes were all over the place and it took a month or two to learn to co-ordinate my limbs. I jumped in at the deep end and that taught me really how to swim. In 1973, I had had the inspiration to write a long poem, A Map Of Time. *The first draft didn't take long, about six to eight months, a year at the most. What became apparent shortly afterwards, however, was that it needed a lot of work on the form because, though I'd got the ideas together, it was a mess. I needed years of craftsmanship to get it into a reasonable shape. I spent the first four years at Brixham revising and re-writing the poem, and from this I learned to order and control my material. With* A Map Of Time *I jumped in at the deep end, too, and it taught me how to swim poetically. I found it hard to get all my strokes right and even now, I'm only satisfied with certain parts of it. It shows all my 'unco-ordinated limb movements' too clearly in places, my inability to match form and content. I found I was wrestling with the problem of finding a common or satisfactory language with which to name and express the innumerable features of the unknown country of the mind. Though at first glance the poem appears a classical epic being divided into books (or Phases) with an argument preceding each, it is much more complex and, finally, circular in form. It begins with a look back to the Eden of childhood, then takes a spiritual journey through my life up to a certain point in time, finishing in another Eden, where love – 'only when with you in perfect days / and nights beside the lighthouse by the sea' – made 'all the contradictions of the world dissolve / Like darkness in a little drop of light.'*

*   *   *   *   *

It is my view that the most sociable encounters are those with thinking people who are prepared to debate more than trivial matters. Mike

Brown, a librarian who lived in Harlow, a well-educated, sensitive but diffident man, was, for many years, just such a companion.

One evening, quite unexpectedly, Mike turned up at The Mount. He was accompanied by a willowy, attractive woman in her twenties. Now, Mike came from Essex; but it appeared his girlfriend was a nurse at Torbay Hospital. After talking in my study for a couple of hours they suddenly announced they were going to get married in a few months' time. Then, as if embarrassed by the drama of the announcement, they prepared to leave.

As I escorted the librarian and his girlfriend down the hill to the bus station, Mike enquired: 'Would you and Patricia come to the wedding?'

I assured them we would, if invited.

'You'd come all the way to London just for a wedding?' He sounded incredulous. But, again, I assured him we would.

However, some months later we received what can only be described as an 'ex-post facto invitation'. This was a printed announcement on a card to the effect that Mike and his girl had married some weeks previously at a church in the Home Counties. I later learned from an American lady: 'We often do this in the States.' But why in Essex I wondered?

From that day, years back, when Mike came to see us, to this, I have rarely had the opportunity for conversation with my old Essex friend whose two most memorable quotes were: 'Hatred is a form of caring'; and 'Old friends, like old wine, are best'. Maybe Mike felt, for all my poet's arguments, that it is possible to become unacceptably 'bookish', and had opted for something different? He was, after all, a librarian.

*   *   *   *   *

During the years 1977 to 1980, there occured a brief flowering of philosophical intensity. I have always been of a philosophical cast of mind, not in the rigidly logical sense of a trained philosopher, but more as an amateur, picking up, thinking over, then absorbing or discarding ideas: more an eclectic reader than a systematic one. I've always felt that a poem, to have any real lasting value, must offer some interpretation of reality, over and above mere description. In any discussion on poetry I am always more concerned with ideas than things. During these years I became obsessed with what I considered a wrong-headed notion that everything could – and should

– be made concrete, and there should be no abstractions. This didn't seem right to me. I remember reading Schopenhauer and Spinoza along with several other philosophers. Then something moved me to put my thoughts down on paper. I remember looking across Torbay one evening, just as the coloured lights came on and having a flash of inspiration about inner and outer perspectives and feeling very excited about it.

All these thoughts, which I carried around in note form and in my head, came to fruition in my two books of philosophy, Of Human Consciousness *and* The Idea And Its Imminence. *The former, written in 1976/7, postulates the existence of an outer world subjected to the laws of physics, and an inner world which is not. Though this separation is useful to discuss perception, the two are not inseparable: think of the conflicts which arise between moral precepts and practical experience! The physical senses are part of this process, they are the first step to opening the door to the inner reality. But what enters after that is a different matter. I've tried to show how we have glimpses of what could enter in my search for Paradise.*

The Idea And Its Imminence *was written in 1978-79 and sub-titled ' a poet's philosophy'. I wrote, 'the only true knowledge is an act of penetration of things by the mind and a union of the two.' But this 'penetration' has to be reciprocal: the 'thing' has also to penetrate the mind. The result is knowledge. Whether a philosopher would agree with this is one thing, but a poet would recognize the workings of the creative imagination – expressed perhaps in somewhat Coleridgean terms. The two twin poles of poetry revolve around love and death and as such poetry will go on. It is necessary. It will only die out in this world if love and death die; if they die, so will poetry.*

*   *   *   *   *

Imaginative excitement. A knock at the front door in The Mount. one rain-threatening day. I open the door and there is a stranger. A tall, lithe figure with floppy, flowing white hair falling half-across his right eye. He has a healthy complexion, a visage with seraphic expression and blue-grey eyes that are the colour of wisdom. Is he an angel, I ask myself? The figure is wearing green corduroy trousers and a pale smock-like jersey. With the utmost naturalness in the world he asks, 'Are you William Oxley?'

I admit my identity, then he says, 'I'm John Gurney. You may remember you published some poems of mine in *Littack* about a dozen years ago ...?' I do remember vaguely; and invite him in. And for the next three hours he addresses Patricia and me on everything from Jacob Boehm to Baked Beans, with only the briefest pause in his monologue to decline a meal with us on the grounds that he cannot eat food until he has done 'at least an hour's yoga first'. Abruptly, at the end of three hours, Gurney departs, even more dramatically than he arrived. I open the door for him and observe, 'It's raining! You'll have to hurry to your car, wherever you've parked it.'

It was as if my words acted as a starting pistol. For John promptly broke into the most incredible run from our house, literally bolting down the lane and disappearing from sight in seconds. He had the turn of speed of an Olympic sprinter and he left Patricia and myself not only bemused at his many words and ideas, but wondering what the neighbours might imagine at the sight of a fifty-year old man fleeing from our house at such a great rate. No one else has ever fled our company so quickly!

From John Gurney's flood of words, however, we gleaned some facts about this unusual man. After calling on Harry Chambers, the editor of Peterloo Poets, whose house, according to Gurney, 'hangs on the lip of a disused quarry in Cornwall', John had thought of calling on us. We also found out that he was an ex-fighter-pilot-turned-teacher; but who considered his main calling in life was writing poetry and verse dramas ... ceaselessly.

And I mean ceaselessly! John must be the most prolific poet now writing in the British Isles for not only has he written thousands of poems, including a sixteen-thousand-line epic called *War*, but nearly thirty verse plays as well. An illustration of his amazing productivity and metrical facility: a year or two later, John took Patricia and me to visit William Cowper's house at Olney. While she and I were absorbed in the exhibits there, John managed to pen nearly two hundred lines of blank verse on Cowper's life. I remember opening a door in an upper room of the old house to find John seated at a table surrounded by the remains of Cowper's library and scribbling away furiously. We also subsequently, and more fully, learned that John is a yoga adept who claims to practise levitation, a spiritualist and a keen vegetarian. He is as forceful an advert as could be wished for the creative and energising properties of a sound diet. It is true, that since ceasing to be an R.A.F. pilot, John has had a history of mental traumas. But these he has gradually overcome by the regular practice of transcendental meditation coupled with a careful diet. Thus it was that 'the Bard of Bedford' entered our life like the whirlwind of Isaiah, did no damage, and stayed. He is probably the most spiritual person I know and has become a constant source of that imaginative excitement which I believe – all arguments about diet, etc. aside – to be the true source of health.

*   *   *   *   *

After the philosophy, I also put together and corrected a huge book which had been hanging around since the Sixties. As early as January 1968 I'd been sending father long screeds filled with poetic theory: it was a practice I was to continue throughout our correspondence. These ideas were altered, modified or strengthened with the passage of time, more reading, further thought and, hopefully, a little more poetic wisdom! But in 1982, Dr. James Hogg of Salzburg University was coming to visit us, and had specifically asked if I had anything for publication. The Notebook Of Hephaestos *(published in 1981) had taken all my shorter poems and, as yet, I didn't feel ready to offer* A Map Of Time. *So I spent the spring revising once again the essays and writings which became* The Cauldron Of Inspiration. *Having been written over a number of years, these prose pieces were, of necessity, in differing styles which no amount of correction – save entire rewrites – could iron out. It opens with the portentous words: 'In essence this book is an Odyssey of the mind: a journey that I have always known, as a poet, I would have to make sooner or later.' In essence, it is a cross between Graves's* The White Goddess *and Coleridge's* Biographia Literaria. *It charts my journeys through Celtic myth, the concept of the Logos, what I felt poetry to be, ideas on craft, style, imagination and, finally, a chapter on my 'poetic heroes' of the early eighties. Glyn Pursglove, on reading it, said that 'no academic could have written it' meaning, I hope, it was too much of a rag-bag for an academic work. It was described by* Orbis *as 'Oxley's book of English prose' – no doubt referring to its differing styles. I think in some respects both were too kind. It is a book I'd like to correct (again) and up-date ...*

*   *   *   *   *

As the years have gone by the 'trickle' of visitors to The Mount, both expected and otherwise, has increased. Most, I have to say, have had an artistic slant; such as the poet-novelist, jazz and cricket buff, Alexis Lykiard, or his friend Rupert Loydell, who is a painter, publisher and poet. An ebullient and, to many people, an abrasive young man, with whom I have always enjoyed a plain-speaking relationship, I am indebted to Rupert for his radical ideas on art, his 'experimentalist' outlook, and his youthfully brash risk-taking coupled with a genuine openness to new ideas, all of which has helped, I feel, to keep me young. Rupert runs Stride Publications in Exeter, a small but hyperactive press that grew out of *Stride Magazine*, first published while Rupert and his wife, Sue, were students at art school. It was through my old friend, the poet and novelist, Brian Louis Pearce of Twickenham that I first got to know of Rupert. And it was around the time he accepted my book, *Mad Tom On Tower Hill*, that Rupert made his first visit to The Mount. If not his first visit – for he comes two or three times a year, not, I suspect, for the 'arty ambience of the Oxleys', but Patricia's excellent puddings – certainly it was his most memorable, if only for the mode of his and Alexis's departure.

We had invited them over to make the acquaintance of Glyn Pursglove – who had recently taken over as Patricia's reviews' editor on *Acumen*. Glyn and his Persian wife Parvin, plus their two daughters, were staying with us for a few days. Rupert, Alexis and Glyn found they got on well together. In fact, such first meetings are often successful in the literary world because the participants frequently know of the work and reputation of each other long before making acquaintance 'in the flesh'. Although Glyn is an academic from Swansea, his knowledge of the poetry world and its sustaining humus of little magazines and small presses is second to none.

The talk lasted well into the small hours and the wine lake spilled its banks. Finally, Rupert, and Alexis who was driving, decided they must, somewhat regretfully, depart. However, the narrow gravelled lane which serves all the houses of The Mount is an unlit cul-de-sac. The last view any of us had of them was of Alexis negotiating his way out of the lane backwards, with Rupert stood reversed on the front passenger seat, his head out of the sun-roof, shouting instructions as they slowly dissolved away into the black Devonshire night.

Such are some of the ways in which one's art gets translated into one's way of life. And I do not think that Yeats was right when he said we have to choose between 'perfection of the art or perfection of the life'. Life, even for poets, isn't as cut and dried as that.

CHAPTER SIXTEEN
Excursions out of Paradise

The poem 'The Lane', one of the first written at Brixham, some years later found its way into my collection, *The Notebook of Hephaestus*, published in, of all places, Scotland. How this came about is both a happy and a sad tale; and it illustrates that though I have dwelt in Brixham since May 1976, many have been the sorties I have made from the port, for one reason or another.

Among those with whom I corresponded was Leonard Clark. Leonard was a stockily built, owl-like, rather bouncy figure of a man who hailed from Gloucestershire. A country boy at heart, Leonard was a compatriot of Ivor Gurney, Laurie Lee and F.W. Harvey, all Cotswold poets, each of whom he greatly admired. Leonard had made a career as an H.M.'s Schools' Inspector like the great Matthew Arnold before him.

Leonard and I had an agreeable, if fitful, correspondence for a number of years. Then, around 1979, as I was putting together my latest collection, I wrote and asked Leonard if he would consider writing a foreword. With his customary generosity he said he would, but added modestly, 'I doubt, though, if your poems need any compère.' In due course, he read the typescript and wrote a splendid introduction.

Because I lived in Devon and he in North London, Leonard and I did not often meet. But around a year after he'd written the foreword to my book, knowing I was in London on business, he invited me to his house for afternoon tea. Upon arriving in leafy Highgate, I found myself ushered briskly into a spacious, if dark, hallway; my coat was virtually lifted off my back; and I was whisked into a large front drawing room which doubled as Leonard's study. He guided me to a deep leather armchair with the words, 'Sit there. It's still warm from where Ted Hughes was sitting till five minutes ago!' A remark, together with the booklined walls, the photographs of Leonard with John Masefield, Andrew Young and Edmund Blunden, calculated to impress. And it did! Leonard exuded the air of a genuine man-of-letters: the old-fashioned worker among words. He was a genuine poet, too, and one very different from that modern breed which Robert

Graves derisively called 'career poets'. (I wonder what either would make of some poets of the late Nineties?) Leonard had what I can only describe as a friendly abruptness. Pouring me a glass of sherry he demanded, 'Have you found a publisher for your book yet?'

With a slightly embarrassed air, recalling the mounting rejection slips the manuscript was receiving from publishers on whom I had tried it, I mumbled, 'Well, no, er, I'm afraid I haven't.'

'Well, I think I have!' he replied promptly, with an air of almost off-handedness.

I felt both exalted and dumbfounded. This almost immediately gave way to a sense of the generosity of the man. Here was a well-known and distinguished poet prepared to trouble himself to find a publisher for a relatively unknown and, because of *Littack*, notorious young man. It was very gratifying. In that well-lit but soberly decorated study, I felt that I was encountering in Leonard Clark that all-too-rare disinterestedness and generosity of spirit of the true poet: one who never made the mistake of confusing the artist and his art, the workman and his work.

And so it came about. The press Leonard had 'found' for me accepted the collection, and the wheel of publication began slowly to turn. Over the next six months I found myself working towards the intimate shaping for public consumption of *The Notebook of Hephaestus & Other Poems*. Working with a sympathetic and meticulous editor called Leslie Cook who was also the proprietor of The Lomond Press in Kinross, Scotland. A happy experience that was, alas, to be marred by tragedy.

In his foreword to the volume Leonard wrote: 'William Oxley ... will further develop his undoubted gifts, and, through trial and error, eventually arrive at the point when he will be more fully recognised for the genuine poet he is. I hope that I live long enough to see that happen.' So, as the book moved through 1981 towards publication, Leonard kept a weather eye on its progress, both by letter and when we dined together occasionally in the Tottenham Court Road. The book's development seemed to interest him almost as much as it did me. It was arranged, too, that Leonard would spend a week's holiday with us in Devon that August: where he hoped to have the pleasure of 'tasting some Brixham lobster' and, perhaps, be with us 'when the book comes out'.

But as August drew near a vague note of uncertainty began to creep into his letters – an uncertainty concerning not the book but the feasibility of the Brixham holiday. At first, I thought he had merely lost his appetite for travel, for he had only recently made a trip to the Holy Land. And he was, by now, an elderly man. I suspected there were other difficulties, but had no idea what the problems were. I still have no idea really, but the upshot was that he did not come to Brixham. Instead, in early September, Patricia and I were summoned to see him at Weston-super-Mare – a visit in answer to urgent appeals from him.

Before we even arrived at the rather sombre house in a road of uniformly grey, turn-of-the-century dwellings, Leonard's letters had informed us that he was staying at a nursing home: an ominous sign. So when a matronly figure opened the door and asked, in reply to our request to see Mr. Clark as we were friends, 'How long is it since you've seen your friend?' I felt a strange sense of foreboding.

After admitting that I had not seen Leonard for some six months, the lady sighed, 'Oh dear! In that case you should be prepared to find him much altered.'

The man we discovered in a neat upper room looking out over Weston towards a hint of sea was indeed changed. Looking crumpled and pallid, Leonard was slumped in a bedside chair. He was up and dressed, wearing a brownish suit and waistcoat, but gone was all his natural ebullience. Soon, too, we discovered how little conversation was left in a now wandering mind, and he looked as though he had suffered a partial stroke. Leonard scarcely recognised me, and Patricia not at all. His pipe and notebook lay sadly unused; a meal was untouched. 'I can't eat!' he moaned; and he stared vaguely, wildly about, seeing little or nothing. Worst of all, there soon came an alarming and pitiful request to be helped to the toilet.

As I all but carried Leonard along to the bathroom, I realised that he had scarcely any strength left in his body, and I found myself having to perform the offices of a nurse. Saddest of all, though, was the way he kept re-iterating through the remainder of our stay that he 'would never forget what you have done for me today'. As poignant and heart-rending a comment as it is possible to receive from an obviously dying man.

Soon the conversation had all but ceased so, leaving Leonard to nod in his chair, we went downstairs to see the matron. She told us how Leonard had arrived by taxi, apparently quite well, but within a day or two had declined rapidly, refusing food and concerned only about the proofs of a book of poems he was expecting. Eventually these had arrived, but by this time Leonard had been so weak that the Matron and her husband had had to help him with the corrections before sending them back to the publishers.

At my urging, the Matron rang Leonard's wife who was on holiday in the north. She said she would drive down to Weston immediately to collect Leonard and take him back to Highgate. Then, not much reassured – feeling this was the last time we would ever see Leonard – and in a very dispirited frame of mind, Patricia and I took the train back to Devon.

Within three days a phone call informed me that Leonard Clark had died. The following week, Patricia and I and the children attended Leonard's funeral at St. Bartholomew the Great in Smithfield.

At the very last minute a footnote to Leonard's foreword of my book was added by the publisher: 'Leonard Clark died on 10th September 1981, while this book was in the press'. His wish to see my work 'more fully recognized' was not granted. Neither was mine to have him see the book. Sadly.

*   *   *   *   *

Everything traditional, even death itself, is constantly under threat in our times. When I first lived in London, it was close to the famous Highgate cemetery, and in those days it was possible to wander freely through the mysterious and necrophilic groves of the old cemetery by oneself. One could enter deserted tombs, their doors creaking in the wind. One could creep along strange paths through undergrowth where lurked stone angels like giant trapped condors or come face to face with mighty moss-covered crosses. Yes, then, one was quite free to be spooked if one wished.

Today, however it is necessary to pay an entrance fee and submit to being chaperoned on this Boot Hill of North London. And all because – but for the timely intervention of the Friends of Highgate Cemetery – the developers and their bulldozers would have moved in. Nothing being sacred in our time but money, even death is under threat.

I returned to Old Highgate Cemetery with John Gurney in order to hunt up the grave of Samuel Taylor Coleridge. Not long before, I had visited Coleridge's birthplace at Ottery St. Mary in Devon and I had had a sudden desire to bring the experience of Ottery and Coleridge's last resting place at Highgate together. An irrational wish, I suppose, but ...after a confrontation with a High Tory lady of advancing years, who appeared to be the C-in-C Highgate Cemeteries, John and I were apprised not only of the changes (and charges) that the great graveyard had undergone since my (much) younger days, but I was also smartly informed that I had laboured under a grand delusion, namely, that Coleridge was buried in Highgate cemetery.

'He is not!' the lady said.

But beneath this iron lady's exterior lurked a certain charity. She could see from John's angelic, Shelleyan expression – if not from my glazed scowl – that our quest was at least genuinely literary. So she transported us to Highgate village in her car, depositing us at St. Michael's church. And there we encountered a priest with a faintly Irish accent who showed us a faded blue plaque on the floor of the central aisle. When this kind man had turned all the lights on fully we could just make out the words:

> Beneath this stone lies the body of
> SAMUEL TAYLOR COLERIDGE
> Born 21 October 1772 Died 25 July 1834

There was also an epitaph in verse, unreadable in any light save that of a brass rubbing, price £1. We were informed that the bones of S.T.C. had been moved into the church sometime in the 1960s. Till then, Coleridge's remains had lain in the churchyard, the original burial ground, until a new cemetery (now Old Highgate Cemetery) had been established in the 1830s or 40s.

* * * * *

When I worked in London, I'd always felt that I had an ambiguous relationship with the place. But when I moved to Brixham, my abiding love-hate relationship with London became more focussed. So that when Lazards asked me back in times of emergencies for spells of work varying between one to three months, I was not averse to the offer. I have not been ungrateful for their generosity, regarding the temporary employment as worked-for patronage of poetry; something which, given my distaste for state interference and patronage, has proved more agreeable to me – as well as being a source of income. The 'hate' side of my relationship with the City had been made clear when I initially resigned from Lazards, but for all that I said there, I do also 'love' the City: its monuments, its moods, and many of its men and women. Why this should be, I'm not sure, but love London

I do. Perhaps it is that underneath all the dross of systems and day-to-day futilities and triviality, there lurks an indestructable free heart; a heart which shows itself in the intellectual excitement I feel in the places I visit and the friends I meet there. I've already said that nobody in Lazards really understood what it meant to be a poet, and when I returned for one of my stints with the firm, I was often asked, 'Yes, we know you write poems down in Devon, but what do you actually *do*?' This confusing query does express how mystifying people find the idea of anyone writing poetry full time. Nor is it surprising that it was at Lazards that there occured the most hilarious misunderstanding of my new role in life.

It was in the snowy winter of 1978-79 when I was asked back for another stint and while there was invited to a staff farewell party. It was one of the better, more sumptuous affairs held in the plush directors' dining room which was packed to overflowing with after-work cocktailers; men in city suits and women in anything which, within the bounds of the firm's propriety, allowed them to emphasise their sexuality. Soon, well-primed with food and wine, I began to circulate among the guests and renew old acquaintances. It was while I was thus engaged that I encountered two middle-aged women from our section talking to a third whom I did not know. One of women promptly yanked me over to join them and, shouting above the hubbub to make herself heard, introduced me as, 'This is Bill Oxley – he's a poet and chartered accountant. He lives in Devon but comes back now and again to help us out with the annual accounts.'

Now I ought to emphasise that the noise level was very high, but that I was sober enough to note clearly the queer look that spread over the face of the recipient of this information about my life. It was the sort of look one might have expected on being introduced as a self-confessed murderer. I assumed it was the idea of me being a poet that had caused such a transformation.

Nothing, however, was said by the woman; she merely continued to give me furtive yet ever more puzzled glances. Then, abruptly, she looked me full in the face and said, 'I didn't think there were many left in the world?'

As can be imagined, I was not at all prepared for such a remark. For while true poets may be few in number, they are not quite the extinct species that she seemed to be suggesting. All I could manage in reply was, 'Er, well ... ?"

My reaction seemed to further embolden the lady and she added, more mystifyingly still, 'Mind you, there used to be a lot of them in your part of the world, didn't there?'

I grasped that by 'your part of the world' she meant Devon. But I was rather flummoxed in that I can't honestly say that Devon had ever boasted an abundance of poets. Sheep, yes; tourists, yes; but poets, no. By this time the two other women had also begun to think that the conversation was rapidly growing crazy; but it was the mystified woman herself who eventually resolved the situation. Suddenly turning to the others she asked sharply, 'You did say he was a chartered accountant and *pirate*, didn't you?'

*   *   *   *   *

Harry Kemp, the last living disciple of Robert Graves, defined poetry as 'Telling what it is like to be alive'. When Kemp moved to Crediton from Cumbria in his septuagenarian days, he invited Patricia and me to lunch. His first words to us as he opened the door were a gleeful, 'Don't you think this is a marvellously ugly house I live in?' That is how poets see things. And how they make us see things: not necessarily as ugly or beautiful, but *afresh* even in their ugliness or beauty.

To say that Harry's critical clock had stopped years ago is not intended to be unkind. It is to suggest that in his engaging out-of-dateness he had become, in a way, timeless. Early publication of his poems by Graves and Laura Riding in Majorca in the Thirties; his contributions to their magazine *Epilogue* (dusty copies of which he proudly showed me); his admission to their charmed circle of exiles, had all been too much for Harry. Finally he had made a cult of the Muse. The Muse, however, is not a cult-figure. She is a goddess: and Graves knew the distinction. But I fear Harry, a mathematics teacher from Ulverston, did not.

Neither Patricia nor I met Harry Kemp again because, for some reason, he started sending me long and querulous epistles. I say 'for some reason' because I couldn't think what I had done to deserve them. But relationships often end in this oddly abrupt way in the literary world, mostly without lawyers or blows, thank goodness!

*   *   *   *   *

I've already mentioned that John Gurney took Patricia and me to Olney, to visit the home of William Cowper. Cowper's home, now a museum – like the village of Olney itself – still speaks what Cowper thought it spoke in his lifetime, namely, rural dullness. A place where the discovery of an adder in the garden was just about *the* event of the year. A place, too, where the Reverend William Bull would arrive and smoke a hugely noxious pipe in a tiny summerhouse and talk all day with the poet. And where the reformed slave trader, the equally Reverend John Newton, would visit periodically and inflate Cowper's already huge sense of sin and guilt; then, afterwards, join the poet in composing devotional hymns. A place where lack of event and sheer boredom caused William Cowper to send forth a stream of letters, year by year, that are some of the most interesting and literary epistles ever penned. Thus proving, yet again, one need not lead a life of Hemingway-like action to be a great writer: pace Cowper, pace Emily Brontë, above all, pace William Blake, the humble engraver who out of a life of nothingness became one of the world's great visionaries.

Nevertheless, we do all write out of our experience, be that experience wide or narrow, high or low, and whether or not we regard it as being of sacred or profane origin. The inner experience is primary; the outer secondary: though that is perhaps only convenient critical categorizing. For when we write well, in a trance of concentration, both inner and outer experience are fused into one. The truth is that all experience is really one and unified. Throw a stone in a pond and the ripples go everywhere. Or, to reverse the metaphor, what we call 'our experience' comes from everywhere: is drawn to one centre, ourselves, which is already its own experience of being alive.

*   *   *   *   *

Friends introduce us to many things without which our lives would be considerably impoverished. Their being and unique way of seeing the world enters our consciousness forever, and the smallest and most insignificant moments with them become invested with an unforgettable glamour.

My friend Glyn is the son of a Yorkshire miner. But, despite that, he is no snob. Some may think this an odd remark? Just let me say that I have come across far too much inverted snobbery among people who sentimentalize a 'working-class background'. Of course, the 'middle-class' – and most of us are now members of this muddled class – is guilty of snobbery as well, but I don't like snobbery of any kind, feeling it is essentially 'cheap'. So when I encounter another human being who has no 'side' to him – who does not drag status or background or wealth or politics into the discussion at every opportunity – I delight in that person. Call him or her 'genuine'. A genuine human being. And such a one is Glyn Pursglove of Swansea.

Of middling height, swift of walk, swifter of talk – a bustle mixed with an expansiveness and, paradoxically, much patience – physically he resembles an owl that is beginning to bald. An unacademic academic, Glyn is a lecturer at Swansea University. He is very bright, too; yet for me it is his sensitivity towards the needs and feelings of others, especially his friends, plus his sheer generosity of spirit, that matters most.

Never shall I forget walking through Singleton Park, Swansea with Glyn and his two small daughters, and having my attention drawn to my first sight of a redwing that was like a bloodstained leaf blown among the swirl of autumn's twigs and branches. Nor that first walk to Mumbles with Glyn and his Persian wife Parvin, when they took Patricia and me to a coffee shop called *Treasures*. It was like a genteel cave that smelt of dry spices and herbs and roasted coffee beans.

Mumbles – there's a place now; and entirely owed to friendship. Mumbles, with its sea that is a white swirl around its famous lighthouse, and a grey swaggering sky, or clear blue as porcelain; with its colourful and quaint houses, its little local shops, and immense 'heron-priested shore' of golden Swansea Bay. There, too, in Mumbles are the forever brooding, mutually inimical presences of Dylan Thomas and Thomas Bowdler. The latter is buried in Mumbles' churchyard, but his old house is slap-bang opposite Glyn's place a few miles away in Brynmill, Swansea. Yes, scarcely believable to think that the greatest censor in the history of English literature dwelt just across the road from that of the so-liberal Glyn Pursglove ...

Brynmill is the suburb of Swansea where Dylan Thomas was born and grew up. Brynmill Primary School is where the poet received his early education and where Glyn's children received their primary schooling. I remember my feelings as I went with them there one day, then afterwards went off to visit Cwndonkin Drive and the house where Dylan was born. Like so many others, I guess, I walked in the park opposite, 'a lonely mister' thinking of his 'hunchback in the park', and of the kids in Dylan's childhood cruelly teasing one old cripple. I recalled, too, the marvellous letters that passed between Dylan and his fellow Swansea poet, Vernon Watkins. An unequalled correspondence on the craft of verse: letters awesome in their literary wisdom, as well as being redolent of the almost magical spirit of

Swansea. I remembered, too, having read somewhere that Dylan's parents had retired to Brixham and I wondered how it had come about.

Yet everything 'comes about', this interconnection between things. And I believe it to be because we humans are all – both the living and the dead – united in a vast single memory which only the imagination can really tap.

Such things and occasions are memorable to me; and many are owed to Glyn the hospitable, and to the learned Parvin, who inveigled me into translating with her the ghazals of Hafiz, the greatest of all Persian poets, which despite Parvin's scholarship remains mostly unpublished. For all things are connected, from Persia to Porthcawl, from place to place, from person to person. In our hearts the beat of a universal heart. Memories. Ideas. Dreams. Reflections. Those categories of the imaginative life to which I am always seeking to give expression, however inadequately.

Yes, with the passage of time, our debts to Glyn Pursglove have been many. I'll specify just two more. To him Patricia owes an amazing debt of gratitude for his many hours of work as the reviews' editor of her magazine *Acumen*. Despite all the many other calls on his time, he has never failed to meet a deadline for the magazine. And to him, too, is owed our friendship with Christopher J.P. Smith, the Southey scholar and poet. Although Chris, and his partner Julie, are no longer denizens of 'the Swansea scene' having moved to Sheffield, we see them in Devon and elsewhere. A tall, well-built, Gravesian figure of a man (more Byronic than Gravesian when we first met him), Chris has a very English insouciance coupled with a delightfully deliberate sense of irony. Slow to 'open up' with strangers, with friends he is just about the finest late-night drinker and talker one could wish for. And, like I say, it's down to Glyn that Chris has become such a good friend.

*   *   *   *   *

It wasn't until the late eighties that we travelled even further westward out of Torbay and crossed the Tamar into Cornwall. Dave Woolley lived there then, with the delightful Sylvia, and they had organised a reading by contributors to an anthology he was publishing in celebration of the work of Barbara Hepworth. For us, this involved a trip to Liskeard, then to an arts centre at Upton Cross and an overnight stay in their rural farmhouse at Callington. The house is situated in a niche of a hill with a view over a chequered, dreaming landscape of fields all the way to Brentor Church on the southern edge of Dartmoor. The white farmhouse, the meadows, the animals: it was an idyllic place. It was also my first encounter with Mercer Simpson, that amiable bluff Englishman who resides in Wales, writes poems and has edited the Welsh Academy's magazine. A wonderful day that ended with a candlelit meal in the octagonal conservatory with moths circling the table and the sound of crickets rubbing their knees in the bushes outside the open windows.

*   *   *   *   *

Even after Patricia's four hectic years at college had ended, as witness the next chapter, we were constantly meeting our metropolitan friends and creating opportunities to do so. Once she had given up her studies and was expanding her publishing interests into books, she, too began to organise launches. Her first was at Dillons Art Bookshop in Long Acre. As well as some Poetry Society people, far more with no connection with the Society and its difficulties came; friends and acquaintances and many more poets, as well as non-poets, and even readers' friends turned up.

Danielle Hope, our newest doctor-poet, came with her poetic 'mentor' Feyyaz Fergar: two people with an especial place in our affections. Both Danielle and Feyyaz had been correspondents of mine ever since Danielle had run her magazine *Zenos* in Nottingham. Danielle, an attractive blond-haired lady, has always appealed by her combination of intellectual maturity and sense of fun. There is, too, a balance in her and a lack of neurosis. She is a good poet who applies herself with unusual alertness to the many difficulties of that most problematic of crafts.

But how do I begin to describe Feyyaz, who is, alas, now no longer with us? In his seventies, with wild but beautiful white hair and, *pace* Danielle, 'polar bear eyes': a beard like that of a Napoleonic hussar coupled with a grand moustache, he was a short, stocky Turk; talkative, hard-drinking, with a personality that wrapped itself round you. I knew his poetry, and I had his letters; and his style was gesture that shaped all his utterance. Knowing exactly where to end the short verse-line with the same infallible instinct with which that other great free-versifier D.H. Lawrence knew exactly where to end the long line. A poet who could combine surreal imagery with a vertebrae of meaningful utterance precisely. A romantic soul who was disciplined in his craft, joyous yet sceptical in his ideas. That night Feyyaz slid

into the large gathering and, for me, dominated it. Patricia, David
Perman – Feyyaz's and my publisher – and myself will never forget
how we ended this grand occasion around the white table in Dannie
Abse's home in Golders Green utterly absorbed in the Anglo-Turkish
poet. Drinking, eating, and celebrating poetry and eternal things in
an atmosphere of practical conviviality. The following day Feyyaz
composed these lines to Patricia and posted them to Brixham:

> EVENTAIL (fan)
> for Patricia Oxley
>
> The sun came to borrow
> your intricate lips
> But William was not
> in a lending mood.

In Shakespeare's words 'This was a man.'

And what of David Perman? David is one of those people who
have style but style without eccentricity or pretentiousness. He has
character too. David is the local historian of Ware; a publisher; and
an antiquary who has restored a famous 18th century grotto. He once
interviewed the Ayatollah Khomeini for the BBC World Service, but
now is into less safe pursuits like publishing a whole motley crew of
poets, myself included. His charm and energy, which sometimes
degenerates into restlessness, has made him into the most impressive
and dynamic addition to the small but select band of British poetry
publishers. And one of whom it can be said, without reservations, he
is 'good to his authors'.

Epping in Essex was paradise – above, views of the town and, below, William among the campion and parsley in 'Magic Lane' leading to Theydon Garnon Church in 1971 – now the junction of the M11 and M25.

With Robert Graves at Deya on Majorca in October 1972 and, below, with Dannie Abse during a convivial meal with the doctor-poet in London in 1983.

William with Kathleen Raine, poet and Blakean scholar, at her Chelsea home in the early 1990s. Below: with Peter Russell on leave from his home in Tuscany in February 1996.

With John Heath-Stubbs at his flat in Notting Hill in August 1987. Below:
the Gang of Four at The Mount, Brixham, in 1995 – William and Patricia
Oxley, David Perman and Danielle Hope.

CHAPTER SEVENTEEN
College Capers

Still on the subject of poetry publishers for a moment. In one of my notebooks I have this entry dated 22nd September 1988: 'I went to Paignton in the afternoon and met Roy Lewis off the train. He brought me fifty copies of *The Mansands' Trilogy*, and some two hundred fliers to be dispatched with *Acumen*. Patricia laid on a spread for him and we drank the bottle of claret that has waited, unopened, for 15 months in my study for just this day. Roy was on good form and very expansive, giving us much of his sociologically-oriented views on the novel. He has a dome of a head that looms between two persistent clumps of silver grey hair, and a face that is all pouches and whorls of flesh with a very modest doublechin. He appears a professor rather than a publisher-journalist- printer: though the latter is what he was and is. A great devotee of "the unconscious"; an admirer of Wells and Freud; I haven't traced his genuine love of poetry to its source. But his visit certainly rounded off what Patricia and I feel is something of a partial ending of our Brixham exile.'

A partial ending of our Brixham 'exile' was due to two things. Firstly in 1985, Patricia had decided to launch the literary magazine, *Acumen*. Then, as if that did not involve enough responsibility, she decided to do a mature student's degree. In 1988 she obtained a place at London University (Westfield College). So, gone was our work as part-time gardeners at an old folks' home; and soon to go was my part-time book-keeping job. Nor would there be any more 'charing' for Patricia at the local Post Office which she had been doing for several years to 'help out' financially. And though our principal home remains in Brixham to this day, much was to flow from our various periods of residence in West Hampstead, Fortune Green, and Golders Green.

The next entry in my notebook, dated 2nd October 1988, recorded how it began: 'Travelled up to London to begin our "new life": Patricia at university, me as her "minder". Early afternoon moved into the Abses' house in Golders Green. Joan looked well; Dannie not so much. They are off on a reading-lecturing tour of Czechoslovakia for the next two weeks; we are to look after the cat. An easy, good

conversational day spent in their company; much looking over their
good library. Dannie thinks the growing insipidity of much Anglo-
Welsh writing due to the decline not of "Celtic influence" but in Bible
reading. Both the Abses are a couple characterised by gentleness.
Their garden is long, secluded and overgrown – a mite "jungly" –
and Joan says Dannie has "never been to the bottom of it".'

*   *   *   *   *

The first place we had of our own was in Westbere Road, West
Hampstead; a wide suburban road backing onto a railway line and
lined with Victorian villas now all converted into flats and bed-sits.
For £84 a week we had a large, airy double room overlooking the
street and use of a shared bathroom and kitchen. The house, relatively
clean and dry for rentland, was divided into half a dozen bedsits,
each occupied by a changing population of restless beings. As
everyone there went out to work except me and an unemployable
young Irishman, the 'restlessness' only became a problem at night.
Night meant drunkenness, marital accord and discord, loud T.V.,
endless banging of car doors in the street and bedroom doors in the
house, the sudden rush-rattle of trains and the thundery enormity of
jets lumbering overhead, cries in the night that always sounded like
murder, and the unrhythmic slurp and talk of water in heating systems.
Day meant peace (for me) and the occasional visit of the middle-aged
landlady who wore tinted lenses and dyed hair and dressed like a
fashionable teenager. She came either for rent or to bawl out the
young Irishman for a thousand sins of which she was convinced only
the Irish are guilty.

Our next place of similarly temporary abode was a damp and dingy
flat at the back of a disused shop in Fortune Green Road. This 'flat'
consisted of a bedsit-living room, a kitchen and bathroom. It was
heated by a single gas fire, smelled perpetually like a cellar, had worse
décor than an Inland Revenue office, and opened onto a backyard
full of junk and rats – the latter which sought to scratch holes in our
door at night. At night, too, the Greek family above switched the
washing machine on, and brother-and-sister quarrels were conducted
fiercely for hours with the diminutive mother acting as screaming
referee. The bathroom, having a stone-flagged floor, was stone-cold,
and the toilet had no seat until an Oxford friend of ours, Tony Morris,
brought us a second-hand one ('Thanks, Tony, you were a pal!')
instead of the customary bottle of wine. But, nevertheless, it was

technically a flat, and if less salubrious than our place in Westbere Road, it represented a 'step-up'; for the privilege of which we paid £90 a week instead of a mere £84.

Between times – and apart from when we returned to Brixham – we would look after the Abses' house at Golders Green, which was a welcome luxury after these two places. Equally, when we finally moved into one of the dozen or so large houses fronting onto the Finchley Road and backing onto the Westfield College campus, that seemed like luxury too. Being, as we were, in a large room at the rear of the house which opened, through french windows, onto a garden of lawns and trees, the prospect seemed one of unalloyed delight in every way. But, alas, totally unalloyed nothing ever can be, and especially not on a university campus. Although we saw out our time there – dwelling in the place for two years – and enjoyed facilities as good as student life could expect to have, the rumbustious, the wild, and far from scholarly behaviour of the student population made it far from a comfortable existence. Suffice it to say, though, that – as with our dwellings on Westbere Road and Fortune Green Road – our main problem was shortage of sleep involuntarily induced by people's lack of consideration for others.

Nevertheless, it was because of these three (four if you include the Abses') temporary pieds-à-terre, that two provincials were able to enjoy something of the trials and tribulations, the pleasures and pains, of academic and literary life in what has always been their favourite city: London.

*   *   *   *   *

Seated close to the big fountain in Regent's Park, the poet John Gurney produced two packs of sandwiches put up for us by his wife Sally. A very thoughtful thing to do on her part, I observed. Said John: 'Well, Sally knows you're even poorer than me! Now that Patricia's at college.'

Scarcely had I opened my packet when I felt a gentle but firm tap on my shoulder. I looked round to discover, to my amazement, right up against my neck and on the backrest of the bench, a grey squirrel with filmy, bushy tail and big, impenetrable brown eyes. I took only one bite of my sandwich before the polite tap occurred again; so I gave this all-too-human squirrel a morsel of crust, which it took from me and, moving to the arm rest of the bench, proceeded to devour it.

So there we were: three animals, seated side by side, all eating bread. No sooner had Mr. Squirrel, however, consumed his piece than he repeated his shoulder-tapping performance, to which I responded, and the first sandwich was very soon finished. I then indicated he should be satisfied and leave. But not a bit of it. The squirrel came down onto my knee and began to unpack the rest of the sandwiches from their cling film. This I only prevented by a bigger bribe.

By this time I was joined also by a crowd of sparrows who arranged themselves alongside me on the bench, on my arms, my shoulders and anywhere else they chose to. It is, of course, well known that the animals in London's parks are incredibly tame, but when the sparrows and squirrel were joined by four Canada geese, a mallard, some pigeons including one with a broken leg, and, finally, a moorhen – that timidest of all pond fowl – things were clearly getting out of hand. So bold were the sparrows in particular that one balanced on the sandwich and pecked it even as I ate.

Oddly, though, almost none of the birds, nor the squirrel, bothered at all with John, who was seated scarcely six inches away from me. 'It's because they sense the discontent in me, but the peace in you, that they flock to you,' was his explanation. Then spoilt the idea by adding, 'Besides, they recognise you as a soft touch!'

*   *   *   *   *

Something in literary life breeds anecdotes: perhaps the overspill of creative imagination into 'real life'? Whatever, Patricia and I once went to a reception while she was at college where I met Patricia Pogson and Geoffrey Holloway, husband and wife, who lived in Cumbria. Patricia I'd never met, and Geoffrey only once twenty years before. Of course, I'd encountered them both in print and sometimes communicated by letter, but never together face to face. But I had the best opening line ever with a woman:

Me: Bet you don't know who I am?
She: No.
Me: I'm your husband!
She: Ah, in that case, you must be William Oxley.

Her real husband – to whom this conversation must have sounded crazy, to say the least – looked amazed; until we enlightened him with the story behind our conversation. Both his wife and myself had had poems printed in the same issue of *Iron* magazine. Its 'notes on contributors' had said: 'William Oxley is married to Patricia Pogson, the poet and editor'; though it had corrected the mistake in the following issue saying that I was married to 'Patricia Oxley, editor of *Acumen*'. But it is not the sort of mistake a writer forgets, and Patricia Pogson certainly hadn't forgotten it.

Even so, her husband – de-mystified – promptly contrived a brief, but equally as memorable a conversation with me straight away. As I said, he and I had not met for around twenty years, and he asked me how old I was. 'Guess?' I replied. Geoffrey paused for a moment. 'Around 64 I suppose.' '64!' I echoed, 'I'm, just fifty!'.

'Fifty!' he exclaimed, 'God, my eyesight is getting worse and worse!'

I also remember another literary occasion that turned progressively anecdotal. It was at Bernard Stone's old bookshop in Lamb's Conduit Street, and was one of the least well-attended book launches I ever went to at Bernard's during all the years Patricia was at college. Michael Ivens had had to go far afield to find a publisher who, in this case, turned out to be my old friend, the gardener, small press publisher and poet, Fred Beake.

Fred Beake – the Bard of Bath – comes across as a true man-of-letters. In his shambling, hairy, endearing Calibanic way, Fred is totally absorbed in poetry and life, when he is not out earning his living as a gardener. More sympathetically avant gardist than myself, Fred's ear is tuned to the prosaic but subtle rhythms of modern Americans like Pound and William Carlos Williams. But, equally, he is at home with poets such as Shelley and the medieval poets. A solid man with a face that peers through a huge bush of a beard like a surprised lion, the slow, battered integrity and humanity of the genuine poet shines in Fred Beake. At times, Fred mumbles his words, and his pearls of wisdom can get badly chewed in their passage through his small but strong teeth. But he is a remarkable reader of his own poetry, having an unforgettable style of vocalisation.

After the somewhat sparsely-attended reading, Michael Ivens invited everyone to join him and his wife for a meal at Bernard's favourite Italian ristorante – a two minute walk away from the shop. And a splendid meal we all had which went on until around 11.30pm.

After the meal was over, the thank-you's said, we all dispersed our separate ways; Patricia and myself moving off with Eddie Linden towards Southampton Row. We hadn't gone very far when we were accosted by a man who turned out to be an ex-convict. He solemnly informed us that the 'most shunned members of society' were ex-prisoners. I, who had had plenty to drink along with the excellent meal, suddenly desired to challenge his statement. Somewhat foolishly, I said there was a 'more shunned species in society than prisoners', adding pompously it, too, 'began with a "p".'

The ex-convict, after looking puzzled for a moment, came back with, 'Oh Yeah? An' what's that then?' to which I answered, 'A poet.'

At this there followed an aggressive pause; then he demanded to know if I was a poet? I admitted I was. And almost immediately a look of great uncertainty crossed his face and a glazed look appeared in his eyes. Then, a second later, he turned on his heel and walked rapidly away.

'He only wanted some money for a cup of coffee,' admonished Patricia sternly, (she doesn't like me drinking too much!) 'not a lecture!'

* * * * *

Talking of Bernard's bookshop ... Bernard Stone was a bookseller: the doyen among booksellers of contemporary poetry. No one, in the entire United Kingdom, quite occupied a position like his.

An orotund and benevolent figure, short of stature, Bernard wore strong ground lenses behind which his eyes flickered and moved like alert goldfish. Like all businessmen he exuded an exact mixture of melancholy and cheerfulness. Though how far so generous a human being could be a genuine businessman is an open question. It is probably best to describe him as a patron-businessman who happened to specialize in the world's most unprofitable line of trade: poetry. Yet, unprofitable though poetry is, Bernard always paid cash-on-the-nail for anything he bought in his shop.

His shop? In my time Bernard has had four shops successively: the first was in Kensington Church Walk and was like a long, book-lined cavern; the second in Floral Street behind Covent Garden Opera House was a cramped affair; the third in Lamb's Conduit Street in the heart of Bloomsbury; and the last in Great Queen Street, just opposite the Masonic Temple.

It was for these last two that I have the greatest affection, knowing their book-deluged and awkward interiors best. It was there I attended many of his most memorable, after-hours, book-launch parties. There some poets *à-la-mode* like Jeremy Reed or Wendy Cope, or a T.V.

'personality' and novelist like Sandy Gall, or a magazine editor like the perennial Dr. Martin Bax of *Ambit*, would be the centre of one of Bernard's 'events'.

Each such function would, of course, attract its particular coterie. But, in addition all kinds of non-coterie folk and 'droppers-in' like Ken Smith the 'prisoners' poet' (now *he* would have known an ex-con only wanted money for a drink!), or Donald Davie the transatlantic critic from Barnsley, or Peter Jay the Anvil Press publisher from Greenwich, or William Cookson one of the two editorial pillars of *Agenda*, or myself, would be invited or just turn up. When I say 'non-coterie' folk, I mean persons who do not necessarily belong to the particular gang organising the evening. For one must always remember the poetry world, like most other worlds, has its groups and its gangs – often engaged in violent conflict.

Bernard Stone and his broad-minded narrow book den with its life-sized wax model of Sigmund Freud 'serving' at the counter ... to the shock of many an innocent customer who tried to buy a book from it. It was a shop chockful of contemporary poetic ephemera plus many of the great classic works of poetry, with portraits of poets high on its walls, and Bernard's office at the rear where he and a telephone lurked among a bombed site of files, manuscripts, commercial paperwork and review books. Somewhere, too, in that apology for an office there was a desk under masses of paper; and on the walls an array of remarkable items from titillating postcards of nude girls to beautiful poems on posters.

There, amidst this bibliophilic chaos, dominated by sensuously evil drawings by Ralph Steadman, one was likely to find the proprietor in conversation with the likes of Christopher Logue, Laurie Lee or Adrian Mitchell; or embroiled in earnest, long distance phone-chats with Lawrence Durrell, or Anthony Burgess or another of his literary 'big-shots'. Even so, there was no side to Bernard at all. He would greet the nervous and unknown scribbler, the aspiring poet, like an old friend and open the discreetly hidden fridge to offer a glass of white wine. A marvellously hospitable man, making marvellously hospitable gestures at all times of the day: his wine and vodka day.

There was also Bernard Stone the publisher, seen sometimes wearing a hat inscribed with his publishing imprint – and name of his shop – 'Turret Books'. I never quite penetrated to the core of Bernard's taste in poetry: it was as mysterious as his generosity. He has published everyone from Roy Fuller to Fiona Pitt-Kethley, both the decorous and indecorous. He has published famous international poets like the Austrian, Erich Fried, and strictly local poets like Rosaleen Cooper of Teignmouth in Devon. This latter lady, who happened to be Robert Graves' younger sister, Bernard published in her ninetieth year. This large-hearted little man was catholic in his taste: something not all that common in the narrow, faction-ridden demi-monde of contemporary poetry.

Once when, for a short period, Patricia and I lived in Westbere Road, off Mill Lane in West Hampstead, I remember Bernard telling us that he, too, had lived 'just off Mill Lane as a young man'. In those days he still dwelt with his parents and he told us his father was so fanatical about punctuality that, 'If I didn't get home dead on time to the minute for my evening meal, I was not allowed to have any at all. It didn't matter if the train had been held up, or anything. No excuses were allowed.' A sad little tale, told in Bernard's slightly breathless voice to the accompaniment of something like melancholic mirth. A brief glimpse of loneliness? But what made this fleeting touch of autobiography memorable was that Bernard Stone brought anything but loneliness to the lives of his poets. Indeed, whether one was a poet whom he had published or not, such was Bernard's largesse of spirit, as well as his practical generosity, that all were, in a sense, *his* poets. At least, all – and there have been hundreds over the years – who frequented the Turret Bookshop.

Alas, Bernard has now gone, forced to quit through illness and financial problems, and there is a gap in the London literary scene, an empty seat on that merry-go-round which will never be filled.

*   *   *   *   *

Reason chops up reality into ever more exiguous and discrete strips; the imagination builds and unifies. As such, it is a noticeable feature of literary life how easily – no matter in how small a way – everything connects.

One day, somewhat hungover from an evening of socializing during our time on the Hampstead campus, I fell asleep after breakfast, Patricia having gone off to do some work at the computer centre. While I can't claim that I dreamed of Graves' *White Goddess*, I was certainly in that twilight zone where his, and mine, and all poets' dreams, and dreams of poems, are born.

At what I took to be nine-thirty I was awoken by a knocking at the door. I still felt queasy but circumstances forced me to snap to. On

opening the door there stood Chrys Salt, the actress and occasional
poet. She was carrying a bunch of flowers that jostled vividly in her
hand, and she was dressed like a diminutive rainbow in multi-coloured
tights and top. Not a sight exactly for the hung-over to appreciate but
... Chrys is a pretty, bubbly, bright-minded, amusing lady and seeing
her there was like drawing back a curtain to let in sunlight. She, at
least, looked fresh and attractive.

Chrys bounced into the room waving the flowers, saying, 'Ah ha!
You'd forgotten I was coming?' Her tone was merry-but-accusative.
I mumbled that of course I hadn't forgotten but it was only nine-thirty
and ...

'It's ten-thirty, William. And we agreed on ten-thirty.' Then she
asked where Patricia was. I told her Patricia was also expecting her
and would be back around eleven as she had some urgent work to do.

Soon the somewhat painful act of simply making coffee began to
lift my hangover. And in the course of conversation I made the
discovery that Chrys had been one of Robert Graves' 'muses'. Graves'
concept, which I knew from reading *The White Goddess*, had been
built up from a certain amount of theory plus some very concrete
experiences with earthly forms: one of which I was now entertaining
to morning coffee.

Chrys told me she had met Graves when he was at St. John's
College, Oxford; she had been nineteen and he was in residence
there as Professor of Poetry. Said Chrys, 'I went and bearded the lion
in his den, and thrust some of my poems in his hand saying "Read
these please". And he did and was quite kind about them. He used to
take me about Oxford by taxi and introduce me to people: really to
show me off to friends. he was an old goat you know. But after I left
Oxford we corresponded for many years. In fact, I met him right up
to his last years, when he came to London on a final visit. But he had
gone very gaga by then and we met at a party, but he didn't really
know me. He was a wonderful man: like a great statue of a Greek
god and he had such presence ...'

As she had never visited him in Mallorca, Chrys was very interested
to hear about our visit there. By this time Patricia had returned and
was able to add details as well. Chrys didn't know that *The White
Goddess* had first been drafted while he lived at Galmpton near
Brixham: it came as a surprise to her, as it does to many. I made her
laugh when I related how I had been invited to give a lecture on
Graves to the Devon Society, and though I had been told it would be

given in a library, nobody thought fit to tell me it was the library at Paignton Zoo!

*   *   *   *   *

Patricia organised some half dozen poetry readings for her fellow students at College. Little things stand out. Ken Smith seated in our room drinking wine under a poster of himself on our walls: a head and shoulders picture of the guy like a gunslinger out of a Western movie – square jaw, droopy moustache, stetson and sun-glasses.

Then there was the moment at the end of Dannie Abse's reading when Patricia invited the audience to 'ask the poet questions'. Which invitation, as is so often the case, resulted in everyone clamming up. So Dannie suddenly leaned forward and said to a girl student in the front row: 'Ask me a question.' And this set the ball rolling most effectively.

We usually entertained the guest poet in our room first and, often when the reading was over, we went back there with all who cared for more poetry. The evening John Heath-Stubbs came to college ended that way, and I recall the 'limerick reciting contest' between my City friend, Quenten Lane, and John. They capped each other, limerick for limerick, witty, erudite or scatological, until each had recited around fifty. Both were prepared to go on, but the 'audience' proclaimed it an honourable draw.

For years John Heath-Stubbs lived in Notting Hill. Physically, a gangling giant of a man, he is in some ways like an overgrown schoolboy still. John's physical stature towers ever higher because of his enormous mental stature. Blind, or near blind for much of his life, this pallid giant with large square cranium is the figure whom, in my poem about Leonard Clark's funeral, I described as 'a blind-eyed statue'. For John is like one of those damaged Greek statues out of some classical museum, or a mythical figure that has stepped out of a niche of the Poets' Pantheon which he so wittily describes in his long poem 'The Triumph of the Muse'. And such a description is no insult; for there is something profoundly monumental about John Heath-Stubbs.

Without doubt, save possibly for Peter Russell, the most capacious brain in English poetry, John's blindness appears to have afforded him the compensation of ready access to a large, well-stocked memory. His knowledge of history, natural science, Christian theology, folklore, mythology, literature in general and poetry in particular, is immense.

Despite his accomplishments, which have included the publication of many books over the last fifty years, he has always seemed a lonely figure on the edge of literary life. It is, of course, true that many poets lead a marginalized existence, peripheral to the main fashions of the day, sometimes by choice, sometimes for geographical or other reasons. But John's brooding, rather ironical, and fiercely independent presence has always haunted the salons and functions, the poetry readings and art exhibitions, the publishers' launches and so on which make up the metropolitan cultural circuit. And it has always seemed to me that he has been a representative embodiment of neglected poets, despite the fact that he has mostly dwelt in London.

Someone once described John Heath-Stubbs as 'an insider who was not preferred'. This is very true. For though honours have been latterly showered upon him, including the Queen's Gold Medal for Poetry; and the O.B.E., following the publication of his magnificent *Collected Poems* at the age of 70, his work has been mostly ignored since the Forties.

Nearly the whole time I have known John – a period of twenty years – he has lived in a flat which contains all the essential ingredients for the understanding of chaos, everything, in fact, which one could think of to exemplify poverty and a life of discomfort and danger. Danger is the best exemplification of the hazards of this stoical life: a life endured courageously by a blind poet who has lived alone since leaving his parents' home as a young undergraduate. A proud, self-reliant soul who has always insisted on doing for himself, save for the typing of his manuscripts, for when composing John dictates his poems into a tape-recorder for others to type out for him.

John, like all poets of integrity, will offer his services at readings for students at well below the normal rates, and was happy to read to the few students at Westfields who attended regularly.

I remember, too, the reading I gave with Peter Dale at college, and how, after it was over, Patricia's colleague Sarah asked me in a surprised voice, 'Is he *really* a friend of yours?' She was referring to Peter's saturnine temperament: a temperament I am both used to, and find a healthy corrective to my own, perhaps too romantic, outlook. Sarah couldn't understand how I could possibly enjoy Peter's company or be his friend. Neither do I, of course – sometimes. But poets will be poets; and, as Keats said, they all must have a degree of negative capability in their make-up.

Lastly I think of Brian Louis Pearce in the first of those readings.

Brian, a gentle, hesitant and diffident fellow – yet the amazing transformation which occurs when he reads or lectures. Something I did not discover until the night of the Westfield reading; such flowering into self-assuredness seemed impossible. But it happened.

*   *   *   *   *

Poetry and wealth. Patricia and I were invited to an evening at a compact but gracious and elegant house in Hampstead that was once the home of the Victorian actor Gerald du Maurier, father of the Cornish novelist Daphne. This very fetching house had played host in its great years to many famous figures from the world of literature and elsewhere – Henry James was one name mentioned, and I think Dickens – and now a wealthy American lady had the idea of staging poetical and musical entertainments there. Because we had a vague connection with a group of such entertainers called 'Angels of Fire', we'd received an invitation. The whole evening was genteel, almost out of Jane Austen, with the performers reciting from memory and often to musical accompaniment. They were all very friendly and far more respectful of their guests than we were at Westfields. Yet which, finally, did the most for poetry? A group of students in a seminar room, or the reading before a small, drawing-room audience in more select surroundings? But it was an enjoyable night. The beauty of the house I can't begin to describe in detail, but the main room had a small minstrels' gallery, and there can't be many of those left in private houses in England.

*   *   *   *   *

Because, in my youth I had done some serious acting with the Manchester Shakespearean Players, I was offered two small parts in a play about John Clare. This proved traumatic in several ways, beginning with my difficulty of learning someone else's lines after being only used to composing my own. Also, as the play took place at the Central School of Speech and Drama at Swiss Cottage, it was performed before a highly expert audience which, I believed, would make no allowance for my inexperience. I was cast to play Lord Radstock, one of John Clare's patrons, who was notorious for presuming to lecture Clare on how to write his poems. Sarah, the director, also thought I had the perfect 'aristocratic presence for the part' – which boiled down to the fact that she thought I had no difficulty in appearing pompous!

For several weeks we rehearsed this resumé of the play, *The Fool* by Edward Bond. For those college students taking a degree in English & Drama, it was a necessary requirement they put on such a play under the rigorous auspices of Central School.

Sarah was a great expert on theatre and a niece of the late Edmund Blunden. This was her second time round at university, having done social anthropology – or something like that – the first time.

The 'star' of the play, believe it or not, was Andrew, a young full-blooded American in his twenties. He played John Clare, the Northamptonshire peasant poet; and, amazingly, in just three weeks managed to transform his thick yankee accent into something approaching that of a convincing English rustic. If he had one weakness, this young man whose ambition was to become a Hollywood star, it was that he could not project emotion too well which resulted, at times, in a certain blandness. But he was very handsome and professional in his approach and, of course, the girls were falling over themselves to attract his attention – something which led to the more amusing aspects of rehearsals.

Wednesday: the day of the dreaded dress rehearsal at which we were to appear before an audience composed mainly of the actors from the other five play-scenes, plus a few members of the public who were not able to come to the official performance. The tension was terrific.

I was on the balcony immediately over-looking the theatre's back area which looked like a builder's yard full of portacabins and rubbish skips. Actors and actresses in all manner of fantasy's dress were constantly coming up and down the flight of around thirty stone steps. I was leaning against the bright blue rails and attired in frock coat, grey waistcoat, white Beau Brummel shirt and black cravat. Suddenly Dannie Abse appeared at the foot of the steps in his winter overcoat and bright red scarf, waving and shouting to me. All the cast equally as suddenly appeared on the balcony and, after having introduced Dannie to my fellow actors (my only private audience apart from Patricia who knew the cast and Joan who hadn't arrived yet), we all went into Studio One.

Like I say, I played this pompous retired admiral and, had I more confidence in my abilities as an actor, would have enjoyed strutting about the stage lecturing John Clare about the shortcomings of his poetry. As it was, I was far too nervous to enjoy anything, being merely in a sweated state of hyper-concentration trying to avoid forgetting to say or do anything.

After it was over Dannie – who has also written plays as well as poetry – thought I'd done well. But the strain had been enormous and got worse and worse as it was increasingly borne in on me that this was not just any old play but an integral part of Sarah's finals' examination.

The next night, however, was the really important occasion. Not only would the college's senior drama tutor be present, solemn pen and clipboard at the ready, but a whole array of external examiners as well, plus around 200 extra other people as audience. And as we couldn't be in the audience ourselves, we actors had to skulk around the dressing room or sip 'orange juice only' in the Swiss Cottage. (I risked one glass of Beaujolis; got caught; claimed it was blackcurrent juice but wasn't believed and earned a telling-off from Sarah!).

Imagine a room as big as an aircraft hanger with black draped curtains around the walls and batteries of stage lights miles overhead. Imagine figures in circular pools of orange or purple or yellow or blue or pink or pure white light. Imagine figures attired in all sorts of costumes from the elegant to the tawdry, colourful or dull, moving through imaginary scenes. And see rows of seated persons, and people standing or squatting on the floor like spectators at an overfull sports' arena, around three sides of the auditorium. Imagine this and the dusty claustrophobic heat and you'll get some idea of Studio One on that big night. An occasion that was wonderful, magical and absolutely harrowing for the actors.

Did anything go wrong on that all-important evening? For me? Only one thing. It was a very serious audience. Everybody who came up to the dressing rooms after having given of their best said that: it was a very serious audience. No one laughed, or even tittered. No one ... until Admiral Lord Radstock managed to raise a giggle on his penultimate line of the first scene. At which event His Lordship was so astonished he quite forgot his lines and 'dried' (as we say in showbiz!) for a full fifteen seconds which seemed like a lifetime until he pulled his noble self together. I shall never forget the barrage of hissed promptings needed to get me going again.

Fortunately, my second part as Lord Milton (John Clare's other patron) was both smaller and later. So I had a full five minutes to get a hold of my emotions before I was on stage again. And through sheer strength of character which I never knew I possessed, I was able to survive the rest of the play without more ado.

Yet our beloved and skilful director, Sarah, appeared very downcast. But when a short while later, 'the dreaded Mr. X' signalled his approval of our performance, she went quite hysterical with joy. So everything wasn't so bad after all. Even Patricia's friend Christine, another mature student who'd sat with Patricia throughout the play, helped when she confessed she had thought (until she'd seen the anguished expression on Patricia's face) that I was only 'pausing for effect'. Some effect!

In the end Sarah did get a 'First', and is now researching drama at Oxford. I like to kid myself that my small acting role helped; but I don't suppose it did!

*   *   *   *   *

During Patricia's college years we entertained many interesting folk in our room on the Finchley Road. But our last guest, before we moved back to Brixham, was by no means the least entertaining. It was the Australian poet Peter Porter who came for lunch and to be interviewed for *Acumen*. A tall, slightly academic-looking and fresh-faced man, Peter is, in fact, far from academical: 'I loathe libraries; they give me claustrophobia. All those dead writers hung up like corpses in a meat factory.' Yet he is both clever and learned and a good poet – if, at times, a mite too realist and socially-conscious for my taste. Though there has been a deal of suffering in his life, he is famed for his affable manner, he's a good talker and is full of interesting insights

He said he was 'pressed for time' and, in any case, 'I'm not a great eater, especially at lunch, so I won't stay long.' In fact, he stayed for lunch and shared a full bottle of wine; then left a whole hour later than his expressed intention, and was manifestly reluctant to leave. As Patricia said, 'That's typical of a poet!'. The two good things, you might say, about poets are that, mostly, they are convivial beings who make lively company and do, from time to time, write some good poems. But as the world has long known, poets are not much use for anything else – unless it is making trouble for repressive governments ... and institutions, even poetry societies.

CHAPTER EIGHTEEN
The Poetry Society

In the autumn of 1990, during Patricia's second year at university, I was invited to become a member of the recently revamped General Council of the Poetry Society of Great Britain. This meant, amongst other things, I rapidly became a close observer of what may best be termed 'establishment literary politics'; whose chief imaginative virtue lies in its comicality. But, as one person put it, it gave me 'something to do'! – my claim to being either 'a student's assistant' or a poet pure and simple, being considered little short of pure idleness.

The Poetry Society, founded in 1909 by William Galloway-Kyle, has been an institution in this country for ninety years; and for much of that time subject to great controversy. Never more so than during my two years on its council. There is much to tell about this turbulent period, a deal of which cannot be told without risk of libel, and most of which grew so complex that it could only be sorted out with much research and considerable hindsight.

I'd first been drawn into its activities in the late 1960s. Though still a poetic greenhorn feeling my way round the literary world, I'd soon discovered a number of things about the Society which had repelled me; especially the same sort of crass egotism that I had encountered in the acting world. Indeed, a thrusting and petty self-importance was almost the order of the day. Everywhere I'd found people not being themselves but acting horribly gimmicky and artificial roles, turning life into a sort of frenetic masked ball which, while it might be colourful, actually achieved nothing.

What I did not fully appreciate, though, was just how such interested parties were actually motivated by non-artistic considerations ... fame, power and money. In my romantic and idealistic way I had assumed that poetry, at least, was beyond financial exploitation. Many people who worked for the Society seemed not to care what standards were sacrificed so long as poetry was made into populist propaganda. It had to be 'Taken to the People', made to 'Reach a wider audience', shoved down to 'the grassroots'. Such were the phrases never off unsubtle lips when I first became associated with Earls Court Square and the Poetry Society under the chairmanship of Norman Hidden.

My new encounters with the Society began after an intermission of fifteen years. Firstly, I went to an Extraordinary General Meeting called to change the Society's name – a motion that was soundly defeated after a lengthy and orderly debate. I met John Cotton and John Loveday. Tony Whittome was there: he always had a glitter in his eyes like a twinkle of humour, an oddly distinctive man; and I talked briefly with Alan Brownjohn with whom I had not held speech for nearly 20 years. John Mole and Sebastian Barker were present too, but I wasn't able to speak to either; or with Hilary Davies who turned up looking harassed and laughed a lot – at what I'm not sure unless it was the proceedings! John Heath-Stubbs was there, following the events avidly and interrupting from time to time.

John Heath-Stubbs is a proud and independent man. One day, drinking cider from cans and settled in facing armchairs in his flat, I told him I had been asked to be a nominee for the General Council. He urged me to accept. 'We need new blood,' he said. John, himself, had been a member of the council for many years. I agreed to do so, and that was the vital step towards my closer involvement with the Poetry Society.

When I became a member of the General Council, Sebastian Barker and Hilary Davies were Chairman and Vice Chairman, respectively. Sebastian I knew well, having had the privilege of working through various drafts of his literary *tour de force, The Dream of Intelligence* – a long poem based on the life of the philosopher-poet Nietzsche. They'd been to our flat on the campus in the spring before I'd joined the Society's governing body; but I made them laugh when he and Hilary came to visit us that Autumn. 'Last time you came, Sebastian,' I told him, 'I was dining with a fellow poet; now it's like having the boss to dinner!'

Increasingly in the poetry world, Sebastian was coming to resemble a kind of Caesar; but I hoped he would not turn into a dictator! When I first met him I knew nothing of this literary political world in which he moved, but soon realised what he was taking on, with the aid of the Society's new director, Chris Green. Certainly a lot of fresh air needed letting into the place, but a great and fundamental drama was underway at its Earl's Court premises centred round the far-from-unopposed proposal to sell the building there and move to a smaller, central location. A simple enough proposal, it might have seemed, but I rapidly began to appreciate it had untold ramifications.

But whatever the pro's and con's of the great debate that consumed all of my two years on the General Council, one thing – with hindsight – is beyond question: during that same period the Society put on many excellent literary events ... all at its soon-to-be former headquarters.

*   *   *   *   *

From my notebook, Autumn, 1988: 'It was an odd experience me talking to George MacBeth after all these years. He has bought a house in Galway and is moving over there. It is no longer the Sixties' George MacBeth, he of yellow suits and "flash gear", but a more tweedy figure: the bucolic George straight out of Crabbe country but shorn of the disagreeable "real life" of the peasantry. He still has his buck teeth and moustache, his eager spectacles and his rangey figure.

'Ted Hughes, by contrast, is a rather craggy, be-cardigan'd figure, around my height and of stocky build. Lank hair hangs down beside an angular face: he is a sort of plainer Geoffrey Boycott, and resembles nothing so much as your average, middle-aged, Yorkshire cricket supporter. There is a deeper glow of geniality about him these days, it seems.

'This evening Charles Causley read his poems to an audience of perhaps a hundred people. I thought the poems he chose to read accessible, amusing, but a bit limp in places – which surprised me because, at a reading he gave with Graves in the early Seventies, I had found Causley excellent.

'Sometimes something happens which is scarcely credible. Just a year ago Patricia and I went to the seventieth birthday party for Charles Causley at Exeter University where two women fainted – one of them Patricia. Since then that occasion has become half-legend, half-joke between us. To my shock-horror, this evening, just before the end of Causley's reading, Patricia had to leave the room because she was again feeling unwell. In the bar afterwards – Patricia having miraculously recovered away from the poetry – I reminded Ted Hughes and Charles Causley of the previous year's happening. Ted came up with the theory that Patricia is a person who "draws all the poetic vibrations in a place" into her and "is overcome by them". He told us a story of how, at another reading, the "vibes" had shattered a cut glass decanter on a table near the reader.'

Who else was there that evening? Hilary Davies, dressed in her much favoured red, was as pert as ever; Robert Greacen, with his rosy face, was fresh back from a successful visit to some American campus.   And Eddie Linden was wandering around looking very glum, his neck in a plastic halter.

Robert is a jolly civil-service sort of man from a minor Belfast public school, with a square, pinkish face and a quietly affable manner. He went to Trinity College, Dublin which he describes as 'a sort of Irish Oxbridge'. A Northern Irish Protestant of Scottish ancestry, he gives no hint of violent prejudice, having, or appearing to have, a nature bordering on serenity. In his poetry he is fond of the character sketch. His sense of humour is light and without irony, but it is there: a good-natured glow devoid of exaggeration.   He has this current Irish notion that the 'English strain' in poetry is best represented by the likes of Hardy, Edward Thomas or Larkin: a sort of non-dramatic, passionless ironic wit. In conversation with him, I countered this by suggesting such a definition of Englishness automatically excludes the likes of Milton, Shakespeare or Chaucer. To which he smilingly retorted, 'Ah, well, you know, I always thought Shakespeare was an Irishman!'.

Not long after, alas, Robert returned to Dublin for good. Though we renewed our acquaintanceship there in 1995.

Eddie Linden.   Where would the poetry scene in London and elsewhere over the last quarter of a century have been without Eddie? That wee, aggressive Scot who has pulled himself up by his tartan bootstraps to be the editor of *Aquarius*, an irregular but good quality and never dull literary periodical. Eddie, too, has generously acted as the eyes of the blind poet Heath-Stubbs for many years; and I first remember Eddie as a wiry, stooped figure of a man given to suddenly straightening up, nay springing up, in the middle of poetry functions in the Sixties. Eddie, a whole 'happening' in himself. And he was always there, selling copies of *Aquarius* out of a plastic carrier bag on the street corners of literary life as if it wasn't a poetry magazine but the London *Evening Standard*.

In those days Eddie had a mop of red hair and would sometimes wear a kilt. In addition to copies of his magazine, Eddie carried with him everywhere he went his 'mini-epic' about Glasgow life called 'City o' Razors'. This poem-sequence he would declaim in flats, in pubs, in cafes ... anywhere he could find an audience: I am told he even read it on the Tube to startled strap-hangers. It was a poem about *his* Glasgow, and he would preface every recitation with the words: 'This pome is aboot Glasgie and it's called "City o' Razors".

An' by Christ it *is* a city o'razors!' Sometimes too, he would display scars as proof of his assertion. Though I think he gave up this old soldier's act after someone claimed that his wounds were made with a red biro.

In the end, Eddie's reward, and a sort of recognition, came in the form of a book written about him by Sebastian Barker called, unoriginally, *Who Is Eddie Linden?* Some felt the book a masterly exercise in failed hype; but at least it gave the world, insofar as the world cared to take any notice of it, a portrait of the editor of *Aquarius*, one of the abiding 'characters' of contemporary literature, a character we all know and, if not exactly love, certainly would not be without.

That particular evening flowed on, and with it the white wine – the obvious cause, in my view, of Patricia's undoing, never mind the 'vibes' – and the usual cheerful atmosphere prevailed. Such events at Earl's Court Square were what the 'old' Poetry Society did best; for in those days the Society still had some aspirations to being a Society and providing good opportunities for the meeting of like minds.

*   *   *   *   *

I attended my first meeting of the General Council of the Poetry Society on 1st October 1990. Alan Brownjohn looked hunched and frail after his heart attack: his voice a whole octave down. The editor of *Agenda* magazine, William Cookson dragged himself up the stairs and crossed the room shakily carrying a cup of coffee. There again, too, was Eddie Linden, elected at last to the executive committee 'after tryin' ti get on it for twenty yeer!'

During the meeting John Loveday was displaced – and looked displeased to be displaced – as Vice Chairman by Hilary Davies. Sebastian appeared increasingly uneasy as the evening wore on. It was a sensibly conducted meeting – yet a meeting that ended with a great row between Sebastian and Alan Brownjohn. I couldn't make out what it was all about, and neither could several others. I went home in a taxi with John Heath-Stubbs feeling depressed. Later, Patricia's demands to know 'how it went' didn't help to elucidate the proceedings and I went to bed feeling even more downcast.

*   *   *   *   *

I learned afterwards that the mysterious row involved the two honorary deputy presidents, Alan Brownjohn and Clifford Simmons and the question as to whether they had an *ex officio* right to attend Executive Committee meetings – which latter constitute the real power in the Poetry Society. Almost the whole of the second meeting I attended was taken up in discussion of a possible compromise, involving a constitutional amendment, which made things 'rather boring', as Dannie Abse, who was seated next to me, suggested. But just about everyone who attended wanted to put in their two pennyworth.

Sebastian Barker presided over this fairly tense meeting that never quite broke out into open hostilities – though it came close more than once. News came at the beginning that P.J. Kavangh, poetry editor of *The Spectator*, had resigned from the council; as had Gavin Ewart, the latter's reason being, 'to make way for younger men' – a not unreasonable attitude when one is 75.

Eventually, it being decided there was not going to be enough time to complete the business for which the meeting had been called, Dannie and I left and he ran me back to Finchley Road in his car ...

The most important 'unfinished business' of that meeting, in fact, took many months to resolve – namely, the forcing and/or persuading of Alan Brownjohn to cease attending meetings of the Executive Committee. And this matter, plus the even longer running saga of the projected sale of the Poetry Society's headquarters in Earl's Court, was to consume most of the Society's energies during my two years in office. I have to say that – though a participant in many important meetings, as well as privy to nearly all that went on involving not only the various council members, but the Literature Panel of the Arts Council as well – I was someone caught very much in the middle of all the tensions. For I came to the council as a friend of Sebastian Barker and Dannie Abse, and I also grew to like Alan Brownjohn. A situation which became increasingly difficult for me as the split between the committed Barker and Brownjohn factions widened by the day. How close I was to both of the protagonists, quite leaving aside my even closer relationship with Dannie Abse, would appear as time went on.

*   *   *   *   *

Dannie Abse: what can I say about him? It seems almost an *embarrass de richesses* having known him so long and so well.

Let us start with appearances. Though he has lost some of his extreme handsomeness of youth, Dannie's face has mellowed into a sort of angular Jewish gentleness dominated by dark eyes that glance about in quick, bright merriment; a face which, beneath a mass of grey tousled hair, can sometimes look very tired; sometimes take on that peculiarly Jewish look of historical suffering. Mostly though, it wears an outwardgoing, friendly expression, quizzical, even impish at times.

At the time his first book was published, Dannie was still a medical student at Westminster Hospital. Subsequently, he has never been entirely out of that scrutinous thing called 'the Public Eye'. A modest self-publicist, and one who after a brief excursion into poetic polemics in the Fifties, has managed to enjoy the goodwill of virtually everyone in the literary world. More importantly, through all the years a steady stream of varied, well-written and fairly accessible poems, plays, short stories and novels have flowed from his pen. Never a deliberate entertainer, nor a mere journalist, Dannie's prose works have a straightforward and plain elegance mixed with a dose of dry Jewish humour; work of a wide but not quite 'best-seller' appeal.

His poetry is another matter. It, too, has reached a respectable-sized audience, though nothing like that of a Betjeman or a Larkin. It has always had a certain serious and anguished depth to it. Freudian, matter-of-fact, slightly philosophical, down-to-earth, compassionate, vaguely politically-committed, slice-of-life, medical, beautiful, ugly, and capable of sudden surprising expressions ... such are some of the features of Dannie Abse's poetry. Yet he is also a poet of mystical flashes (glimpses of Paradise?), coruscations of the deeply implanted memories of his Judaic background. A Jew? Not entirely. A Welsh-Jew? By birth, certainly. An Englishman? By domicile, yes. By choice? It is difficult to completely untangle the cultural threads that make up Dannie Abse. Often the struggle to do so makes one lose sight of the sheer Englishness of him.

For Dannie and I the interaction has been one of fruitful intellectual intercourse in which English, Welsh and Jewish cultural resonances have played a creative, rather than a de-creative, part. Also, Dannie's greater poetic experience – especially on the technical level – has helped me, the younger poet, in its clarifying of my ideas concerning the craft of verse-writing. I hope I have given something in return, both in the field of poetry and of human sympathy.

*   *   *   *   *

In October 1991 the Arts Council decided to intervene in the troubled affairs of the Poetry Society, something which, as the Society's 'principal shareholder' so to speak, it was entitled to do. A long letter outlining certain perceived shortcomings of the Society was delivered that month to Chris Green and Sebastian Barker, as Director and Chairman respectively, and it formed the topic of discussion at the current meeting of the General Council. The substance of the letter was a far-reaching and detailed critique of 'the complacent Poetry Society', concluding with a veiled threat to cut-off the Society's subsidy in a year's time if 'things hadn't improved'. Loss of the subsidy – the Poetry Society being the Arts Council's biggest literature client – would almost certainly have meant the end of the Society: something which, of course, many poets and poetasters and poetry watchers from the late Ezra Pound to, ironically, at least one of my then fellow council members, would have considered the best thing that could happen to poetry.

The conclusion – and for once there was a clear-cut conclusion – was that this 'insulting' letter should be 'answered firmly', which meant 'totally rejected', and a committee was formed to write the reply.

*   *   *   *   *

On 20th January 1992 I went to Alan Brownjohn's house in Belsize Park for afternoon tea. He had asked me round to discuss a set of figures produced by the management of the Poetry Society in advance of the crucial meeting later that day. A veritable pillar of the Society over the last forty years, Alan headed the crucial opposition to the Progressives at 21 Earl's Court Square; and the meeting that evening was to have been 'The trial of Alan Brownjohn' as I dubbed it. It was a complicated story leading to his proposed 'impeachment', involving literary politics, Arts Council threats, flaming rows, recriminations, libellous utterances, near-fisticuffs, walkouts, outbursts of petty egotism, accusations of financial incompetence, and, on Alan's part, at least one heart attack.

The basic problem with regard to Alan was, owing to his passionate attachment to the elegant headquarters of the Society in Earl's Court, he did not seem to trust Chris Green, Sebastian Barker and all the rest of the Society's management who wished to sell the Earl's Court building to get us out of the dreadful financial mess the Society was in. Because of Alan's attitude, and the endless acrimony his criticisms (often, but not always, justified) caused, a movement developed to have him excluded from all meetings of the Executive and

Management Committee: something which was technically impossible without a resolution of the General Council. So, finally, that evening a resolution – backed by a many-paged document of indictment – was to have been put to the meeting. But two days previously an 'out-of-court-settlement', as it were, had been reached through the diplomatic efforts of Dannie Abse and John Loveday, in which Alan had finally agreed not to attend any more meetings of the Executive in return for his 'impeachment' being withdrawn. Despite this, however, Alan wasn't giving up his struggle to save the Earl's Court building ... which was why I was having tea with him in Belsize Park. I was being canvassed.

The chief difficulty for the General Council members lay not in any refusal to acknowledge the dire financial plight of the Society – even Alan was agreed about that – but over the matter of getting a new building adequate to the purposes of the Society as laid down in its constitution. Unlike Alan, few thought there was any way out but to sell the Earl's Court building and buy a cheaper building, using any surplus to pay off the Society's debts. But no one seemed to wish for us to move to a building that would not be suitable enough to carry on all its constitutionally required activities. Though it has to be said that, as time went on, there seemed to grow a willingness – possibly backed by the Arts Council? – on the part of some members and staff to settle for a new building of office premises alone: thus retaining the professional and administrative side at the expense of the social side of the Society.

As a result, the meeting that same January evening proved a very stormy affair and it had to be adjourned, no decision having been made on which of the new buildings on offer to take, only on the sale of 21 Earl's Court Square. That night and the following morning, Patricia and I had lengthy discussions about the situation with the President Dannie Abse; then we went off home to Brixham. Two days later Dannie rang to tell us that he had resigned as President. Evidently he, at least, had had quite enough.

*   *   *   *   *

Great were the tensions created at these meetings, and the following little anecdote seems very representative of those turbulent, rumour-ridden days at the Poetry Society, as well as bearing all the hallmarks of absurdity which so characterises literary life normally.

One day, I was having a quiet drink with a fellow member of the Council and I asked casually, of another member, 'How does he survive?' By which I meant, of course, financially.

I was told, 'He has a small disability pension: he's a registered psychopath you know?'

I had never heard of a 'registered psychopath', but well knew the particular member's intemperate utterances (intemperate even by Poetry Society standards). Then my colleague went on to describe how the subject of our discussion had just been mugged, 'He had no money, but his attackers stole his bus pass.' And, even more surprisingly, he added, 'You know, of course, he bears this great grudge against ...' and he mentioned yet another member of the Society's council. 'He keeps ringing the poor fellow up at all times of the day and night and abusing him; and he's not a well man. Finally, he's had to get police protection. It's terrible but...' and he named the persecutor, 'he's so unreasonable...'

*   *   *   *   *

With Dannie gone as president, 21 Earl's Court Square – that spacious Georgian building with white marble Adam fireplaces – sold, and the Council moved into more cramped but not wholly impossible quarters in Covent Garden, it looked for a few weeks as though things might settle down. But Alan Brownjohn continued his opposition; and I had increasing doubts concerning not only questions of financial competence but, also, as to who, exactly, was running the Society. Throughout the summer and autumn of 1992 intense politicking by members of the Society's Executive and General Council led to a series of both official and secret meetings at which plots were hatched and unhatched, motions won and lost, letters exchanged and documents churned out. Various parties, myself included, were summoned to the offices of the Arts Council. It all became very complex and, finally, very disagreeable to me.

I'd always felt that, at bottom, the problem had always been that the Society had been run by people concerned about money but with little understanding of that commodity. I only seemed to exacerbate the situation because, as both a poet *and* chartered accountant, I insisted that the management called all the figures quoted in documents by their correct terms – i.e. called a loss a loss and not merely a debt – in order to prevent the practice, deliberate or otherwise, of what I call 'subjective accounting'. To anyone not a poet or artist (or politician?) such demand for precision probably makes sense; but to the management of the Poetry Society it was either 'nit-picking', 'heresy' or 'siding with the Brownjohn faction'.

By October of 1992 I was asking myself the question: 'What is *really* going on at the Poetry Society? What is the "hidden agenda"?' There was a feeling that there was a cleansing of the white middle-class stratum by the Arts Council, a drive for 'political correctness' underway; and, absurd as it may seem, a decision on the part of that bureaucracy to get rid of the poets from the Society's management. I was convinced that the Society had become a two-headed monster, one of which belonged to the Arts Council. And when the Society received yet another lengthy missive from the Arts Council listing its short-comings (a copy of which document I actually received on 5th October, though it was dated 11th September); and when, a few hours after I'd read it I received a phone call from a journalist on *The Guardian* newspaper asking if the Society was being criticised 'for not being politically correct', I knew the time had come for me to resign. Dimly, I began to see why so many 'decisions' had, or had not been made; or having been made had not been implemented. The legally-elected representatives were no longer 'calling the shots', as the Americans say. So I followed Dannie into the wilderness out of the lions' den. Alan Brownjohn resigned shortly afterwards. And that was that.

CHAPTER NINETEEN
Poetry Readings and other Friends

Poetry readings? Poetry readings are not always magical occasions for their audiences, though they can be. But for poets, despite the nervous tension beforehand, they are almost always magical, especially in retrospect. In my own case, most of the magic comes from meeting people and visiting new or odd places, than from any satisfaction I might derive from the actual reading. So it was an 'odd' experience to be invited to give a reading in Harlow at, of all places, the staff bar at Pearson Longman's publishers. David Woolley's idea – he was literature officer at Harlow College at the time – was that I should read my Epping Forest sequence in my old Essex stamping ground. I'd read in bars before but this was the first time by sober invitation! Although the reading was intended as lunchtime entertainment for the staff, it was open to the public, so my old friend, the former Epping librarian, Mike Brown turned up. Eccentrically, while waiting for David to arrive in the glass foyer of the Longman's building, I was seated in front of a large photographic triptych quite oblivious to the fact that it consisted of blow-ups of the illustrations to my book!

After, David ran me back to Golders Green where Patricia offered him supper. As he was desirous of making the acquaintance of some of the famous Hampstead public houses, we went on pub-crawl – all of which resulted in David having too much to drink to drive back to Harlow and having to curl up in a sleeping bag in the Abses' spare room. As the sleeping bag was conveniently in his car boot, one wonders how many times this had happened to him ... ?

*   *   *   *   *

It had been the custom, from 1988 onwards for Patricia and myself to stay, from time to time, at the Abses' house in Golders Green, often while Dannie and Joan have been at their cottage in Wales or elsewhere. This was primarily to look after the Abses' cat, a ginger female called 'Caitlin' – a rather aristocratic puss of somewhat noticeably refined manners. Once when we were there and had been socially very active for a couple of days, I was just saying to Patricia at breakfast that 'today, at least, should be a very quiet day' when, inevitably, the phone rang. I answered, expecting the call to be for Dannie. But a strong American voice collided with my ear: 'Can I speak with William Ahkslee?'

Having confessed to being 'Ahkslee', the voice friendlied: 'Great! Hi! This is Richard O'Connell from Florida. Beryl 'n me're in the U.K. for a few days. Can we meet?' Who was Beryl? I was obviously supposed to know. I met the two Floridans at the entrance to Golders Green Underground Station and brought them to the Abses' place where Patricia had knocked together a lunch. No need for great detail about the convivial time we spent with this blue-eyed American and his wife; nor need to describe the stroll we took later in Golders Hill Park. Sufficient to say that O'Connell proved an intelligent and delightful companion at this first, and at subsequent, meetings. He was also a man full of anecdotes, retailing many, both literary and scatalogical, during our encounter – including one about being accused of 'flashing' in deepest Wales one freezing winter's evening... 'Me, a flasher an' in that weather, Jesus!'

Our 'quiet day' in Golders Green falls easily into two tales, the second of which, in fact, ran on to more than that day. After spending most of the day with us, Richard O'Connell – the only poet to have lost his academic post at an American university for publishing poems in *Playboy* magazine, – and his wife left us. Scarcely had Patricia returned to her studies and I to watching a boxing match on TV, when the telephone rang again. Still it was not for Dannie. The conversation, brief but potent, went like this:

Caller: 'May I speak to Meester William Oxley, pliss?'

Me: 'Speaking.'

Caller: 'Goot! At last I find you! I haf been ringing you everywhere. Dis is Miron Grindea of *Adam*. You haf heard of *Adam*, yes? ... Your long poem, I vud like to publish eet.'

Adam, an international literary magazine, was nearly fifty years old; and it was one of the most prestigious journals published in England this century. Its contributors had included the likes of Maxim Gorky, H.G. Wells, Bertrand Russell, Sir Winston Churchill, T.S. Eliot, Robert Graves, Jean Cocteau, Albert Camus and a host of other literary luminaries, as well as having been illustrated by famous artists like Chagall and Picasso. So I was naturally a bit stunned to have the editor chasing me, a mere poet from the provinces. He continued:

Editor: 'Goot! Now tell me, has dis long poem of yoors ever been published before?'

Me: 'Er, no, not really. Just a section of it in a Belgian magazine.'

Editor: 'Dat is goot. *Adam* only likes to publish vork dat has never been published before.'

Me: 'I understand that.'

Editor: 'Are you staying in London?'

Me: 'Yes.'

Editor: 'Splendid! Can you come and see me?'

Me: 'Certainly. When?'

Editor: 'Immediately! Tomorrow morning. 11 o'clock, yes?'

Me: (mentally cancelling all appointments.) 'I, er, well, yes. Of course.'

Editor: (about to ring off but has afterthought): 'How old are yoo, Meester Oxley?'

Me: 'Forty nine.'

Editor: 'Forty nine? Ah, a mere child! Vell, I shall see yoo tomorrow. Gootbye!'

Later, watching the great Sugar Ray Leonard beat Donny Lalonde on T.V., I felt quite 'phone- drunk', uplifted, and slightly suspicious that my life was in danger of ceasing to be my own.

The following day found me pressing the front doorbell of a large house in Emperor's Gate, a very enclosed square on the borders of Chelsea and Knightsbridge. The door almost immediately opened to reveal a young Chinaman. He asked me in impeccable and quiet English whom it was that I wished to see. Mr. Grindea, the editor of *Adam*, I told him. At which, inviting me into the darkened hallway but leaving the front door open, the Chinese youth tripped to the foot of a narrow flight of stairs. Abruptly, and shockingly, this hitherto quietly-spoken oriental bellowed like a yellow-visaged Ian Paisley: 'MR GRINDEA! YOU HAVE A VISITOR!' A tiny frail voice drifted back down the stairs in reply, telling the youth to show me into the drawing room. This the Chinese lad did, before departing himself through the front door and closing it behind him.

The room was very large, high-ceilinged and somewhat Victorian in style and atmosphere. One tall window was draped with enormous velvet curtains which, though drawn back, seemed somehow not to encourage daylight. Though spacious, it was crowded with memorabilia, books and paintings. It had a grand piano blocking the fireplace; one armchair with a tall back; and a sofa covered with much punished cushions.   However, it was the paintings and photographs which most attracted.   There were sketches by Picasso, Matisse, Chagal, Jean Cocteau; as well as signed photographs from people like Camus and Stravinsky. A photograph of Miron Grindea with Jean Cocteau, the latter in his dressing-gown and obviously very old, stood on the mantlepiece ...

But I got no further with my inspection as I was interrupted by a small square man with fierce white hair who looked like a cross between Albert Einstein and an older Hugh MacDiarmid.   After glaring at me for a moment, Grindea threw himself theatrically into the high-backed armchair.   There he sat facing me and began to ask questions. He first asked, somewhat unbelievably, 'Where iss Devon?' After I told him it was in the West Country, he demanded to know if it was 'near Exeter?' I informed him that Exeter was a part of Devon, a town some thirty miles from where I lived.

Next, he told me that though *Adam* magazine was the 'oldest literary journal in the U.K.' it had 'always been eegnored by the Establishment!'   A fact which, judging by its long list of highly distinguished contributors, and the many laudatory notices it had received over the years, was hard to credit.   Therefore I ventured a mild demur.   But this only provoked him into a fierce denunciation of someone whose name he couldn't quite recall, yet who he said had written 'dat book on the Forties, you know, and eet never once mention *Adam*! How is dis possible?'

At this vague piece of information all I could do was frown and allow Grindea to fume on. 'You know, yes you do ... dat man it vas ... you know, he had involvement wiz dat woman who became a Catholic?' This enabled me to establish that the woman he meant was now a famous novelist; and the guilty author none other than my old friend Derek Stanford, whom Miron Grindea referred to at first as 'Derek Stainforth'. Without admitting any connection with Derek, I tactfully suggested that the omission must have been an oversight. To avoid pursuing this sensitive topic further, I glanced away from the extraordinary figure before me, and gazed at the pictures on the walls.   This immediately called for a further, far from modest observation from the editor of *Adam*. Said he, 'I am de only man in der British Isles who has been drawn by Picasso!' Wow! I thought. How else could I respond to this flourish of ego?

I was saved further comment by the arrival of Mrs Grindea bearing a tray of coffee and biscuits.   She stayed only long enough to be introduced. Over coffee, Miron enquired about Patricia's work with *Acumen*. He was also desirous of knowing what subjects she lectured on at London University. I explained she was not on the staff but was, at that time, 'a mature student' doing a degree in English. But he seemed unable to comprehend how anyone bright enough – and old enough – to edit a magazine like *Acumen*, which he had seen, could only be a mere student.

Another round of what my mother would have called 'boasting' followed, as Grindea felt it important to tell me that Stravinsky had played the piano, as well as composed, many times 'in dis very room'. He also told me how he had been a close friend of the late Jean Cocteau: 'A genius, a magician, you know?' Then, abruptly, he ordered, 'You moost come to my lecture on Jean!'

'Gladly,' I replied brightly, 'when is it?'

'Eet iss next Wednesday.'

That was a bit awkward. I was supposed to be going to the Arts Council with Patricia and then on to lunch with Anna and Norman Adams. Still, one can easily get about London by tube or taxi – so I decided, it should be easy enough to fit in a lecture.

'Okay. Where are you giving it?'

'In Brighton,' he replied promptly. 'You moost come ... I vant all my friends to come!'

'I, er ...?' (So I was a friend already?)'You drive?' he demanded, 'You haf a car? Eet iss only one hour to Brighton by car.'

'I'm afraid I don't drive ...'

'Ha! zat iss difficult, yes?' He paused, then said, 'Never mind, eet iss not a problem. I weel find you a car. You shall haf a lift to Brighton. Goot! Eet iss settled, yes? I vill ring you later.'

Shortly afterwards, having staggered bemusedly out of the grand house, I realised we had hardly discussed the proposal to publish my long poem, 'Swansong for a Golden Age'. Grindea had merely said at the start of the interview, 'I haf been looking for a long poem for sometime. I wish to publish a long poem. I vill publish yours.' And that was that. He'd spent more time trying to establish where exactly in the world Devon was. But he did publish the poem finally.

Around five that afternoon, back at Golders Green, the phone rang again. This time it had got to be for Dannie surely? But no. It was Miron Grindea again. In a loud, but oddly soothing voice, he said, 'Meester Oxley, I haf found you a car! Pliss ring dis number and ask for Katie ...' He then dictated a telephone number, adding, 'Say dat

Miron told you to ring her, okay? She will be driving to Brighton for my lecture. I look forward to seeing you there. Gootbye!' He put the phone down abruptly.

I gave in and rang the number. But, as it turned out, Katie, an American woman with a small baby and husband, did not seem all that enthusiastic about sharing her car with a total stranger or, for that matter, going to Brighton at all. Whether she actually went or not I have no means of knowing. I went. On the train.

*   *   *   *   *

It was while we were staying at Golders Green that David Perman, ex-BBC producer turned publisher, set up a reading in Ware ... of 'Great Bed' fame. Ware, a delightful old town, is built on the banks of the River Lea and is full of old warped houses, pubs and remarkable buildings on the river bank called 'gazebos'. The arts centre there is a former malting. Many people came to the reading, locals and friends from farther afield. Patricia gave a brief talk on *Acumen*, and I read poetry for three quarters of an hour. David Woolley came too, and afterwards, much of the audience repaired to a local inn to carry on the experience, an 'experience' which went on after closing time and far into the night in David Perman's small cottage. I fell asleep that night – as I have done after many such occasions – full of the fresh images of poetry which fine hospitality and new surroundings always provide.

*   *   *   *   *

Our first meeting with the late Jonathan Griffin, a tall, skeletally thin, old gentleman, was in an Italian restaurant after a reading somewhere. I sat opposite this 84 year old poet whose habit was to lean forward and talk to one in an excited urgent whisper. We discussed the Franco-African poet Senghor, and Roy Campbell in the context of Camöens. Griffin thought Campbell a superb poet and translator and had 'no time at all' for the fashionable, politically-correct anti-Campbell view of so many of the literati ... Jonathan was a man who exuded great gentleness and sweetness of being. In his lifetime he had been a diplomat and a controller at the BBC and there was an overwhelming sense of high-civilization about him. Unhappily, he died while Patricia was still at college, but we had begun to get to know him before that sad event.

It seemed appropriate, somehow, that he and his wife – the strong and lucid Kate – should have lived in a narrow but tall and elegant house close to Primrose Hill. A house full of priceless books that included such treasures as an original *Chronicles* by Holinshed, plus other Renaissance early editions, all acquired when it was still possible to purchase such things in ordinary second-hand bookshops.

But the best memory I have is of the octogenarian translator of Pessoa staggering across the over-filled first floor living room with the huge volume of Holinshed and depositing it on Patricia's lap with the whispered words, 'This may well have been the very volume Shakespeare used when writing his historical plays – look at the annotations!' There was something extraordinary boyish about Jonathan; a kind of eternal and gentle youthfulness. And it was, again, this cool web of language that brought us together. As it has done with so many others ...

*   *   *   *   *

'A small, birdlike figure' as Virginia Woolfe once described her, Kathleen Raine has always been something of a grandmotherly lady to me. I remember the first day she opened her front door to me at Paulton's Square, Chelsea and said: 'Ah, William, how nice to meet you at last'; and I recall being struck by the sheer femininity of her cool blue eyes despite an already aging face. Yet it was a face in which the lines of suffering, and a woman's ever-unwelcome wrinkles, were offset by the sort of spiritual placidness one most often associates with the faces of nuns.

It was an interesting, lively yet calm, face the more one viewed it in various lights and at various times. At a party, it could be mysterious and withdrawn; or it could be solemn, almost pietistic at receptions, especially if any of the clergy were in evidence. Such was the face I saw when, with the actor Edward Fox, Kathleen gave a reading in the crypt of St. Paul's Cathedral.

Though Kathleen and I continued to meet, it was rarely at poetry readings – though she gave a marvellous one at the Blue Nose venue for Patricia – for by this time she was always insisting that she wasn't interested in poetry any longer 'Only in Truth, William, only in Truth!'

Then would come the rather haughty look one saw in argument; or, if the haughty look appeared when the conversation took a turn of which she disapproved, Kathleen bore an uncanny resemblance to another, even more famous, lady at her most determined and argumentative. I remember being in the Old Corn Exchange at Cambridge where Kathleen, David Gascoyne and Peter Russell were giving a poetry reading. Behind me sat a famous translator and his companion. The latter remarked, 'Don't you think Kathleen Raine reminds you of Margaret Thatcher?' To which the former responded sharply, 'Where do you think Thatcher learned her style?' A jesting remark perhaps, but there was a certain resemblance between the Silver Lady of Poetry and the Iron Lady of Politics.

A more frequent side to Kathleen which I encountered, especially when taking tea with her, was that seen when she wore her more homely face. Mostly her demeanour, though, was benign and wise: a face in which womanly compassion softened austerity. There was, of course, another, earlier Kathleen Raine that I never knew. One that she spoke of as a stranger to her when she looked back or read the poems of this younger self. This earlier being was the Kathleen Raine who was a beautiful young woman. She had the visage of the Muse in nymphlike aspect. But that 'face' I only came upon by accident in an old photograph.

What had drawn me initially to Kathleen Raine was, I suppose, the quality of her mind. That, and our shared spiritual experiences. We seemed to agree on many things in that, finally crucial, area of personal and philosophical beliefs ... or so it seemed in the beginning. Kathleen was something of a Platonist; was interested in Blake and Berkeley; and we both believed that the central deficiency of modern poetry derived from its lack of metaphysical concern.

I admired Kathleen, too, for having stood out against the pressures of fashionable materialist theories, and against an establishment, central to which were lifelong friends of hers like William Empson, who would have had her conform to the nihilist creed of a secular age. Though I was never entirely in awe of her intellect, I greatly admired it.

Now and again, she would introduce me to friends of hers. Like the day the two of us were dining at the PEN club, then in Glebe Place, Chelsea, and a sad-looking, rather clerkly figure passed our table. He could have been the club's bookkeeper but was, in fact, the painter Cecil Collins. Then, I had only heard of him because Kathleen had paintings on the walls of her house in Paulton's Square. It was not until years later that I learned from a T.V. film about Collins, shown after his death, that he and his wife actually lived in the same house as Kathleen, in a flat upstairs.

For all the years that I had been visiting her, I had never realised
that she shared the house with anyone else; even though I had often
climbed the stairs to the bathroom, passing many paintings by Cecil
Collins on the way. But at least I did realise that each time I visited
that same bathroom it contained the very bath in which Gavin Maxwell
had kept his famous otters when he and Kathleen had been living
together. For I had read her oblique, but sufficiently revealing,
autobiography *The Lion's Mouth* as well as Maxwell's *Ring of Bright
Water* which takes its title from a poem of hers.

We often lose touch, for one reason or another, even with people
we have known well. For a time, Kathleen and I still wrote to each
other occasionally; but I confess it was, finally, more or less down to
Christmas cards. This saddened me, and did so more than I can say.
But all that is history now, and largely beyond untangling as far as I
can see. However the essential differences between Kathleen and I
ought to be noted.

While I remain a staunch admirer of her poetry and her life of
absolute dedication to the truth as she sees it, philosophically I believe
I have passed both the stage of rigid neoplatonism and my own 'Blake
period'. Again, Kathleen believes absolutely in 'the Fall' and the
idea of Original Sin; whereas I am nearer to the 'Pelagian Heresy' in
my ideas. Finally, and on a more personal level, the more I grew
acquainted with this remarkable woman, the more of a puzzle she
became to me – puzzled too by the fact that many well-known literati
had an ambivalent attitude towards Kathleen Raine. She is probably
the most famous – and fame counts a great deal in getting published
– poet in England never to have been consistently published by a
major poetry publisher. Something which struck me as very odd.

Much later, discussing Kathleen with another literary lady, it was
pointed out to me that due to her involvement with certain aspects of
Indian vedantic teaching, her brush with the New Age movements
and the like, she was widely regarded as 'something of a cult figure'.
I suddenly realised that I had been viewing Kathleen simply as a fellow
poet and judging her exclusively in that light, whereas there was a
side to her which I had failed to take into account, a side which was
bound to effect both her verse and her poetic status. Many of the
seemingly strange remarks she'd made over the years suddenly began
to appear in a fresh light, and at last I could begin to understand what
Kathleen, whom I had always thought of as a dedicated poet, meant
when she kept saying, 'I am not interested in poetry, only truth'.

As clearly as I had misjudged her, perhaps she had misjudged me. One evening when giving one of her rare readings in the basement of an Islington bookshop, on hearing some louts entering clearly intent upon starting a fracas with the proprietor, it was me she turned to, rather than any of the other males present. Calmly she said, 'Your father was a boxer, William. You go upstairs and get rid of them.'

That I did climb the short flight of stairs to confront the intruders did not mean that Kathleen Raine was right; nor that I was other than mightily relieved to find the potential troublemakers had fled!

*   *   *   *   *

On the death of the veteran editor and pillar of poetic society Howard Sergeant, the abrasive Roland John inherited *Outposts,* Britain's oldest poetry magazine. Direct as a navvie but more refined in his tastes, Roland John has long, haphazardly greying locks, a powerful straggle of a beard and leonine features. He has about him a touch of the Sixties in his attire. I have several warm memories to call upon concerning Roland. I recall, for example, a wonderful candlelit dinner at his house in Sutton where, along with Patricia, Peter Dale and others, I enjoyed a mini-banquet of chicken and red wine that developed into a great contest of verbal wit. Then there was an equally rich evening spent with Roland in John Skelton's pub The Running Horse at Leatherhead. Perhaps most romantic of all given its setting of a barn beside a lake, was Roland's fiftieth birthday party at Carshalton – a fine do. Not long after, Roland upped sticks and shifted his base of operations from the metropolitan fringes to the wilds of Somerset.

Not a man to be put upon, Roland has matured into sound taste with age: even if, like us all, he has his blind spots. For years he was an ex-officio member of the lovable, if not always loved, 'Agenda clique' as it is known to its enemies. It was through his association with *Agenda* that Roland acquired a good knowledge of editing and intimate acquaintanceship with the literary politics of our time.

Mention of *Agenda*, a distinguished contemporary magazine devoted to the memory of Ezra Pound, involves thoughts not only of the durable William Cookson, its founder, but of its erstwhile co-editor, the remarkable, and remarkably critical, Peter Dale. A good poet, Peter Dale has a most vigorous and unsentimental mind. After leaving one lengthy and stimulating session with Peter in the coffee bar at the South Bank, Patricia demanded to know: 'Is there any poet Peter Dale actually *likes*?' Which might sound an unfair question except that, like Geoffrey Grigson before him, Peter tends to tear poetic reputations to shreds almost as much for reasons of anti-fashion as anything else. And in an age of so much pretentiousness I, for one, find his attitude refreshing – in small doses. Of average size, pinkish complexioned with tidy silver hair, Peter is a bit schoolmasterish at times in his manner – but that was his profession for many years. Philosophically an existentialist, I regard Peter as a secular dogmatist, a description he should not find displeasing. He is also a masterly verse technician and a fine poet in his own right so his not-a-little-prejudiced criticism is an experience not to be missed and I usually welcome the imaginative excitement of it. And it seems not to matter a jot that I disagree with most of his sillier judgements ...

*   *   *   *   *

If words have any value at all, it is in enabling us to see better the essential humanity of others, even those we may dislike. Hugo Manning taught me this as we sat in a seedy cafe in Camden Town drinking turgid coffee after coffee. Hugo, who resembled nothing so much as a ruined Old Testament Prophet, was dying of every illness imaginable. But in that great head, with its smouldering visionary eyes, a fierce wisdom burned on. Speaking of Roy Campbell – that supreme *bête noir* of the poetry scene throughout the Thirties and Forties – Hugo observed, 'A man who, by all accounts, I should have loathed. Yet I found him a gentle giant full of humanity...'

It is that essential humanity, and human identity, of many wordsmiths that comes through in their art – even in those one differs from greatly in belief. It is this humanity which I want to convey here as briefly as possible.

Anna Adams is a poet, editor, ceramist and wife of the distinguished Royal Academician, Norman Adams. A long-time correspondent, it was not until Patricia started *Acumen* that either of us actually met Anna. And we might not have made her acquaintance even then but for the fact that she moved from her abode in that sheep country through which runs the famed and beautiful Settle to Carlisle railway, to a flat situated, of all places, on the top floor of Burlington House, Piccadilly – because Norman became Head of Schools there. And it was in the midst of a bright chaos of paint brushes, pallets, stacked canvases and back copies of *Apollo* and *The Poetry Review* that we first encountered Anna.

A poet with a determined metrical ear and commonsense views on the craft of poetry, my earliest impression of Anna, on seeing her seated at a small table in a high-windowed studio room, was of a woman of calmness. Her complexion was smooth; her hair silver-grey and bobbed short; and there was something peasantly artistic about the way she dressed. Anna, though London-born, had 'gone native' in northern sheep country to the extent that she is frequently described as 'a nature poet': an epithet which does not please her! For this much-talented lady is no mere bucolic scribbler. She draws her inspiration from many sources, writing about urban as well as rural things. Admittedly, one of her volumes of poetry was entitled *Sheep Country*; but another was in celebration of Van Gogh, much of it penned in Provence and lovingly called *Dear Vincent*; while a more recent volume bears the ambiguous title of *Angels of Soho*. So this quietly spoken lady, with a pragmatic mind, has 'considerable range'. What strikes one most immediately about Anna is that she is a person who knows her own mind; and, soon, one realises it is a mind worth knowing.

* * * * *

John Taylor, who, besides being the editor of Keats and Shelley, was also the editor of John Clare must, judging from Clare's letters and journals, have been the ideal editor of a poet. Why? Because it would appear he had a genuine – but discriminating – interest in the poetry he published. Now most editors, even if they cannot be kind, are at least tactful in dealing with one's work. Of all the magazine editors I have had dealings with, Richard Mayne of *Encounter* was the most often unfailingly both. Unique in my experience of dealing with many dozens of magazines, Richard was the only one with the sensitivity to realise how poets dread the sealed return envelope coming through the front door, and he would – when appropriate – write on the outside of the envelope 'acceptance inside'. Richard also holds, along with Tony Rudolf, the distinction of being one of the only two editors voluntarily to place my work in periodicals other than those they edited.

I wouldn't want, in any way, to sound ungrateful to my several book editors – especially the patient and thoughtful Leslie Cook, or

the abrasive but fair Rupert Loydell, or, above all, to Dr. James Hogg
of Salzburg who has invested so much time and money in many
publications by me over the last dozen years – but with all the book
editors with whom I have had dealings David Perman comes closest
to Richard Mayne's high standards. Indeed, David performed a small
miracle with my volume *In The Drift of Words* when it was published
in November 1992 in getting the printer to correct an horrendous
mistake in an almost impossibly short time. Less than a week before
the launch, it was discovered that, by printer's error, a quarter of the
poems included in my book were by someone else!

*   *   *   *   *

A few years ago the magazine *Aquarius* run by Eddie Linden, that
self confessed 'gay, socialist and Catholic', asked the question Who
would be the first poet to die of Aids? I never forgot that, nor the
feeling I had that somehow the answer would be connected with the
magazine that asked it. Now, although Eddie is the official editor of
Aquarius, John Heath-Stubbs was its unofficial *eminence gris*; and
it was John who introduced me to a young friend of his, Adam
Johnson.

Adam was a charming young man, of slight build and with a
tendency to favour blazers and snappy suits which were pretentious
but never vulgar. There was a touch of elegance in Adam's make-up
and he had an indefinable gift for friendship so that, at a young age,
he was, like my dead friend Tom whom he physically resembled, the
centre of a personal web of breathtaking proportions. Adam was a
poet and became a good friend of Patricia and myself; we met him in
London on various occasions and Patricia published his first book of
poetry – as distinct from his first pamphlet which was published by
John Rety who ran, and still runs, that remarkable poetry venue which
goes by the name of Torriano. It was at Torriano, one November
evening, that Adam gave his first poetry reading with John Heath-
Stubbs.

Adam was so nervous that he drank a whole bottle of red wine
beforehand. But he shouldn't have bothered, for he was a very
personable young man and a good and entertaining reader. When it
was over he relaxed by insisting Patricia join him at the piano; and
while she fingered one end of the keyboard (she can't play a note!),
he composed several amusing ditties – with the help of Heath-Stubbs
or myself who shouted out when he seemed stuck for a rhyme. Then,

in his inimitable way, John Rety suggested a festive end to the evening with his usual 'We can all have a glass of wine ... if some of you go to the off-licence on the corner and buy some!' So, as always, the evening at Torriano was ... quite individual.

I never knew when, exactly, Adams was told he was 'HIV positive'; but I have to say that long before it was official, and long before its terrible conclusion in Putney Cemetery, I somehow kept associating Adam in my mind with that question first posed in *Aquarius* magazine in the early Eighties.

* * * * *

In every walk of life – and poetry is no exception – there have been, and probably always will be, those 'unsung heroes' who perform a vital function in, as it were, oiling the wheels of whatever they embrace. One such is John Rety.

John Rety is a small, bearded, Central European refugee whom, I believe, came to reside in Britain as a result of Communist persecutions in Europe. For over ten years he has run the ex-Friends' meeting house in Torriano Avenue as a cultural centre supported by the fairly 'fundamentalist' Camden Council. A somewhat seedy, run-down ground floor room (which I described as 'a Comrades' hall' in a poem), the place is used mainly for poetry readings and allied events; it also acts as a down-market art gallery for the work of Rety's daughter Emily who is a fine book illustrator and artist. The 'family' team is completed by the seemingly long-suffering Susan who, it must be said, appears to do a hell of a lot of the work in running the place.

Torriano is a startling place in which events can very easily turn into what were known in the Sixties as 'happenings'. This is partly because John Rety, an avowed anarchist, is frequently on the side of chaos and disorder, or so it often seems. The first time Patricia and I went there, Dannie Abse was the main reader. After many readers 'from the floor' – myself included – Dannie had just stood up to start his reading when an elderly gentleman suddenly stormed out of the place shouting, 'I didn't come here to listen to other people read but to read myself!'

Since that first evening I have been there both as audience and, on a number of occasions, as guest reader. Rarely are the events there unmemorable, though not always for the poetry read! What was billed as Stephen Spender's last reading turned out to be a fine and very crowded occasion, except that Spender was prevented for a while from getting to the raised dais at the front, not only by the sardine-like crowding, but by a very fierce black dog that didn't look at all friendly towards poets. In fact, the same dog was at my first solo reading there, but it had broken its leg and was more subdued, though it still managed to walk up and down on the bare floor boards during the reading, its plaster-of-paris leg clicking out of time to the rhythm of my poems.

It is an especial place, too, for meeting old, and making new, friends. I first met David Perman there, who became my publisher. And it was through Torriano that Patricia and I got to know Danielle Hope and the late Arthur Jacobs well.

Then there is the unconscious humour the place generates, as when Dinah Livingstone, at a Torriano Christmas party, asked me what I thought of Arthur, our mutual friend standing not two yards from us and able to hear every word. 'I like him – he's a good friend,' I replied truthfully.

'But he's a stubborn man!'

I demurred. 'No, not stubborn, just a bit shy.'

'But stubborn also.'

'Why do you say he's stubborn?'

To which Dinah answered, 'Well there was that business over his teeth. You know, when Rety wanted to organise a benefit reading for Arthur's teeth.'

'Pardon?' I said with great emphasis.

'Oh you must have noticed Arthur's bad teeth? Well John wanted to organise a poetry reading to raise some money so Arthur could have his teeth fixed. But Arthur wouldn't hear of it. He's so stubborn.'

Another occasion: John's 60th birthday. People brought quantities of wine, there was french bread, olives, taramasalata, other nibbles. A diminutive birthday cake, almost as flat as a pancake, was on display adorned with 4 candles, no more being available apparently. John even had great difficulty blowing out four! Someone read a poem specially composed for John's birthday, but which, as far as anyone could understand it, appeared to have no relevance to the occasion. Then John went from guest to guest handing out beautifully printed rules for a party game. Unfortunately no one, not even John himself, could understand them so he then went from guest to guest lamenting ... And that was the same occasion on which John Rety made one of his unforgettable pronouncements. A young poet, having drunk too much, vomited in one corner of the room. On being informed of this

Rety exclaimed, 'Sick? Sick? Impossible! Nobody has ever been sick at Torriano!'

There are some I know – unsubtle, bourgeois minds – who would deny the spiritual, or even the cultural, contributions of a place like Torriano. But not only do I believe a man like John Rety helps oil the wheels of poetry, a place like Torriano makes a vital contribution to the spiritual and cultural life of the community.

*   *   *   *   *

It was through a poetry reading that I came to know the Scottish poet Hugh MacDiarmid. I had first heard him read in 1969 but was unimpressed by what little of his work I then knew. But when I heard him again in 1971, it proved to be the most affecting reading I had yet attended. MacDiarmid was a small, solid, thistle of a man – all grey and prickly; until one met him when he seemed surprisingly gentle. It was following another similar occasion at the Institute for Contemporary Arts in the Mall, that I really got to know the man.

He'd been participating in a debate with Allen Ginsburg and Al Alvarez on 'Poetry and Politics' – that perennial obsession of Sixties' literati – a lively and somewhat acrimonious affair and I was there with Patricia and my two friends, David Beugger and Quenten Lane.

Afterwards I introduced myself to MacDiarmid and his wife, Valda, and suggested we all had a drink together. As we ambled along to The Old Shades in Whitehall, MacDiarmid and I discussed his 'Sangshaw' lyrics, the poems written in Lallans which had so moved me when I had heard them read.

Considering MacDiarmid was 81 years old, his vitality of mind and physical condition were amazing; as was his dry humour: 'On ma 80th birthday, I had a major oper-ration! Afterwards, the doctor wes examinin' me an' he said I had the organs of a mon 30 years ma junior, an' that I wud probably live ti a hundred. Which didna please the wife, I can tell ye!'

The chief impression I gathered of the man on this occasion was of a certain Englishness of humour: a strong sense of ironical understatement combined with a limitless capacity to laugh at himself. He would have killed me for this view, of course; for as he once wrote, 'The English lack that essential seriousness necessary to produce great art.' And he listed 'anglophobia' as his chief hobby in *Who's Who*. 'D'ye ken,' he said, 'I wes born juist six miles fra' the border? Anither six miles an' I'd've bin an Englishman ... a fate worse than daith!' Even so, his was an open, quick and friendly wit I found.

Considering that he was, to judge from his published writings, the greatest of egotists, he proved as good a listener as a talker; so that I had one of the best two-way conversations I had had since my father died. We discussed MacDiarmid's own poetry, and especially 'On a Raised Beach' which I have a high regard for, and this led him to confess he had published over 135 books and that 'I've written so much poetry, I don't know what I've written. Fra time ti time people confront me wi a poem I'm supposed ti have written and, honestly, I dinna ken whether it's mine or no?'

I was editing *Littack* at the time, and we discussed the making of enemies. MacDiarmid said, 'I've thoosands an' I'm still makin' 'em!' I also discovered, too, that he didn't like 'Graves or his pooetrie!' and added the rider: 'An' I've liked him less still sin' he made such a fool o' himself o'er that new translation of Omar Khayyam.' But he confessed the real source of his dislike for Graves derived from a somewhat impolite postcard 'th'mon sent me 43 year ago!'

Six to eight malt whiskies later, it was time to terminate this fascinating encounter. At length we got him and his wife into a taxi and, after promising faithfully to visit him at his home in Lanarkshire, we despatched them both to their hotel in Bloomsbury.

I finally kept my promise a year later and did visit Hugh MacDiarmid, or Christopher Grieve as his real name was, at his home 'Brownsbank' in Biggar, Lannarkshire. His crofter's cottage was located close to the brow of a small hill and an unpaved lane led up to it from the Biggar-Edinburgh road. It was in the heart of the green Scottish Lowlands with idyllic views in all directions.

The layout of the cottage was simplicity itself. There were two main living rooms, one for him and one for Valda: 'Ti stop us fechtin'!' as he confessed. In addition there was a small kitchen and a bathroom-cum-toilet built on the back. 'Built by students fra' Edinbro' University in 1952. It was the first time we'd had an indoor toilet in oor lives.'

In his wife's room there was a bed, dressing table and a litter of puppies with a bitch; breeding dogs being Valda's hobby, 'Ti keep me sane i' this madhoose wi him!' The more striking room was MacDiarmid's. It was stuffed full of books, photographs, and dominated by a big oil painting of the man himself. Everywhere in the room there were pictures and sketches and busts of MacDiarmid, and he ushered me in with the ironic comment: 'Welcome ti this shrine ti mysel'!'

I'd arrived at their home late in the evening and was immediately given a large glass of whisky and a fried egg sandwich. Then MacDiarmid and I promptly talked for several hours, long after his wife had retired to bed. There was mention of his admiration for the poetry of Peter Russell, John Holloway and, to my then surprise, he also had a liking for Larkin's poetry as well. Then he said of our mutual friend Tom Scott, whom I had just visited in Edinburgh, 'We used ti drink together every Friday night wi Tam an' his wife. But it got so wi Tam that he couldna hold his booze too well, so that in the end he'd be hittin' other customers wi' his beer mug. Noo, ye canna gang doin' that sort o' thing, ye ken. So I havena seen Tam in a dozen years.'

Back at Brownsbank the following morning, after spending the night in a local B. & B., I spent the day talking with the Scottish poet, drinking whisky, nibbling food, and listening to his reminiscences about a long and active life in literature and politics. I heard of how he had travelled as far as China and many other places, to read his poetry, before we finally got down to the serious business of doing an interview with him for *Littack*. I taxed MacDiarmid on his politics and its relationship to his poetry. 'As a political animal, insofar as I am also a poet, I cannot separate these functions – and in any case, I can't agree that any human interest can be excluded from poetry.'

In some ways, though, perhaps the most outstanding thing about MacDiarmid was his humanity and spiritual generosity. Despite his being, at that time, internationally famous with considerable calls on his time, he could interest himself in the progress of a small magazine edited by an unknown poet. And three years after, he even found time to write and wish Patricia and I well when we moved to Brixham, and he continued his expressions of kindness and goodwill towards my wife and myself right up to his death. I have always felt it to be true what Chu Hsi, the Neo-Confucian, said, 'Sincerity is the essence of the real'. To judge from my acquaintance with Hugh MacDiarmid, he was above all sincere, and thus a very real, a very true human being. For one whose reputation in the literary world was frankly fearsome, even shocking, MacDiarmid was in truth a most helpful and kind man.

CHAPTER TWENTY
Foreign Connections

A short distance from the outdoor Shoalstone pool in Brixham, where the shore is a wild mass and mess of broken boulders, of sea-lichened and sea-licked rocks, and a multiplicity of glassy pools, is a small inlet which an Austrian student friend dubbed 'the lagoon'. Above the lagoon is the Berry Head Hotel situated on the edge of a modest-sized cliff where all manner of wild flowers from white sea-campion to pink cyclamen grow. Once upon an age ago, this elegant Georgian mansion was the vicarage (when clerics lived in style) belonging to All Saints Church, Brixham; and was the home of the 19th century minor poet Henry Francis Lyte who wrote the words of the world-famous hymn 'Abide With Me'.

For a while during the Eighties, the lagoon was a frequent resort for Patricia and myself, principally because our Austrian friend took a particular shine to this sheltered coastal spot during several lengthy sojourns he made with us at the expense of the Austrian government. How and why this came about is worthy of note. But first I should mention the admirable Dr. Hogg.

James Hogg, an ex-Carthusian-monk-turned-university-professor and a publisher, came into my life in 1981. He wrote a letter, completely out of the blue, requesting my help in the preparation of a *festschrift* which he wished to publish in celebration of Peter Russell's sixtieth birthday. Russell lived in Venice, and had been a considerable supporter of *Littack*. To cut a long story short, I did assist the redoubtable Dr. Hogg and, in due course, the *festschrift* was published. Then James Hogg wished to publish some of my own unpublished work; something that was not hard to oblige him with as I had plenty of unpublished material. Hogg went on to publish a number of my volumes under the imprint of his 'University of Salzburg Press', ranging from books of poetry to two philosophical texts. He also invited me, on several occasions, to travel to Salzburg to deliver lectures, give poetry readings and to participate in seminars.

Then one day, in his elaborate and parrot-dominated drawing room (James keeps about a dozen parrots distributed throughout his grand chalet-style house – all of which he has 'rescued' from unsuitable owners or habitats!) he introduced me to a young Austrian post-graduate student who had expressed a wish to do a thesis on my poetry. This was Wolfgang Görtschacher: a short, handsome man with something of the look of a Thirties' dance band leader about him. His English was excellent, both in speaking and writing. If he suffered from one (later discovered) fault it was that he was such a scholarly perfectionist it made him a painfully slow worker.

So that was how Wolfgang and I, and sometimes Patricia, came to spend a deal of time sunbathing away hot days at the lagoon, and discussing various aspects of my writing. It was also how the Austrian and I came to spend many days incarcerated in my study: Wolfgang would probe and question me, recording my answers on tape, or make copious extracts from my correspondence and take copies of articles and poems which had appeared over the years in magazines and journals. The days were a mixture of hard-working and hard-idling. In the late evenings we would frequent the pubs around the harbour or, at the end of a particularly strenuous day, merely stroll round the corner to the Northcliffe Hotel (before it was destroyed by fire); and now and then we would cross the fields to the Churston Court Hotel.

If the truth were told, and it should be, though much academic work was done during Wolfgang's visits to Brixham, I guess we must have sampled just about every hostelry in the area: from The Lost and Found at Greenway; to The Manor Inn at Galmpton; all the way to The Waterman's Arms at Brixham St. Mary's – which had, in those days, a clock that went backwards, with the bizarre result that one often had the pleasurable, if somewhat Einsteinian experience, of leaving the pub earlier than one had entered it!

Wolfgang was a charming and talented young man and such was his gregarious nature that he soon became well-known locally, building up quite a circle of friends, many of whom I did not know. This came about because our two daughters were still living at home and we had no spare rooms, so Wolfgang had bed-and-breakfast at a nearby boarding house; an arrangement that gave him ample opportunity to develop his own circle of friends.

Many things occurred during his stay in Brixham. He learned to play cricket in order that he could explain this mysterious game to his fellow countrymen through the pages of a Salzburg newspaper. Then his landlady's sons were assiduous in teaching him the finer points of English beer – something he found easier to grasp than cricket!. I took him to London, Exeter and Brighton so that he could meet and

interview several writer friends of mine. Sometimes, too, Patricia
and I would take him swimming, but he could never quite accustom
himself to the chill of the English sea. On two occasions Wolfgang's
girlfriend Andrea, with whom he had been living for five years, came
to Brixham. They were eventually married, but it was a marriage
destined to end within a year of its being solemnized. A strange
result for one who believed strongly, as Wolfgang did, in the efficacy
of trial marriages to promote domestic harmony!

The very last of Wolfgang's many days spent in Torbay illustrates
best how well this remarkable anglophile had managed to integrate
himself into local society. It was the eve of our younger daughter
Katie's wedding. The ladies of the Oxley household had their hands
full with pre-nuptial arrangements, so it was decided that all the male
overnight guests, many who were staying at the same boarding house
as Wolfgang, should tactfully withdraw for the evening to the bar of
the Northcliffe Hotel. Not a very onerous imposition from our point
of view. This meant that our old and somewhat eccentric friend David
Beugger, my former boss from the City, Michael Whitehead, John
Wilson my childhood friend, and Quenten Lane (if he should turn
up) would repair to the seaview bar. In addition, Wolfgang was
expected to present himself there as well. As many of my friends had
heard of Wolfgang, but only John had met him, his arrival was awaited
eagerly.

However, it was Wolfgang's final evening in Brixham and he was
much in demand everywhere. He had been deluged with presents for
his own impending nuptials from the many local well-wishers who
knew him. Consequently he felt obliged to make something of a tour
of the town to distribute his farewells and thankyous in person. Also,
it was darkly hinted, to receive the tearful farewells of several young
maidens with whom he had become acquainted. So, as the evening
went by and Wolfgang did not appear, I finally resorted to the hotel
phone. Knowing where to ring, I was soon through to the noisy bar
of The Manor Inn down in the town. Above the din, I could hear the
landlord bawling, 'Wolfy – y're wanted on the phone!' And in no
time at all his pals in one bar had put him in a taxi and dispatched him
to his pals in another bar. Thus it was that my friends shared in the
final few 'rounds' of the man who had come all the way from Salzburg,
Austria to investigate contemporary English poetry – but who had
found the attractions of life, even in a small Devon fishing port, almost
more than scholarship could bear.

*   *   *   *   *

The last time I saw Derek Stanford was one summer's day in the gardens beside the Royal Pavilion in Brighton. We'd gone there to accompany Wolfgang who was interviewing Stanford for a book on the history of the small literary periodicals of our time. While investigating my poetry, he'd become fascinated by the English 'little magazine scene' and my poetry had gone west with his enthusiasm to write on this new and more intriguing theme.

Derek, a doyen of the Forties' critical scene and one of its historians, is a richly-textured being: as perceptive a critic in his own way as his great friend and mentor George [G.S.] Fraser. In his snazzy tweeds and waistcoat, looking like a retired colonel balancing a cup of tea on his knees, and sprawling in a striped deckchair, Derek expatiated effortlessly on the literary scene of the last fifty years. A Chelsea bun in one hand, he would gesture with it emphatically to underscore each point he made; and in brief pauses would nibble at the bun and gulp his tea. A blue silk handkerchief in his top pocket, Derek was the very epitome of the old-fashioned man-of- letters. And through each pithy phrase and effortless sentence oozed his humanity, his experience of humanity – all the best there can be in life and letters. Thanks to Wolfgang, I have this abiding memory of a man who, alas, has physically retired from the poetry whirligig, but who, thankfully, still writes poems.

*   *   *   *   *

Somewhat inconveniently, at the very start of Patricia's first term at college, we had to go abroad to Austria. At that time the University of Salzburg was holding seminars on my poetry for its students of English, through the good offices of Dr. James Hogg.

The best attended and most enjoyable poetry reading I ever gave in Salzburg occurred during this visit. The good audience was, in part, due to Wolfgang, now also a part-time journalist, who had contrived a good write-up for the event in the local *Salzburger Völksblatt*. The reading was followed by a reception attended by a number of academics and members of the university's administrative staff, and it was only marred by one thing. A delightful Austrian student, Eva, who had visited us in Brixham and done an interview with me in London, was invited by Patricia and me to the reading and reception. She was, I think, still technically a student of the university, but what neither Patricia nor I appreciated was that students and academics at Austrian universities did not mix socially at that time. Status is a much more rigidly defined affair than in the UK. The upshot was that she was shunned by some other friends there, which rather took the gilt off the evening's gingerbread for us, as well as leaving us feeling a mite awkward in our enjoyment of Wolfgang and his then wife Andrea's magnificent hospitality over the next few days: a free holiday in Carinthia, the wine-growing region close to the Yugoslavian border, as it then was.

In the Styrian wine country we stayed at a *gasthof* known appropriately as 'The Bacchus Keller'; entirely at the expense of Wolfgang and Andrea who wished to repay us for the times they had spent in Brixham. A generous gesture! 27th October 1988: the sole purpose of the day was to meander by car from vineyard to vineyard sampling *stürm*, as the new season's wine was called. First, though, we went into the town of Gamlitz to buy postcards; then on to Ehrhausen and visited the magnificent church with its incredible minaret like a cluster of red eggs on the outside and its crowded golden interior.

In the afternoon we drove up what is known as the *Wienstrasse*, and made our first call at a farm which kept grizzly bears for the public to admire and feed. These were formidable creatures but rather sad-looking: sad to see the great forest on all sides of them yet prevented from reaching it. Patricia looked very upset at their captivity, but admitted that she wouldn't have liked to have met them in the wild. Farmhands sold bread to the tourists with which to feed the bears. These vineyards are really farms that harvest grapes and make their own wine. The first we visited was very like an English traditional farmhouse inside. We sat in a large, table-filled room like a gloomy restaurant and drank copiously of the white wine which, being freshly fermented, was more yellow than white.

Then we drove to a less sombre vineyard, this time in an open air setting. At the roadside a bearded giant of a man was roasting chestnuts by the thousand; an oldish man in Tyrolean hat and dress was playing an accordion; and a woman was selling red *stürm* in half-litre glasses. The chestnut roaster filled a bin with wood, set it alight, then scooped up a big round sieve-full of chestnuts and proceeded to roast them. When they were well done he would toss them all like a chef tossing a pancake, which action would cause the shells to fall out through the sieve. He had become so skilled at this that none of the chestnuts was lost, despite them all falling from the sky like so many autumn leaves.

It was somewhat chilly and misty on the hillside, but everyone was very jolly and friendly – all Austrians seem such friendly people, so courteous, too – even the Yugoslavians seemed a merry lot. This roadside stop was the most naturally indigenous and atmospheric occasion we experienced on our tour of the Styrian wine country: a countryside which was green, mountainous, and tinged with the bright gold of decaying vine leaves in long, necklace-like rows. The locals, using Wolfgang as interpreter, were amazed to discover we had travelled much of the way to Austria by bus. Peasants though they undoubtedly were, they considered it a little mad not to travel such a great distance by aeroplane. But, then, they probably all watched TV and communicated by telephone as well! Equally, however, I was somewhat surprised (and not a little disoriented, seeing as I had just finished reading Hardy's *Mayor of Casterbridge*) to receive the proposal, also via Wolfgang, from the little old *apfelstrudel* of an accordion player to the effect that he 'buy your wife for 200 schillings'!

From this alfresco party we passed on later to yet another vineyard where, indoors and in the gathering dusk, we roistered the time away with a garage owner, a plumber and a joiner before returning tipsily to our *gasthof* for the rest of the evening. There we ate a variety of cold meats and hard black bread and consumed yet more quantities of *stürm*.

It was on this holiday in Carinthia that I saw one of the most beautiful or 'sublime' sights – as Schopenhauer would have called it – I ever saw in Austria, and also encountered the most tasteless and vulgar sight I have seen anywhere. The first came on the following day when Andrea drove us up a mountain so high as to afford us a panoramic view of Styria. However, that was not quite to be. For, as we alighted from the car, it seemed at first we overlooked an immense lake that was perhaps fifty or more miles wide: a lake with islands floating in it. But, almost immediately, we realised that we were, in fact, above the clouds and these 'lakes' were tops of great mountains peeping through the vastitude of seeming white waters. It was an impressive sight.

From this view we descended to a wide valley, coming upon a house whose side wall was covered by a huge blown-up photograph of Elvis Presley – the sublime to the mediocre. Proving, nevertheless and once more, that memories spring always from moments of intensity, happy or otherwise.

*   *   *   *   *

I once wrote a poem dedicated to Patricia called 'To My Harshest Critic'. She sees all my work 'hot off the typewriter', commenting on its defects or, occasionally, praising something. My nearest and dearest critic, she performs a valuable service which one doesn't always expect, or even want, from a wife. But I'm grateful for it. Even when she criticises my work to others, as she has done during many seminars at the University of Salzburg, she is a harsh but just critic and has helped improve my blemishes when 'I have dropped the wand' of poetic creation.

We were both invited in 1996 to a Writers' Conference at Salzburg University; I to deliver a paper on the current state of the long poem; she to talk about editing a contemporary literary journal. The conference was organised by Wolfgang and Professor Holger Klein, an outwardgoing, somewhat histrionic academic of suave agreeable manners who, for twenty years, was a resident lecturer at the University of East Anglia. Between them, they conceived this conference as a fitting farewell party for Dr. James Hogg, as the man who had been the driving force for so many years behind the University of Salzburg Press. As both James and Wolfgang have been good friends to Patricia and myself for a long time, we were more than happy to attend this 'farewell bash'.

Apart from ourselves, there were many poets and editors in evidence including, Peter Mortimer (then still editing *Iron* magazine), Joy Hendry editor of *Chapman*, Fred Beake, Jon Silkin, Patricia's reviews' editor, Glyn Pursglove with his wife, Parvin, and many another making the gathering seem like a 'Who's Who' of the little magazine scene. Not satisfied with poets and editors, there was a large contingent of academics with the result that the conference proved a heady affair both intellectually and alcoholically.

Not since I'd attended the old Poetry Society's summer schools more than twenty-five years ago, had I encountered such a goodly mixture of poetic fellowship and hard intellectual grind. Whether a group of us were whooping it up with Peter Mortimer and Joy Hendry in downtown Salzburg or sitting alone in our room at the St. Rupert House trying to put together a poem for the 'James Hogg Poetry Competition'. Or whether, having downed half a bottle of Anne MacLeod's and Angus Dun's malt whisky late the previous night, endeavouring to deliver a paper at nine-thirty the following morning and trying to hide my fragility! Or finding myself in a taxi with Jon

Silkin heading for Salzburg's fine ancient library in the centre of the old town, discussing Japanese poetry, then us all participating in a mammoth poetry-and-translation session which threatened to go on till four-thirty in the morning. Or travelling to Vienna in a mini-bus to take part in a poetry reading at the English bookshop there, and being on 'Radio Blue Danube'. Or this ... or that! It was all a terrific whirl of image and idea.

Images. Patricia standing on the side of a lake giving Fred Beake his happy-birthday kiss and nearly drowning ... not in the lake but in Fred's beard! James Hogg, carrying a trayload of champagne glasses, walking into a glass door and managing to break but one glass and nothing of himself. Sitting with Jenny Joseph in the student's canteen and hearing her say, 'I can't face talking about poetry much these days!' Glyn Pursglove sitting cross-legged on a table making a speech at the retirement party for James Hogg. Hearing myself on the Austrian radio while in a seminar class with some students who were translating a poem of mine into German. Visiting the Helbrun gardens in a twilight as ominous as all those poems of Trakl, some of which were written there. Then travelling out of the city with Wolfgang to visit an Austrian pub.

I had my last sight of Jon Silkin as he was walking on the banks of the River Salzach with an elderly lady. And stopping to say goodbye, I never thought it would be a last farewell to that great spirit among post-war poets and magazine editors. Soon to die, Jon had whispered to me in a crowded bar at the conference centre, 'I picked out that poem of yours especially for Stand' – which poem was to be the title poem of my next collection, *The Green Crayon Man.*

More images. Sitting in Wolfgang and Sonja's flat in Salzburg with Tom Clyde, the editor of *The Honest Ulsterman*, working our way steadily through eleven different kinds of *schnapps* brewed on Sonja's father's farm ...and Sonja a judge in the Austrian legal system! Climbing a mountain, too, on the last day with Patricia and Fred, 'to off-set the effects of too much self-indulgence' as Patricia put it. Yes, images, images, and ...

Ideas. Jon Silkin reading his poem-sequence *Watersmeet*, symbolising his love of both Japan and the North of England: their rivers, their trees, their hills, their women. John Gurney's amazing lecture-cum-parody of modern academic theory – ironically, so idea-packed as to be somewhat 'over the heads' of his intellectual audience. Peter Barry from Bangor University – or was it Aberystwyth? – giving

a talk on the London writings of Ian Sinclair, Alan Fisher and my
new discovery Aidan Andrew Dun's long poem *Vale Royal*, which I
had also brought up in my lecture. Fred Beake enthusing about the
too-neglected (in Fred's view) Edward Boden Thomas, the Derbyshire
poet. Peter Mortimer, attired throughout the conference as a 'middle-
aged hippie' as someone unkindly said, informing us all how much
of what we were doing was a waste of time.

Then there was Joy Hendry speaking passionately about Scottish
contemporary literature and Scottish nationalism, suggesting that
'Hame Rule' was best for a healthy culture. While Anne MacLeod
and Angus Dun introduced us to contemporary poetry of the Highlands
and Islands.

These, and many other talks, both formal and informal, in the
seminar room, conference hall or bar, produced whole cocktails of
ideas. Or ideas that just came up while that swashbuckling Scot's
editor Joy Hendry and I stood talking in the shadows of the gothic
town hall when we had slipped out from the marathon poetry reading
for a smoke.

As with all good things though, there was just too much image and
idea for any book to contain, for any prose – or even poetry – to
capture. But my abiding image of that highly successful conference
has to be of Dr. James Hogg. A quiet, saintly-seeming man, a diffident
workaholic, who has done so much for those creatures known
collectively as 'the Poets'. A man who, among his friends, is always
most retiring; yet who, should the occasion require, will brighten up
in the company of strangers. My last image is of him in the bookshop
in Vienna , having been dragooned by the manager into introducing
three British poets – John Gurney, Anthony Johnson and myself –
and doing it in exemplary and extemporary fashion. And when it
came to my turn, I found I could not get my briefcase undone so I
also had to extemporise and read from copies of my books on sale in
the shop window. After which, I was congratulated by both James
and Wolfgang on 'devising such an effective Public Relations'
gimmick'!

*   *   *   *   *

I didn't intend to write about Ireland. But then, I hadn't intended to
go there either. David Perman and I were walking back from The
Old Bull and Bush through Golders Hill Park towards Dannie Abse's
house where Patricia and I were staying, when David asked, 'Well,
are you coming or aren't you?'

Having already been away from Brixham for two weeks, David was proposing he and I went off to Southern Ireland at the end of the following week, so there'd be scarcely any time for me 'to turn round' at home before being off again ... so? 'Alright, then.' I replied, just as we were passing the pond where the flamingos used to be. So I went off to Ireland with another of my critics, my publisher, but above all, friend, to spend a few days in the new, less holy Ireland.

Southern Ireland entranced me; and I found the people friendly and loquacious: two qualities which make people easy to live with. Being there I discovered a new sort of dichotomy. For years I had had, as I thought, a fairly precise idea of what Ireland – Eire – was like; and when I got there I recognized everywhere lineaments of that country: priests, holy sites, castles, the odd tinker representing poverty-in-motion, and lots of public drinking of alcohol. Then Dublin with its great Protestant Cathedral where Swift (my hard-hitting hero) had officiated; the greystone-touched-with-black Trinity College; Stephen's lushlovely Green park with swan-sweetened lake under trees; the long roads out of town past Merrion Square and Jury's Hotel; and Sandymount – the Hampstead of Dublin ... all fitted in with my long read-up image of the place. And the Wicklow mountains in the beautiful garden of Ireland – its Kent – then Blarney, Cork, Waterford, and smaller places:

> the villages and towns that sang to themselves
> as the quiet deep evening came on

as I wrote in my 'Irish Suite' poem sequence – which was the unintended piece of writing I wrote out of my experience of eight days in Southern Ireland. We had, in fact, intended to go there for no more than four days – but Irish hospitality took over our plans.

But back to my dichotomy. I saw and recognised the Ireland which I'd dreamed of. But I was not long there before I was hearing Yeats' voice saying, 'Tread softly lest you tread on my dreams'. But I could see that these words, addressed now to the post-de Valera Irish politicians and Europeanisers were not really having an effect anymore. European Community 'dosh' had evidently been pumped into Ireland on a massive scale so that, now, there are two Irelands. One is de Valera's 'Auld Ireland' made 'theme' (which were all the bits I'd recognized). The other was the New Ireland, the Yuppie Ireland, the Ireland that might as well as not have, as one friendly soul put it, 'kicked you English out': the Ireland that, like the rest of us, might just as well have awaited the coming of Maggie Thatcher.

In other words, I perceived the new, free market Ireland; and could not help remembering Yeats again:

> Romantic Ireland's dead and gone,
> It's with O'Leary in the grave.

And I think my 'Irish Suite' poems were, at the deepest level, inspired into being by having felt this dichotomy.

But that is enough of the politics. I hugely enjoyed the New Ireland: whether in the tarted-up, ultra-modern Dubliners' Bar in Joyce's Jury's Hotel, roistering with my old friend Robert Greacen and his friend, the literary impresario Rory Brennan; or seated alone in Davy Burns 'moral bar' (Joyce again);   or, best of all, enjoying the wonderful hospitality bestowed upon David and me by Martina Evans' numerous and warm family in Burnfort. Martina had a sister, Mary, who ran The Conway Bar, where David and I were ... 'fêted' is the only word at all adequate to describe our visit to the tiny village where Martina grew up.

Which, of course, was our – David's – real object in going to Ireland. David was launching Martina's book of poems called *The Inniscara Bar and Cycle Rest*: an excellent first collection of tensely-nervous, mildly exuberant, accessible poems with a clear voice running through, and a delightful touch of that Irish 'jauntiness'. The book was to be launched at Waterstones' bookshop in Cork; but we had arrived first at high noon at The Conway Bar in Burnfort. Mary and her husband greeted us, then Martina and Declan, her husband, appeared and it was 'free drinks for the publisher and senior poet'. I was the 'senior poet' (a mildly disconcerting epithet when first encountered!). Gradually the bar filled up with locals and a host of Martina's relatives who seemed to have made the pilgrimage from all over the South. More swiftly still, David's and my glasses were replenished; and though I never drank anything but red wine, there was no lack of this strictly non-Irish brew. Then, around mid-afternoon, we all trooped into a backroom of the inn where a banquet awaited and we began the serious business of filling our stomachs. There were speeches too, (from David and myself and the local schoolmaster: a handsome giant of a man) and it was much like a wedding reception, even the local priest being in attendance. To an ignorant Englishman such as myself it all looked like 'the Real Ireland'. There were even posed-for photographs which show me looking overweight and boozed; Martina a slender, slightly haunted, beautiful colleen; and David, ever at home in any situation, looking always about to snap into action.

By the time we reached Cork and the crowded book launch and poetry reading by Martina, there were few who were not 'well-oiled' and feeling they carried an amplitude of generous hospitality within them. Later still, back at The Conway Bar we were treated to a full 'Irish Night' which went on to around two in the morning. Here I met Michael Ryan, a local poet, and I recall talking at great length with the local schoolmaster and his wife. It was a great convivial occasion; at the end of which David drove me off into the night to I knew not where. He still recounts how, as we thundered down dark lanes (in the direction of a place called Mallow as it later transpired), I kept enquiring as to how he knew where we were going; and my repetitive voice still sounds in David's after dinner reminiscences of our adventure, as 'Yes – but how do you *know*?' How did he know where to go? How did he know to take us both to this house shrouded in darkness at 2.30 am? How come he had a key to the place? How?

As we approached the front door of this elegant house, with a gentle breeze just disturbing the tall trees, David said, 'Now be quiet, very quiet, William, everyone's asleep'. So I tried; and, once inside, we crept up beautifully decorated and soft-carpeted stairs to reach the first landing. Quietly David opened the right hand door and turned on the light to reveal a veritable bridal suite of a room. Said he, 'This is your room, okay?' To which I boomed in reply, YES, BUT HOW DO YOU *KNOW*?' Shaking his head wearily, he thrust me forcibly into the pink and gold room and was rid of me for the night. Poor David!

That was the highpoint of our trip to Eire: the best guide to the remainder of our visit lies in the sequence of poems I wrote out of it. We stayed on to enjoy at least three days in Dublin, to visit Blarney Castle: *not to kiss the famous Blarney Stone*, for 'Taking you there would be like taking coals to Newcastle!' (David again); to visit Waterford, Wexford, and many another place including some excellent Irish bars ... which, like I say, was one of the main reasons we were delayed in getting back to 'the Island of the Mighty' as England is called in *The Mabinogion,* if not in *The Book of Kells.*

CHAPTER TWENTY ONE
Completing the Picture

W hen my friend Rupert Loydell offered me the chance of 'completing the picture', I seized it eagerly. Sometime in 1993, he'd approached me for 'ideas for an anthology'. I have always wanted to edit three anthologies: an anthology of lyric poetry through the ages, and, ditto, one of dramatic poetry, plus a contemporary one which would draw attention to a number of poets whom I regarded as 'exiles, outsiders or independents'. Poets who had, I felt, been somewhat neglected if not on account of their work, then because of their perceived status. Naturally, Rupert, with his eye for the provocative and different, opted for my third proposal, despite being aware of the fact that my taste in poetry is far more traditional than his.

In a detailed foreword to the anthology, which was published in the autumn of 1995, I sought to analyse the reasons for the 'neglect' of my chosen poets, 'All the poets I have gathered together in this anthology have nothing in common save their individuality and capacity to turn out excellent work ... I am firmly convinced that some variant of exile status has kept all the contributors to this volume a long way off from critical recognition, if not wholly out of the public eye. If I can do anything to lessen their critical marginalisation, then I shall be satisfied.' In addition to the lengthy preface, I wrote a highly personal view of each poet to introduce their selection of poems; while in a brief note on myself as editor – but whose poems were not included – I said, 'Assembling this volume has given me greater pleasure than any of my other works.' This was true, for the whole exercise, which occupied over a year, proved a delightful and fascinating experience of poetic empathy.

My chosen poets ranged widely from long established practitioners of the art like Jack Clemo, John Heath-Stubbs, Kathleen Raine, Harry Guest and Edward Lowbury, to poets like John Cotton, Lotte Kramer and other lesser known figures such as Arthur Jacobs, Francis Warner or Julie Whitby. Other, not unknown poets, like Sally Purcell and Dinah Livingstone, earned their place too; as did some of the poets whom I give mention to in other parts of this autobiography, such as

Brian Louis Pearce, Peter Dale and Sebastian Barker. I was especially pleased to be able to include the son of a friend of my father's, Geoffrey Godbert, a poet whom I first met when my father took me along to see his friend when I was only two years of age: an encounter which I actually recall, though Geoffrey does not.

Recognising that there will always be omissions from any anthology, I gave much hard thought to the matter, even discussing it in my introduction, 'No anthology, even one in some measure "thematic", can hope to include everyone whom it might be thought had a claim for inclusion'. I went on to describe some of the poets whom I might have included then giving my, or my publisher's – for Rupert had a hand in establishing the criteria for inclusion – reasons for not doing so. With hindsight, I would definitely have included James Brockway, a long time exile in Holland from the British poetry scene; should have included Geoffrey Holloway; and, despite my stated reservation in the preface about academic-based poets, Peter Abbs would have got in too. But, unlike with any book of my own poetry, I feel sure I made fewer mistakes with *Completing The Picture* than with any other project I've ever undertaken.

In The Old Shades in Whitehall, friends of the anthology, and some of its contributers like Fred Beake, Douglas Clark and Sebastian Barker, forgathered for the night of the London launch. This was the pub where, all those years ago, I had had my first whiskies with Hugh MacDiarmid; and it was a pub that the sentimentalist in me wished to make literary again. Among the friends who turned up for this pre-launch drinks' party were Tony and Fran Morris from Oxford, while Peter and Diana Carter had travelled from Ledbury in Herefordshire. Fran and Tony deserve mention for their 'patronage of poets'; as do the Carters. Fran and Tony once laid on a memorable poetry reading on Boar's Hill for me – and even chauffered me to it by Rolls Royce! While as visitors to The Mount and hosts at their manorial house in Ledbury, Peter and Diana have proved warm and stimulating friends to Patricia and myself, as to many poets besides. Peter, a larger-than-life South African, and Diana, a very English rose, made a welcome appearance that evening; as did our daughter Elizabeth and son-in-law Barry. The latter are Foreign Office people and live abroad a great deal, so they rarely get to our literary functions. I think it was Elizabeth's first poetry event for over twenty years.

The actual launch of *Completing The Picture* took place at Dillons Bookshop in Long Acre. Eventually, we all trooped up there in the rain to discover that the basement of Dilllons was already crowded. Soon it was packed to overflowing with more than ninety people: the biggest gathering ever for any of my launches. I organized a brief reading by each of those contributors to the anthology who were present; then there were more drinks – courtesy of the bookshop – followed by signings of the anthology. Many people came whom I did not know; and one I did know, Mike Brown, put embarrassingly on his Christmas card later that year, 'Came to your book bash, but couldn't get near enough even to touch the emperor's hem'.

After, around thirty of us repaired to an Italian restaurant across St. Martin's Lane, where, at two long tables, we had a mighty repast. Not all our good friends from The Old Shades joined us – Tony and Fran had a train to catch – but the company was large and convivial including Danielle Hope, Lotte Kramer, John Heath-Stubbs, Hilary Davies, the Oxley relatives and others like Peter Jay, and Harry Guest up from Exeter. Peter Jay is a charming publisher and Harry is as genial a poet as one could meet. And, of course, Peter Carter was still with us, ordering wine by the crateload and almost involving himself with the catering arrangements then, as he had done on a more privately famous occasion when, at a moment's notice, he and Diana had had to step in as surrogate hosts because, unfortunately, the real one had become too inebriated to attend to his guests...but that is another story.

Just as we were leaving the restaurant and about to go our separate ways, Sebastian Barker mentioned to me a further venture that was already underway, one that involved us both – and our dedication to writing long poems.

*   *   *   *   *

As I've already written, I read most of the classical epic authors early in life, Milton, Homer, and Dante in the famous Cary translation. In my late twenties I'd soaked myself in long poems. As well as the poets of the past, Virgil, Spenser, Camöens and Chaucer to name but a further few, I was also looking at twentieth century long poems or poem sequences. In the ten years from 1965 to 1975, I read much of MacDiarmid and his *A Drunk Man Looks at the Thistle* in particular, *Artorius* by John Heath-Stubbs, Pound's *Cantos, The Anathemata* and other long poems by David Jones, and Charles Williams's *Taliesen Through Logres* and *The Region of the Summer Stars*. Many of these works became conscious or subconscious exempla to me during the time I wrote my longest, and probably most considerable poem *A Map of Time*, which I began in 1973.

Summarising my commitment to the long poem for the *Western Morning News*, I described it as 'a symphony in words'. I also said that I believed it allowed for the development of an extended rhythm and a greater range of feeling than the short poem; in fact, that it encompassed the whole mind. It was poetry for the whole mind which I had tried to encourage in *Littack*, and which I had written about as far back as in the letters between my father and myself. I also said I saw it as a challenge to the declining attention span induced by other forms of media, notably the sound-bite style of much of television and, indeed, much modern 'street-wise' poetry.

In 1994, inspired by the example of W.H.Auden (whose *Collected Longer Poems* appeared in the early 1970s), I was able to persuade Dr. James Hogg to publish nineteen of my longer poems, albeit some in abridged form, in a single volume bearing the same title as Auden's. However, my true mentor or inspiration for this harvest of long poems was Hugh MacDiarmid. His influence upon me was direct and exciting, and the 'Hymn to the Sea' passage of 201 lines of iambic pentameter in *A Map of Time* was inspired by MacDiarmid's poem *Stones on a Raised Beach*. The only other inspiration quite as direct as that upon anything I wrote in the field of the long poem derived from my reading of Masefield's *The Widow in the Bye Street*. This latter poem was responsible for my lurch into narrative in *The Playboy* – though that is a poem, save in its narrative properties, far removed from Masefield's superb evocation of rural working-class life.

The reviews of my long poems, whether individually or collected, have always been very mixed. Most often, it seems the reviewers have only dipped into the collected volume – and who can blame them for it is a big work of over 400pp.! Even one of the most considered reviews, which ran to several pages of *The Edge City Review* in America, glossed every poem but *A Map of Time*. However, despite this omission, the reviewer did appear to have understood what I was trying to achieve in these poems, as, for instance:

> Mythology and modernity intertwine again, with still greater power and force, in *Polydorus Redivivus* ... In Oxley's poem, Polydorus epitomises the millions of victims slain by the political horrors of our century... In the journey of the mind that parallels the struggles that Polydorus underwent before he is reclaimed by life, the narrator gradually emerges from this abyss of self-pity, but never ceases to

be apalled by the city's "commercial values' violence / Its unromantic realistic ways / And impersonal working days"... the poem is bold and far-reaching...

Sebastian Barker, seeing the volume from a different perspective, wrote in *Acumen* that 'Oxley's achievement is he lays bare that the new seriousness so obviously to be desired in English poetry has no chance of success if vision reconciling time and eternity, mortality and immortality, is lacking'.

Stride Magazine managed yet another 'angle': 'a constant longing for lost Eden. This ought to be "old hat", but somehow it is deeply involving. It comes in part from Oxley's love-hate relationship with cities ... half of him is deeply at home walking Bunhill Fields with Blake, the other is agonised by the existentialism of modern city life.'

But with most reviews, it was *The Playboy* which received the largest share of review-space. After giving a very brief over-view of the narrative, the American reviewer picked up at the point where the would-be playboy is forced to work in a bank by his rich but puritanical father. I quote:

Hopelessly bored in the Computer Section ("the newest thing yet in human inaction"), he responds to the advances of a girl in the typing pool, with predictable results:

> ... I soon fell victim
> Of that ennui which strikes during overtime.
> And to cut a rude story extremely short
> Tanya and I were eventually caught
> Engaged in the world's most popular sport,
> By the folly of forgetting closed-circuit TV
> That essential part of a bank's security.'

This passage also intrigued other reviewers. Though I expressly state, in both the prose introduction to the poem and within the poem itself ('Whatever is said/In a poem or novel or work philosophical,/ Leaving it to others to be biographical, /In my humble way I'm prepared to allow / A good author can actually create – somehow') that it is *not* the story of my life, many reviewers, in this age of confessional and personal poetry, took the 'I' of the poem to be me. Yes, I have worked in a bank, and yes, I do live in Torbay. But many novelists use well-known locations or specialist knowledge from their own lives and they aren't accused of being the subject of their own books. Yet some of the most amusing reviews arose out of this very misunderstanding. The reviewer in *Stand*, for example, said I was 'the subject as well as the author'.

I had thought I was notorious only as editor of *Littack*, but *Pennine Platform* gave a further twist to my bad character: while praising the 'technically efficient narrative' of *The Playboy*, the reviewer suggested that I was 'possibly the only English poet to have been dismissed for fornication on bank premises in neglect of close circuit TV'

One reviewer who did brave the 400-odd pages of *The Collected Longer Poems* was John Lucas, also in *Stand*. And he was appalled by it. 'How such tripe got into print is beyond me' he complains, adding, 'He has the megalomania of the terminally ungifted'. I thought this a wonderful phrase; and would like to use it on the back of some future book of poetry, but I'm not sure any publisher would agree! In a 'polite' reply, I wrote to the magazine saying how pleased I was that I was 'terminally' ungifted for that meant I could expect any day to become gifted and looked forward to it with enthusiasm.

Patricia was upset by carping references to the fact we lived in Torbay. The poetic persona in *The Playboy* found glimpses of peace and 'green rapture' and the sea off Torbay he described as 'pure but moody sea'. But Lucas wrote 'I've got news for him: it's foul with untreated garbage'. So she went around for days muttering, 'How can it be, when we've got a blue flag – *and* an EC one at that!'

A couple of years prior to the publication of my *Collected Longer Poems*, Sebastian Barker's *The Dream of Intelligence* had appeared from a small press in the North of England. As a friend of Sebastian's, and someone interested in the long poem, I had been privileged to read this long poem based on the life of Nietzsche at various stages in its development. I admired the scope and ambition of the work and felt that its author had gone a stage beyond anything I had achieved in trying to bring some narrative structure back into the modern long poem: a feature that all the great moderns had long since abandoned.

As a consequence it seemed perfectly natural that Sebastian and I, having both given a great deal of time to the long poem, should find ourselves sharing a platform at a literary festival to debate 'The Long Poem'. The event, which took place in the imposing Great Hall as part of the Dartington Literary Festival, was both successful and illuminating. Patricia, having taped the text of the debate, decided to publish an edited version of it in her magazine. And this set me thinking how the 'Epic Revival Debate' might be carried to a wider audience.

One day, after having had my morning swim, while sitting alone on the beach – Patricia being away helping our eldest daughter Elizabeth and her husband in the hectic times after the birth of their second child – I was thinking hard about this problem and it occurred to me that I might start a long poem group. But, apart from Patricia, I knew of no one locally who might be remotely interested in such a venture. However, on one of our visits to London in the autumn of 1994, we met up with Sebastian in The Flask public house in Hampstead. The upshot of which meeting was – apart from consumption of much red wine – the founding of the Long Poem Group and the proposal to publish a newsletter so as to involve as wide a number as possible of those kindred spirits interested in long poems.

This group which, apart from early members like myself, Sebastian and his wife, Hilary Davies, and Patricia, has attracted poets like John Heath-Stubbs, the late Tom Scott, John Gurney, John Greening, Sally Evans, Leah Fritz, Grevel Lindop, Anna Adams, Fred Beake and others, has had a couple of meetings in London, plus a public presentation at the 1997 Ledbury Poetry Festival where it was sponsored, serendipitiously, by the John Masefield Society.

The stated aims of the Long Poem Group, as set out in our first newsletter, were, among other things, 'to encourage the modern epic and the long poem through critical debate...'. Both the event at Ledbury, called 'In Epic Vein', and the more restricted meeting of the group on Kentish Town in July 1996, resulted in good debate and fresh ideas. For example, it had been taken for granted by most members of the group, and many other interested parties, that for several centuries now the function of the epic or long poem had been increasingly taken over by the novel. Not so, argued David Perman at Ledbury, 'It is wrong to compare the long poem with the novel. What we should be comparing it with is the drama. There are fundamental differences in conception, as well as form, between poetry and drama on one hand, and the novel.' And he went on to develop this valuable theory at length.

Even more interesting was the point made by the Manchester poet and academic, Grevel Lindop, at the first full meeting of the group. Lindop said, 'It is possible that questions on how the long poem continues to survive may be looking at things from the wrong end. I would suggest that the long poem's survival doesn't require explanation in itself because the long poem is the norm for poetry...'

He went on to show how, 'historically short poems are unusual', how they only became 'short' following the exigencies of print and space limitations such as on gravestones and other things where short verses were used as inscriptions, and how in older cultures, 'the long poem was the norm'.

Such ideas and observations as these were, and are, precisely the sort of thing the group was founded to bring into the open and put into print. So more significantly, it has produced seven issues of *The Long Poem Group Newsletter*, which has carried the debate to hundreds of other people and institutions both in the U.K. and abroad. It is a newsletter which began by opening out the debate between Sebastian and myself on the theory and practice of the long poem. In more recent issues, the newsletter has attracted contributions from contemporary poets who have also written in this genre: Brendan Kennelly, Jon Silkin, Douglas Oliver, David Constantine, Gavin Bantock, Paul Muldoon and others still in the pipeline.

The first issue of the newsletter carried a faithful report of how the Group came into being, including the financial aspect. One of the considerations made clear was that members attending the meetings would be expected to 'bring a bottle', as the saying is. However, we felt that a more polite way of expressing this would look better in print. After having ignored twenty-one issues of *Acumen* over the previous ten years, the *TLS* decided to notice this 'perhaps about as little as a magazine can be' *Newsletter* with a couple of half columns. I think they felt there was some novelty in what we were doing, for after 'noticing' it with what can only described as 'a straight face hiding a grin', the reviewer ended with 'not only will the Long Poem Group encourage the modern epic ... by holding regular future meetings, but its members will be expected selflessly "to contribute to the catering costs of these meetings in kind or in money".'

Though MacDiarmid held that, 'Short lyrics ... are incapable of measuring up to the requirements of our age'; while *au contraire* Edgar Allen Poe wrote that, 'What we term the long poem is, in fact, merely a succession of brief ones – that is to say, of brief poetic effects'; neither point of view is, I feel, wholly correct. I have written many long poems; but have also penned innumerable short ones. And though I have suffered a bit in recent times from people coming up to me at literary events – even at readings where I've only read short poems! – and saying, 'You're the poet who only writes long poems, aren't you?', the truth of the matter is that the history of poetry is made up of both long and short poems, just as the human race is made up of tall and short people. When I have been asked for my opinion on the difference (beyond the obvious one of length) between a long and a short poem, I have to say that I think the difference is mostly one of scale. I have never set out consciously to write a long poem. My long poems all started life as short poems and simply went on growing. Of course, finally, they had to be shaped and structured, just in the same way that a short story which grew into a novel would have to be shaped into chapters and the like. The long poem, by its nature and size, inevitably is more comprehensive, greater in scope and development, not just structurally, but in terms of its ideas and wealth of imagery,

Finally, the main differences between the short and the long poem lie in scale and degree of narrative, mental or physical, which are employed. And, of course, the good long or short poem will be judged by the actual level of that intangible, but felt, quality called 'poetry' within the constructed pattern of words.

When a mathematician was once asked, 'How long is a piece of string?' he replied, 'As long as necessary'. Both long poems and short poems are necessary to me.

*   *   *   *   *

The more I think about it, the more I realize how ambitious a title was that given to my anthology, and now to this chapter. *Completing the picture* – how on earth can anyone hope to do that? One can't, of course, for there is just too much in life, and in one's own little life, to encompass or, even, to adequately sum it up. Quite apart from the many stories and experiences which space forces one to omit, as well as those less-than-flattering thoughts about others which we all have, there are many things about oneself which one simply does not understand enough to properly articulate. Especially matters of feeling.

For me, feeling is the alpha and omega of all things. Feeling has precedence over everything: I *feel* that it is the heart of life and mainspring of all we do. Our most loved ideas, our most cherished beliefs, all have their beginning in feeling. Indeed, life has its inception in feeling: from somewhere love flows into us and, turning sexual, is how all of us come to be. But beyond even that, I would claim – and I firmly believe – all which we call 'human consciousness' began in a 'big bang' of feeling. And this feeling generations of men and women have gradually, by leaps of that guiding intuition called imagination, rationalized into ideas, associated with external images, and so made articulate. In short, the whole of human reason is the articulation of homo sapiens' vast congeries of feelings. All cognition is preceded by feeling; and from some degree of cognition action follows.

But describing our actions involves choice; it also involves making judgements. And because, at the bottom of everything is feeling, the residium of the ultimate mystery of life, our judgements are neither infallible nor final. So how can I, or anyone, complete the picture? Only God can.

Meanwhile, however, I continue to dwell in Brixham; I read and write poems – the latter when some modicum of inspiration impels me to do so; I have five grandchildren, two daughters and sons-in-law. Elizabeth and Barry are, at present with the diplomatic service based in Nepal; but my other daughter Katie and her husband Richard live less than half a mile from us here in Brixham: so I see one group of my offspring more often than the other. For many years, too, Patricia's mother Evelyn lived with us until her death in 1997; and though having one's mother-in-law living with one for so long guarantees a certain level of daily turbulence, I survived it mostly unscathed: though I do recall once grumbling, 'If Jesus had had a mother-in-law he'd have found it much harder to turn the other cheek!' But that said, like the business of bringing up children, living with one's mother-in-law has a salutary effect upon one's natural inclination towards selfishness.

As will have been gathered from many parts of this autobiography, a deal of our life here is spent out of doors, swimming and walking; frequently we make trips to the capital and elsewhere on 'poetry business', and Patricia's magazine *Acumen* looms large in our domestic arrangements. While, finally, I would claim that my life, and that of Patricia's, is not now, nor with hindsight has ever been, the pursuit of life, liberty and happiness – to borrow the words of the American Constitution – so much as the difficult journey towards finding some truth and understanding.

So is there anything more to say than that? Can there be?

CHAPTER TWENTY TWO
The Missing Chapter

A gracious Regency drawing-room in a town house in Cheltenham. The year 1997 – just forty years since I met Patricia; over thirty since we married. And I am with the only person still alive whom I have known longer continuously than Patricia herself – and that is John Wilson, my friend from the golden years of the Road: now one of the world's leading autograph manuscript dealers.

Leaning back in a deep, shapeless armchair, next to the warm moth-glow of a frilled table lamp, smoking, drinking a claret, I eye him who fills half a big green sofa. Beside him sits Gina, his diminutive, dark-haired American wife. I report, 'The publisher says my autobiography must deal with three things: my childhood years in the Road, the break with my professional career, and my literary life ...'

'And Patricia,' snaps back John. 'What people would want to know would be your childhood in the Road, the break with your professional career, your literary life, *and* Patricia – the last perhaps most of all. She has been the most important influence in your life – your father not withstanding – and she still is ...' Was he right? Would people be 'most of all' interested to know about how Patricia and I had survived the marriage minefield so long, 'loved so long'? After all, among literary friends I could immediately think of several couples who had preserved their coupledom as long or longer – even in the lunatically lecherous literary world – Dannie and Joan Abse, or Brian and Margaret Pearce, for example; then what about Leah and Howard Fritz, Peter and Pauline Dale, or Elaine and Arnold Feinstein...? – the list soon lengthened. Surely ours was no special relationship, save to us?

I mentioned this thought to my tall friend draped on the languid green sofa. He lowered his whisky glass onto the marbled-topped coffee table, rubbed both eyes with his knuckles after pushing up his spectacles, as is his habit, yawned, then demanded, 'Yes, but how many of these poets – as I assume they all are – is married to someone who so closely shares their vocation as does Patricia yours? Does any of them edit a literary magazine like *Acumen* for instance? Are all these wives or partners equally poetry lovers as Patricia is?' (John's love being classical music, not verse.) Reflecting, I guessed that Joan Abse – as art critic and author of a major book on Ruskin – came nearest to matching her husband's achievement, sharing his interest. But, yet, the real question was not one of shared interests at all, but of love. Of a love that has survived from fumbling, moody, tearful teens. How could I really answer that one? Or describe such a relationship? Yet John insisted that I try.

If this part of my life is to be described at all accurately, it has to be said that right from the beginning Patricia was, remains, an unashamed romantic. During the marriage ceremony itself in All Saints Church, Middleton, Lancashire, she changed the words of the service 'till death do us part' to the single word 'forever'. And by that – and many similar gestures – she awakened my clod-like soul to respond.

She was a slender, good-looking teenager of willowy elegance – an Anglo-Saxon *madchen* type. Her background was working-class, but her whole outlook was naturally cultivated, even slightly aristocratic. She educated me in romantic love – it was her overwhelming obsession: she always remembered, right from the start, and still does, everything we've done, and recalls it with amazing clarity. In my turn, I fostered her interest in poetry, shared her hatred of the bad and the ugly things in life – often seeing these things much more clearly than she did. I introduced Patricia to the imaginative and intellectual life of man; she opened up the female heart for me. And this process accelerated the natural, mutual, sexually-awakened love of boy and girl which began in the 'mean streets of a mill town' – she only ever seeing, experiencing the wonderful world of the Road once; and that after the magic had largely gone from it: on the occasion of John Wilson's twenty-first birthday – or was it his sister's? I forget.

Shakespeare wrote in his most famous sonnet:

> Love is not love which alters
> Where it alteration finds ...

and in saying this he touches on the nub of all real, true love. It is also the heart of the difficulty all lovers must encounter, especially when young and faced with the many attractions and temptations. When I was young, I found that not many people – especially males – either sought or believed in true love. And given their basic attitude, not many probably found it. So how explain that Patricia and I did?

From the moment of our first meeting, I recognized in Patricia the eternal woman: that 'all women in one woman' to whose existence writers as diverse as Victor Hugo and Hugh MacDiarmid have eloquently testified. As I put it to Patricia long ago, 'I recognized you before we met'. And I did. I knew I had encountered her somewhere in my spiritual life in advance of our first physical contact. I even recognized her face. And she drew poetry from me; and surprised me by displaying an immediate knowledge, intuition of, and sympathy for the tradition of English poetry. Even less common, but more significant today was, and is, the fact that Patricia is a lover of poetry without being a poet herself – rarely if ever attempting to compose any. So I was not marrying a fellow poet; I was entering into the service of a muse. For the one thing a muse never does is write poetry herself: she inspires it in others.

A part of the inspiring must have gone into the magazine *Acumen* she started in 1985. When I was doing *Littack*, Patricia did a lot of the donkey work, principally the typing and setting up and so on, despite having two young children. But when the children were grown up she felt herself sufficiently free to start *Acumen* – and, as she insisted to all who thought she was merely a front for a revived *Littack*, doing it *her way*. As Patricia isn't a poet, she has no axe to grind and hasn't any position to compromise. She's doing things with *Acumen* I couldn't possibly have done with *Littack* for I was a poet and hadn't her detachment. Never appearing late in thirty-three issues, it has quietly developed and altered during its life; altered often as Patricia herself has altered, learned more still about poetry – and poets. She's a genuine editor and tries hard to get the best poetry she can within her financial means. I've watched her scrutinizing her submissions carefully, gradually building up a fund of possible poems. I've seen her spend days finally going over and over the poems in the short-list, until she's tracked down the few which finally make it into each issue. Then there are her polite rejection notes, often with short words of encouragement to some aspiring poet, or saying how she liked the poem and short-listed it but space has prevented her publishing it. An inspirer, a muse.

This muse I recall in a thousand situations and places. I see her today in her editorial office, her now silvered hair bound in curls and coils, face directed to a vivid computer screen as she typesets some poems to go into *Acumen*. I see her – still beautifully elegant – in short dark skirt at the Jackson Lane Theatre, Highgate, introducing, by turns, a galaxy of women poets on 'Woman's Poetry Day' in 1996. I call back evenings in long gone cinemas – Roxys or Odeons – in North Manchester when we were 'courting', my arm round her slender shoulders, holding to me her lovely face, breathing in fresh scent which mingled with the scent of her being. I recall her as the capable loving mother of our children, and as both a Brown Owl and Girl Guide Captain; or wearing her white laboratory coat when she was – in an earlier, more scientific incarnation – employed as an analytical chemist. Then working assiduously late at night over her books to get 'a first' at Queen Mary and Westfield College, London, in the early 1990s.

I see her swimming, a nereid in cobalt blue waters of one of the many coves around Brixham – say, Churston or Shoalstone – or walking by my side between Bolt Head and Bolt Tail on our most memorable long walk in the South Hams; or, years back, strolling the disused railway track from La Moye to St Aubyns in Jersey. I see her in the model-seeming landscape around Seeham-Fraham or framed in an evening window in Dr. Hogg's chalet in the same Austrian village.

She is with me, too, in innumerable beds from Epping in our Essex days, to Venice, Paris, Kilburn, Ware, Corbière, Brixham ... and many a time at that hospitable abode of the Abses in Golders Green. She was faithful to the end at her dying mother's bedside for six excruciating weeks, her loving undimmed. She was with me – and John and Gina – at a mini-market beside the windy Cheltenham Race Course, and went walking the high, dry clifflike perimeter of Leckhampton Hill to admire that panoramic plain and hill which Housman must have delighted in too, and where William Langland had his dream visions of Piers Plowman on the far off Malverns. Then in London, at parties and literary receptions, poetry readings and book launches without number I have watched her: a cool English rose blown about among the sweat and excitement generated by the poets and their female bacchæ. Yes, still she attracts me and startles me every way in all manner of place! I can write of her in no other way than as now (save in poems), nor answer John's questions in no wise other than I have done. An ordinary woman, a housewife, a teenage girl, a good-looker, normal ... yet she became, has become in my eyes a being extraordinary. A sort of goddess. And as my muse, a goddess in truth.

What are her faults? After all, even goddesses have some

shortcomings. Stubbornness; a not always worthy pride; sometimes misplaced impatience and intolerance; a capacity to be too easily distracted, sometimes away from more to less important things; and, though, by most women's standards not an insecure woman, she will put her head too much in the sand: especially where death is concerned, or where necessary moral confrontations are concerned (she is very English in not liking trouble of any kind!).

Her virtues are implicit in what has gone before; but I have not mentioned her sharp and perceptive intellect. A light, most often under a bushel. Though she would hate to be labelled an intellectual (for no creature, save only the outright philistine, is more hateful to the poet, the muse, and the genuine lover of poetry). I do mention her swift, strong intellect because it is there, but rarely seen. Rarely seen because – though she is not needlessly or falsely modest (nor immodest neither) – Patricia has never, for a moment, been inclined to 'show off', especially intellectually ('unlike her husband!' some would whisper exclaimingly). She is not a person who aggressively engages in debate; nor shouts others down; easily gets shouted down herself; prefers the quiet one-to-one conversation and will only come forward sharply if unduly provoked or asked for her opinion. She has not one single drop of captiousness in her veins. Likes humour, yet is more serious than humorist in herself – though not at all lacking in wit; but, again, as comedians are essentially show-offs, she is more a happy person than a comical one.

So there, John Wilson and John Doe, I have done as suggested; tried to describe this unique spouse and muse of mine. She is, as Churchill said of his wife, 'Someone with whom I have been proud to walk through life'. More than that I cannot say; she has my love, and much as I have described her has come through the knowledge gained by loving her. Only God can disclose more about her, and about our life together.

Given the burden of my friend John's initial question, 'Yes, but how many of these poets have a relationship with someone like Patricia who so closely shares your interest?', I suspect a big part of the answer to my, and our, constancy to one another does, indeed, have much to do with what John infers: 'How many of these poets are married to someone who so closely shares their vocation?' Only the real question is 'How many poets wed their muse?' Not many, as Graves so abundantly proved: chasing one earthly muse-illusion after another.

But, to parody Jane Eyre, I think I can say about my muse, 'Reader, I married her.'